Adobe®
After Effects® 4.0
Classroom in a Book®

Adobe

Contents

Station Identification

Getting Started

Welcome to Adobe® After Effects®—a powerful software tool for visual-effects and motion graphics. From commercial video and motion picture postproduction to CD-ROM title development, Adobe After Effects provides the tools you need to create dynamic designs. You can composite multiple layers, animate an unlimited number of elements, and apply visual effects.

About Classroom in a Book

Adobe After Effects 4.0 Classroom in a Book® is part of the official training series for Adobe graphics and publishing software developed by experts at Adobe Systems. The lessons are designed to help you learn at your own pace. If you're new to Adobe After Effects, you'll understand the fundamental concepts and features you'll need to master the program. If you've been using After Effects for a while, you'll find *Adobe After Effects 4.0 Classroom in a Book* teaches many advanced features, including tips and techniques for using this latest version.

Although each lesson provides step-by-step instructions for creating a specific project, there's room for exploration and experimentation. You can follow the book from start to finish, or do only the lessons that correspond to your interests and needs. Each lesson concludes with a review section summarizing what you've covered.

Prerequisites

Before beginning to use *Adobe After Effects 4.0 Classroom in a Book*, you should have a working knowledge of your computer and its operating conventions. You should know how to use the mouse and standard menus and commands. You should also know how to open, save, and close files. If you need to review these techniques, see the documentation that comes with your system.

Although it is not necessary, you will find it helpful if you have experience with Adobe Illustrator®, Adobe Photoshop®, and Adobe Premiere®.

Checking system requirements

To complete the lessons in After Effects Classroom in a Book, your system must meet or exceed the following requirements.

Windows system requirements

For Windows systems, you should have the following components:

• Intel® Pentium® processor.

• Microsoft® Windows® 98 or later version or Windows NT® 4.0 or later.

• At least 32 MB of random-access memory (RAM) for Windows 98 and at least 64 MB of RAM for Windows NT.

• At least 80 MB of available hard disk space for installation. You'll need additional space to work with large files.

• 16-bit (or greater) color display adapter.

• Double-speed or faster CD-ROM drive.

• QuickTime® 3.0 (or a later version).

The following are recommended:

• Pentium II or multiprocessor system (Windows NT only).

• Windows NT 4.0 (or a later version).

• 64 MB or more of RAM.

• 500 MB or larger hard disk or hard disk array.

• Video capture card.

• 24-bit (or greater) color display adapter.

• A sound card (if your video capture card does not contain on-board sound circuitry).

Note: To complete Lesson 7, which involves very large files, you will need at least 128 MB of RAM installed on your Windows system.

Mac OS system requirements

For a Mac OS system, you should have the following components:

- Apple® Power Macintosh® computer.
- Mac OS version 7.6.1 (or a later version).
- At least 32 MB of application RAM.
- At least 80 MB of available hard disk space for installation. You'll need additional space to work with large files.
- 16-bit (or greater) color display adapter.
- Double-speed or faster CD-ROM drive.
- QuickTime 3.0 (or a later version).

The following are recommended:

- 64 MB or more of application RAM.
- 500 MB or larger hard disk or hard disk array.
- Video capture card.
- 24-bit color display adapter.
- Two monitors with accelerated 24-bit video.

Installing Adobe After Effects

You must purchase the Adobe After Effects software separately. To install the application, follow the instructions in "Getting Started" in the *Adobe After Effects 4.0 User Guide*.

Adobe After Effects 4.0 is sold in two different configurations: The standard version of After Effects 4.0, and the Adobe After Effects 4.0 Production Bundle, which includes everything in the standard version, plus additional plug-ins tailored specifically for film and video professionals. These plug-ins include more advanced motion controls, keying effects, distortion effects, and device controls. The Production Bundle comes with a hardware key, which is required for using the Production Bundle software.

Installing Production Bundle plug-ins

If you haven't purchased the Production Bundle version of Adobe After Effects, the After Effects Classroom in a Book CD-ROM contains several samples of professional plug-ins for you to try during the course of the lessons. You will need to install these in your Adobe After Effects Plug-ins folder. These plug-ins do not require a hardware key.

Do not install the sample plug-ins if you are using the Production Bundle version of Adobe After Effects.

To install the sample plug-ins:

Copy the contents of the Plug_ins folder from the After Effects Classroom in a Book CD-ROM to the Plug-ins\Standard\Effects folder in the folder in which you installed After Effects on your hard disk.

Installing QuickTime 3.0 (or later) and MoviePlayer 2.1 (or later)

QuickTime 3.0 is required to play the QuickTime movies you create in Adobe After Effects on both Macintosh and Windows systems. To play sound on a Windows system, you need a sound card and speakers.

If QuickTime is not already on your system, see "Getting Started" in the *Adobe After Effects 4.0 User Guide* for instructions on locating and installing the application. QuickTime is included on the Adobe After Effects application CD-ROM.

Note: You must install QuickTime to play the final movies you create in the After Effects Classroom in a Book.

Using the Classroom in a Book files

The After Effects Classroom in a Book CD-ROM includes folders containing all the electronic files for the After Effects Classroom in a Book lessons. Each lesson has its own folder.

You should first try going through the lessons without copying files from the CD-ROM to your hard disk. If you find that some actions are too slow, you can copy the files from that particular lesson to your hard disk.

The size of each lesson folder is listed below so that you can make sure sufficient disk space is available before you copy them.

Projects	Size
Tour	42.5 MB
01Lesson	22.2 MB
02Lesson	13.5 MB
03Lesson	12.2 MB
04Lesson	64.6 MB
05Lesson	59.8 MB
06Lesson	14.9 MB
07Lesson	394.0 MB

To install the After Effects Classroom in a Book folders:

1 Create a folder on your hard disk, and name it Adobe After Effects CIB.

2 Copy the lesson folders from the CD-ROM into this folder.

Completed project files

Each lesson folder contains a completed project file for the lesson. Use these files as a reference if you get stuck in any part of the project. Every project file is locked to prevent you from accidentally making any changes to it. When you open a project file, you may see a prompt that some of the files have changed. This occurs if you copied the files to your hard disk. Simply click OK to open the project.

In addition, each lesson folder contains the completed QuickTime movie for the lesson. To play the movie, double-click the file to open MoviePlayer®.

Creating a Projects folder for work files

Create a folder called Projects on your hard disk. Each lesson in this book includes directions for creating a work file and saving it in this folder. This keeps your work files separate from the project elements.

Image files

The image files on the After Effects Classroom in a Book CD-ROM are all under copyright and may not be distributed.

Restoring default preferences

The preferences file controls how palettes and command settings appear on your screen when you open the Adobe After Effects program. Each time you exit from Adobe After Effects, the position of the palettes and certain command settings are recorded in the preferences file. If you want to restore the palettes to their original default settings, you can delete the current Adobe After Effects preferences file. (Adobe After Effects creates a preferences file if one doesn't already exist the next time you start the program and save a file.)

Important: If you want to save the current settings, rename the preferences file rather than throwing it away. When you are ready to restore the settings, change the name back and make sure that the file is located in the Prefs folder in the folder in which you installed After Effects (Windows) or the Preferences folder in the System folder (Mac OS).

1 Locate the AEPrefs.txt file in the Prefs folder in the folder in which you installed After Effects (Windows) or the After Effects Prefs file in the Preferences folder in the System folder (Mac OS).

If you can't find the file, choose Find from the Start menu and then choose Files or Folders (Windows), or choose Find from the desktop File menu (Mac OS). Type **AEPrefs** or **After Effects Prefs** in the text box, and click Find Now (Windows) or Find (Mac OS).

Note: If you still can't find the file, you probably haven't started Adobe After Effects for the first time yet. The preferences file is created after you quit the program the first time, and it's updated thereafter.

2 Delete or rename the AEPrefs.txt file (Windows) or the After Effects Prefs file (Mac OS).

3 Start Adobe After Effects.

To locate and delete the After Effects preferences file quickly each time you begin a new project, create a shortcut (Windows) or an alias (Mac OS) for the appropriate folder.

Lesson strategies

You may find it helpful to read through the entire lesson before you begin creating the project. Several of the projects are quite complex, so you may also want to arrange your time so that you can complete an entire lesson in one sitting.

Rendering QuickTime movies

At the end of each lesson, you will have a complete project that is ready to be *rendered*, or compiled, into a QuickTime movie. Rendering a movie can take anywhere from a couple of minutes to many hours, depending on the size of the files, the complexity of the project, the type of computer you are working on, the amount of RAM you have, and the compression method you are using.

Because of this, you should structure your time so that you can finish a lesson and then leave your computer free to render the movie, possibly overnight or while you are away from your system. You can work in other applications while a movie is rendering, but it will reduce the speed of your system.

Several lessons provide instructions on how to create a *draft* movie, a smaller, lower-quality movie that renders faster, and allows you to see quicker results. Each lesson folder also contains a completed movie file.

Special bonus section

At the end of the After Effects Classroom in a Book is an appendix called "Technical Information," which includes information on many of the technical aspects of preparing and rendering movies for video and film. It includes detailed information on video interlacing, frame rate, audio, film, and more. Read it at your leisure, or refer to it as you make your way through the lessons in the After Effects Classroom in a Book.

Additional resources

Adobe After Effects 4.0 Classroom in a Book is not meant to replace documentation provided with the program. Only the commands and options used in the lessons are explained in this book. For comprehensive information about program features, refer to these resources:

• *Adobe After Effects 4.0 User Guide*. All aspects of the application are covered in detail.

• *After Effects 4.0 Production Bundle Guide* (if you have purchased the Production Bundle version of After Effects).

• After Effects Tour Movie, available on the Classroom in a Book CD-ROM.

• Quick Reference Card, a useful companion as you work through the lessons in this book.

Adobe certification

The Adobe Training and Certification Programs are designed to help Adobe customers improve and promote their product proficiency skills. The Adobe Certified Expert (ACE) program is designed to recognize the high-level skills of expert users. Adobe Certified Training Providers (ACTP) use only Adobe Certified Experts to teach Adobe software classes. Available in either ACTP classrooms or on site, the ACE program is the best way to master Adobe products. For Adobe Certified Training Programs information, visit the Partnering with Adobe Web site at partners.adobe.com.

A Quick Tour of Adobe After Effects

This tour gives you an overview of the basic concepts and features of Adobe After Effects. It takes about an hour to complete.

You'll create an After Effects project using Adobe Photoshop files, Adobe Illustrator files, and an After Effects composition. You'll learn how to import footage files, set up a composition, animate footage layers, apply visual effects, and render the final project as a QuickTime movie.

If you'd like to see a finished version of the movie, locate 01_b.mov in the Adobe After Effects 4.0\Tour folder. You can play it using any QuickTime movie-playing application, or import it into an After Effects project and play it in the QuickTime Footage window.

For detailed information about any feature, command, or window used in this tour, refer to the index in this book.

Freeze frames of the animated effects you'll create in this project.

Getting started with your project

A project in After Effects is a file that stores references to your footage and all layout and animation information. To begin working in After Effects, you create a new project and import footage items. But first you'll need to restore the default preferences for Adobe After Effects.

1 To ensure that the tools and palettes function exactly as described in this lesson, delete or deactivate (by renaming) the After Effects preferences file. See "Restoring default preferences" on page 6.

For best results, allocate as much RAM as possible to After Effects. For information on allocating more memory to After Effects, see the online Help.

2 Start After Effects. After Effects opens with an untitled Project window. The first time you start the application, the standard palettes are open by default. You can arrange them to fit your work style. The new arrangement becomes the new default.

3 Choose File > Save As, locate the Adobe After Effects 4.0\Tour folder, and then name the project **01_a.aep.** Click Save.

Importing footage items

You can import a wide variety of file formats into After Effects including Adobe Photoshop files, Adobe Premiere projects, and QuickTime and AVI movies. For information on importing footage, see Chapter 3 in the *Adobe After Effects 4.0 User Guide*.

Now you'll import all your footage files.

1 Choose File > Import > Footage Files. Locate the Adobe After Effects 4.0\Tour folder, select L.psd, and then click Open. This file contains an alpha channel, so the Interpret Footage dialog box appears. Click OK to accept the default option of Treat as Straight. The Import Footage dialog box reappears so you can continue to import footage.

2 Select M.psd and click Open. Because this Adobe Photoshop file contains layers, the Import Photoshop File dialog box appears, allowing you to choose the layers you want to import. Select Merged Layers, and then click OK.

3 Continue selecting the remaining files: N.ai, O.mov, and P.aif. Then click Done.

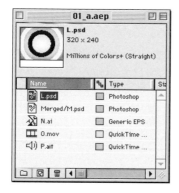

All the files appear in the Project window. When you select a file in the Project window, you'll see a thumbnail image of the file at the top of the window, as well as size and color mode information. Each footage file is also assigned a color, which represents the file type class; for example, a still image file is pink and a moving image file is yellow. For information on customizing the Project window, see "Project window" on page 37.

Setting up a composition

The next step when working in After Effects is to set up a composition. A composition provides the framework for you to add, arrange, and animate your footage. Compositions exist only within a project. You can have multiple compositions in a project; you can even have compositions within compositions. When you set up a composition, you establish the layout, including frame size, duration, and resolution for your final output.

Each footage file you add to a composition becomes a layer that you can animate and manipulate with effects. At any time, you can change any aspect of the composition. For example, you can delete or replace a footage item, adjust an effect or animation setting, or even change the duration for your final output. Remember, the animations you create in After Effects are reversible; everything is adjustable. For more information on Compositions, see Chapter 4 in the *Adobe After Effects 4.0 User Guide*.

1 Click the center icon (between the folder icon and the trash can icon) at the bottom of the Project window, or choose Composition > New Composition to open the Composition Settings dialog box.

2 In the Composition Settings dialog box, leave **Comp 1** for the Composition Name. Select Medium, 320 x 240 from the Frame Size pop-up menu. Verify that Square Pixels is selected for Pixel Aspect Ratio, and that Full is selected for Resolution. Type **15** for Frame Rate and **13:00** for Duration (After Effects automatically sets the first three numbers to 0). Click OK.

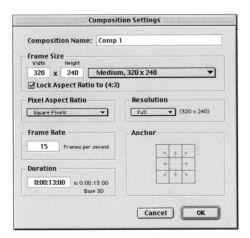

When you create a new composition, a Composition window and a Time Layout window appear. The Composition window provides a visual preview of your footage and all the effects and animations you apply for a given point in time. The Time Layout window provides a visual overview of the composition time, as well as access to layer settings, such as Masks, Effects, and Transform properties.

Now you'll add a footage item to the composition.

3 Drag L.psd from the Project window into the Time Layout window. When you add a footage file to a composition by dragging it to the Time Layout window, the footage automatically appears centered in the Composition window.

Note: You can also add a footage item to a composition by dragging it to the Composition window or to the composition icon in the Project window.

L.psd is now a layer in the composition and appears in both the Composition and Time Layout windows. The layer's duration is indicated by the pink bar under the timeline. The color of this bar initially represents the type of file contained in the layer—in this case, a still image.

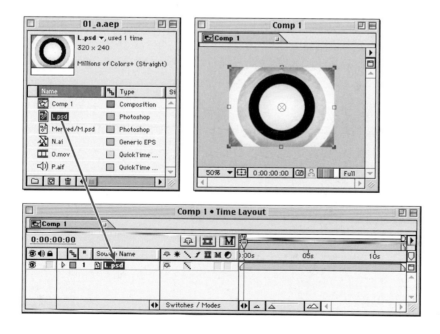

Setting layer keyframes

In After Effects, you can animate layers by setting two or more keyframes for the layer's properties at different points in time. Keyframes mark the point in time where you've set layer property values. In order to create a keyframe, you must first click the property stopwatch to activate it. If you don't activate the stopwatch, After Effects does not create new keyframes for the different values you set for a property. Instead, it sets the layer's entire duration to that value.

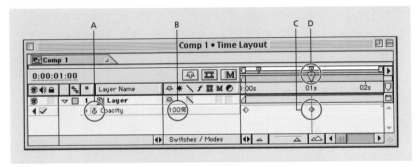

A. *Stopwatch* **B.** *Opacity value* **C.** *Keyframe* **D.** *Current-time marker*

Scaling a layer

You can add an unlimited number of layers to a composition. Each time you add a layer, After Effects assigns the layer a number to help you organize your footage.

You can animate a layer's size by setting keyframes for a layer's Scale property. In this part of the tour, you'll add the N.ai footage file to the composition. Then you'll animate the N.ai layer to make it grow and shrink.

1 Press the Home key on your keyboard to set the current-time marker to the beginning of the composition (0:00). The current-time marker is the blue marker in the Time Layout window's timeline. It indicates the active frame.

2 Drag N.ai from the Project window into the Time Layout window.

3 In the Time Layout window, select the N.ai layer, and click the triangle to the left of the layer name to expand the layer outline. Click the triangle next to Transform to open the transformation properties outline. The Scale property appears.

Note: *You can also press S to open just the Scale property for the selected layer.*

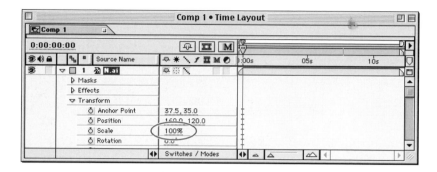

4 Click the underlined Scale value to display the Scale dialog box. Type **0** for Width; the Height value adjusts automatically. Click OK.

5 Click the stopwatch next to Scale to set the first Scale keyframe. Notice the diamond-shaped icon that appears next to the Scale property, in the timeline. Once you activate the stopwatch, whenever you move the current time and change the Scale value, After Effects will automatically create a new keyframe.

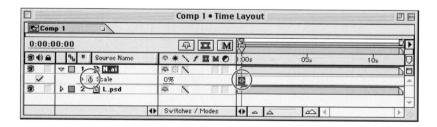

6 In the upper left corner of the Time Layout window, click the underlined current time. In the Go To Time dialog box, type **300** to move the current-time marker to 3:00. Then, click the underlined Scale value again. Type **200** for Width and click OK. After Effects automatically sets a new keyframe at the current time.

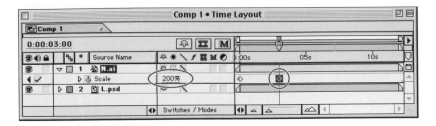

7 Set the current time to 4:10 and click the underlined Scale property. Type **0** for Width and click OK. After Effects automatically sets another new keyframe at the current time.

8 Press the Home key on your keyboard to return to the beginning of the composition, and then press the spacebar to preview the changes.

Continuously rasterizing a layer

Notice how the N.ai layer has jagged edges when it is scaled above 100%. You can make the edges smooth by turning on the Continuously Rasterize switch for the layer.

When you continuously rasterize a layer whose source is an Adobe Illustrator file, After Effects recalculates the footage file's resolution as it transforms, so the edges don't appear jagged. This switch increases display quality, but also increases render and preview time. For more information, see "Layer switches" on page 46.

Layer containing an Adobe Illustrator file with the Continuously Rasterize switch off (left) and on (right)

1 In the Time Layout window, in the panel to the right of the layer name, click the Continuously Rasterize switch (∗) for the N.ai layer.

2 If you want to decrease the time it takes to prepare previews, deselect the switch until it's time to render the project.

3 Press the Home key to return to the beginning of the composition, and press the spacebar to preview the changes.

Copying and pasting keyframes

To save time while designing a project, you can copy and paste keyframes. Here you'll copy the last two Scale keyframes you set and paste them onto the end of the N.ai layer. You'll then apply a keyframe assistant to reverse the order of the keyframes, making the layer zoom in from 0 to 200%.

1 In the Time Layout window, select the Scale keyframe in the N.ai layer at 3:00, and then hold down Shift and select the last keyframe at 4:10. Choose Edit > Copy.

2 Move the current-time marker to 10:00 and choose Edit > Paste. The keyframes are pasted back onto the N.ai layer at 10:00 and 11:10. Notice in the Composition window how the N.ai layer displays 200% at 10:00.

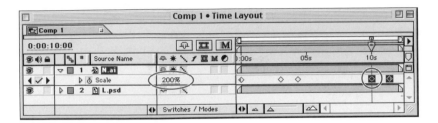

3 With the last two keyframes still selected, choose Layer > Keyframe Assistant > Time Reverse Keyframes. Notice in the Composition window that the N.ai layer now displays 0% at 10:00. You've reversed the two keyframe values, so the value at 10:00 is 0 and the value at 11:10 is 200%.

4 Press the Home key, and then press the spacebar to preview the scale animation.

Rotating a layer

Now you'll set keyframes for the N.ai layer's Rotation property.

1 In the Time Layout window, make sure the N.ai layer is still selected and press R to open the Rotation property outline.

2 Set the current-time marker to the beginning of the composition and click the Rotation stopwatch to set the first keyframe with a Rotation value of 0.

3 Move the current-time marker to 3:00, and then click the underlined Rotation value to open the Rotation dialog box.

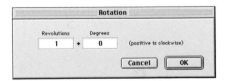

4 Type **1** in the Revolutions box and click OK. A new Rotation keyframe appears at 3:00.

5 Press Home, and then press the spacebar to preview the scale and rotation animations.

6 Click the triangle next to the N.ai layer name to collapse the layer outline.

7 Save the project.

Creating a motion path

A *motion path* illustrates the path along which a layer moves. You can create a motion path in After Effects by moving a layer around the Composition window and setting Position keyframes at different points in time. After Effects can create motion paths using *Bezier* interpolation, with smooth corners and curved lines; or *Linear* interpolation, with straight lines and sharp corners; or a combination of both.

In this part of the tour, you'll add another layer to the composition, and then you'll create a Linear motion path for the layer.

1 Set the current time to 4:00.

2 Drag Merged/M.psd from the Project window into the Time Layout window. Merged/M.psd appears at the top of the Time Layout window outline and centered in the Composition window.

Notice the Merged/M.psd layer starts at 4:00. When you add a layer to a composition, the the layer is inserted at the location of the current-time marker.

3 In the Composition window, select 25% from the magnification pop-up menu so that you can see more of the gray border around the composition's image area. You can move a layer anywhere in the Composition window, but only the portions that appear in the image area will appear in your final rendered output. You're beginning this layer's motion path outside of the image area so that it will gradually come into view.

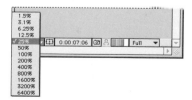

4 Drag the Merged/M.psd layer to the upper left corner of the Composition window, outside of the image area. Make sure you drag inside the layer frame and not a layer handle. Dragging a layer handle resizes the layer.

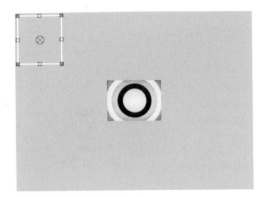

5 In the Time Layout window, select the Merged/M.psd layer and press the letter P on the keyboard to open the Position property. Click the stopwatch next to Position to set the initial Position keyframe.

Note: You can activate the stopwatch either before or after you set the initial property value. The important thing to remember is to activate it before you change the current time.

6 Set the current time to 8:00, and then in the Composition window, drag the Merged/M.psd layer to the center of the frame. After you start dragging the layer, hold down Shift and Alt (Windows) or Shift and Option (Mac OS) to snap the layer to the center of the composition window. After Effects automatically sets another keyframe at 8:00.

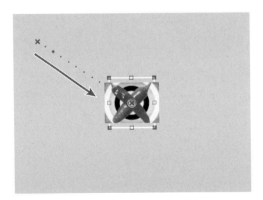

7 Set the current time to 9:00, and then click the keyframe navigator box to create a new, identical Position keyframe. By setting identical keyframes at 8:00 and 9:00, you hold the position steady for one second.

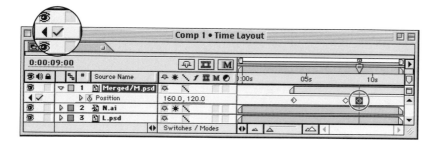

8 Set the current time to 10:00.

9 In the Composition window, drag the Merged/M.psd layer straight up to the top of the Composition window. Make sure you drag outside the layer's center point (X) and not on any of the layer handles; otherwise, the path will bend instead of making a sharp corner. To constrain the path to a 90-degree vertical line, hold down Shift after you begin dragging. Notice that another keyframe was created and appears on both the Time Layout window and the Composition window.

10 Press the Home key on your keyboard. In the Composition window, select 100% from the magnification pop-up menu, and then press the spacebar to preview the motion path.

11 Save the project.

Synchronizing animation

Now you'll set Scale keyframes for the Merged/M.psd layer that are synchronized with the Position value keyframes. By doing this, you'll create the effect of the peppers falling, because they will appear smaller and smaller as they travel toward the center of the background layer.

1 With the Merged/M.psd layer selected in the Time Layout window, press the letter I on the keyboard to move the current-time marker to the beginning of the layer, which is called the layer's *In point*.

2 Hold down Shift and press S to open the Scale property. When you press Shift while opening a layer property, other open properties remain open as well.

3 Click the stopwatch to set the initial Scale keyframe at the default value of 100.

You can easily set the Scale keyframes to the same time as the Position keyframes by clicking the Position keyframe navigator arrows.

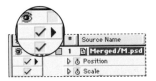

4 Click the right-facing Position keyframe navigator arrow to move the current-time marker to the location of the next Position keyframe (8:00).

5 Change the Scale value to 55. After Effects automatically creates a new Scale keyframe at 8:00.

6 Click the right-facing Position keyframe navigator arrow again to move the current time to 9:00, and then click the Scale keyframe navigator box to create a keyframe identical to the previous keyframe.

7 Click the right-facing Position keyframe navigator arrow one more time to move the current time to 10:00, and then change the Scale value to 100. To determine if you set all the keyframes correctly, compare your Time Layout window to the window below.

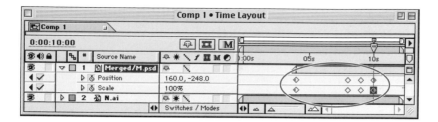

Applying the Drop Shadow effect

You can add any effects to the layers in your composition. You can even apply multiple effects to one layer and animate the effects over time. For more information, see Chapter 9 in the *Adobe After Effects 4.0 User Guide*.

Here, you'll apply the Drop Shadow effect to the Merged/M.psd layer, and synchronize it with the Scale and Position animation. To make the Drop Shadow appear more realistic as the peppers drop to the center of the image area, you'll change values over time for Opacity, Distance, and Softness.

1 With the Merged/M.psd layer still selected in the Time Layout window, press I to move the current time to the layer's In point of 4:00.

2 Choose Effect > Perspective > Drop Shadow. The Effect Controls window appears with the Drop Shadow controls. You can set different values for the effect in either this window or the Time Layout window.

Note: *The sliders that appear in the Effect Controls window do not always display the entire range of values possible. To enter values outside of the range displayed by the slider, you can click the underlined value.*

You'll set the Drop Shadow values in the Time Layout window.

3 With Merged/M.psd layer still selected in the Time Layout window, press E on the keyboard to open the Effects outline. Click the triangle next to Effect, and then click the triangle next to Drop Shadow to further expand the outline.

4 In the Time Layout window, click the underlined Opacity value and type **0** for Value. Click OK.

5 Click the underlined Distance value and type **420**, and click OK.

6 Click the underlined Softness value and type **50**, and click OK.

7 To create initial keyframes for these properties, click the stopwatch next to Opacity, Distance, and Softness.

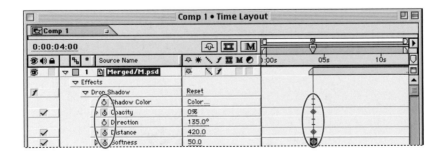

Now you'll navigate to the location of the Position and Scale keyframes so you can set Drop Shadow keyframes at the same points in time.

8 Click the right-facing arrow for the Position keyframe navigator; the current time moves to 8:00.

9 Change the Drop Shadow's Opacity value to 45, the Distance value to 20, and the Softness value to 20. After Effects automatically creates new keyframes for each of these values at 8:00.

10 Click the right-facing arrow for the Position keyframe navigator; the current time moves to 9:00.

11 Click the keyframe navigator box next to Opacity, Distance, and Softness to set new keyframes for each that are identical to the previous keyframe.

12 Click the right-facing arrow for the Position keyframe navigator, moving the current time to 10:00.

13 Change the Opacity value to 0, the Distance value to 225, and the Softness value to 50.

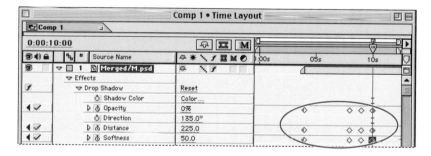

14 Click the arrow next to the Merged/M.psd layer heading to collapse the window outline.

Now you'll preview a wireframe version of the project to view the motion you've created so far.

15 Press the Home key to return the current-time marker to the beginning of the composition.

16 Choose Composition > Preview > Wireframe Preview. The animated layers in your composition display as white outlines on a black background.

17 Save the project.

Adding an adjustment layer

Now you will add an adjustment layer to the composition. An *adjustment layer* is a solid layer to which you apply one or more effects. The effects you apply to this layer affect all layers below it in the Time Layout window, so you can easily apply the same effect to several layers at once. You can also turn an existing footage layer into an adjustment layer.

Once you create the new adjustment layer, you'll apply the Basic 3D effect to simultaneously flip all of the layers in the composition.

1 In the Time Layout window, move the current-time marker to 8:00.

2 Choose Layer > New Adjustment Layer. Adjustment Layer 1 appears in the Time Layout window at the top of the Time Layout window outline, beginning at 8:00. At this location, the adjustment layer modifies all other layers in the composition.

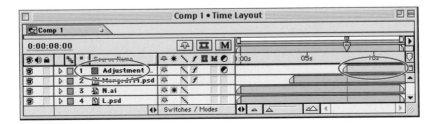

3 With the adjustment layer selected, choose Effect > Perspective > Basic 3D. The Effect Controls window appears. You'll set all the effect values in the Time Layout window.

4 In the Time Layout window, select the adjustment layer and press E to display the Effects outline, and then click the triangle next to Basic 3D to display its properties.

To make all of the layers in the composition spin backwards by one revolution, you'll set two keyframes: one at the default Tilt value of 0, and one at a Tilt value of −1.

5 Make sure the current time is still at 8:00, and then click the stopwatch next to Tilt to create the first Tilt keyframe at the default value of 0.

6 Set the current time to 9:00, and click the underlined Tilt value and type **–1** in the Revolutions box. Notice that another new keyframe appears for the Tilt effect property at 9:00.

7 In the Time Layout window, click the triangle next to the adjustment layer heading to collapse the outline.

8 Press Home on the keyboard, and then preview the effect. Notice how the effect applies to all the layers.

9 Save the project.

Nesting compositions

You can organize your project and create compound effects and animation by nesting compositions. *Nesting* is the process of using a composition as a layer in another composition. Nesting can help you keep layers organized by grouping them together, and it can save time when you need to apply properties to multiple layers at once.

In this lesson you'll nest Comp 1 into a new composition. This process will allow you to add a new layer behind all the layers in Comp 1 and yet leave that new layer unaffected by the adjustment layer. The result will be that as all the layers in Comp 1 flip backwards, the layer in the new composition will remain in place behind all the other layers.

First, you'll create a new composition using the same settings as Comp 1.

1 Choose Composition > New Composition.

2 Leave all settings as they are so they match your first composition, and click OK. Composition settings default to the most recently used settings.

3 Notice how Comp 2 opens as another tab in the Composition window.

4 Drag O.mov from the Project window to the Time Layout window so it snaps to the center of the Comp2 Composition window. The Time Layout window now also has two tabs.

5 Drag Comp 1 from the Project window into the Time Layout window. It is now a layer in Comp 2.

6 Notice how O.mov shows through the black ring in the L.psd layer. The ring represents the alpha channel (transparent area), so any layers placed behind it show through.

7 Press the Home key, and then press the spacebar to preview the nested compositions. Because O.mov is not affected by the adjustment layer, it does not flip backwards with the rest of the layers; instead it appears as the new background.

Using RAM Preview

In After Effects, you can preview your composition at the frames per second (fps) set for your composition using the RAM Preview option. When you use RAM Preview, After Effects renders as many frames as it can given the amount of RAM available on your system. Then, if your system configuration allows, it plays back those frames at the frames per second of your composition.

In the Info palette, After Effects displays the number of frames requested for RAM preview and the number it can render and hold in RAM. To change the number of frames requested, change the size of the work area of your composition. For more information about previewing your composition, see "Previewing the composition" on page 53.

1 Press the Home key to return the current time to the beginning of the composition.

2 In the Time Controls palette, click the RAM Preview button.

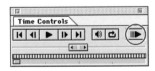

Note the information displayed in the Info palette.

3 If After Effects can't load all the frames for the composition, lower the composition's resolution: in the Composition window, select Half or Quarter from the resolution menu. For optimal results, keep resolution and magnification the same: for magnification select 50% (for Half) or 25% (for Quarter). Then click the RAM Preview button again.

Note: If you turned off the Continuously Rasterize switch for the N.ai layer, it will preview with a somewhat jagged appearance.

Adding and previewing audio

Now you'll add audio to your composition. You can import, edit, and preview audio just as you can any other footage file. You can even apply audio effects and set keyframes for audio layers to animate effect controls. Audio files can consist of any kind of audio, from music to spoken voice. You can also import a file containing both audio and video.

By default, audio previews play for only 4-second intervals. You can change this default in the Preferences dialog box.

1 Make sure the current-time marker is at the beginning of the composition.

2 Drag P.aif from the Project window into the Time Layout window.

3 Press the period (.) on the numeric keypad to preview the audio file.

Note: You can also preview audio and video together using RAM preview by clicking the audio button (◉) in the Time Controls palette, and then clicking the RAM Preview button.

Rendering the project

Rendering converts your final composition into a finished movie, ready for playback on the media of your choice. Rendering speed depends on the complexity of the composition, the speed of your computer, and the render settings you choose. For details about rendering, see Chapter 11 in the *Adobe After Effects 4.0 User Guide*.

1 If you turned off Continuously Rasterize for the N.ai layer, double-click the Comp 1 file in the Project folder and then, in the Time Layout window, click the Continuously Rasterize switch for the N.ai layer to turn it back on.

2 In the Project window, select Comp 2, and choose Composition > Make Movie.

3 Locate and open the Tour folder on your hard disk, and then type **HOT.mov** for the name and click Save.

Note: *After Effects for Windows adds the default file extension .AVI to the name of the movie when you first specify it. In step 7, when you select the QuickTime Movie format, the file extension is automatically changed to .MOV.*

The Render Queue window opens.

4 Choose Custom from the Render Settings pop-up menu. The Render Settings dialog box appears.

5 Choose Best for Quality, and Full for Resolution. Leave all the other settings as they are and click OK.

6 Click the word Lossless to open the Output Module Settings dialog box.

7 Select QuickTime Movie for the format. If you're using After Effects for Windows, a QuickTime dialog box appears. In the dialog box, choose Animation and Millions of Colors. Then click OK.

8 Select Import into Project when done.

9 Choose RGB for Channels, Millions of Colors for Depth, and Premultiplied (With Black) for Color.

10 Select Audio Output, and choose 44.100 KHz from the first pop-up menu in the Audio section. Choose 16-Bit from the second menu and Stereo from the third menu. Click OK.

11 Click Render. When rendering is complete, After Effects chimes and adds the finished movie to the Project window. Simply double-click Hot.mov to play the movie.

Getting to Know the Work Area

This first lesson introduces you to some basic concepts and features of After Effects.

In this lesson, you'll take a look at some basic features of After Effects while viewing a completed project—an inviting opener for a promotional videotape being produced for a performing-arts center. This opener includes music provided by the fictional client as well as backgrounds and textures originated by you or culled from your stock library. During this lesson, you will examine windows, features, and the files that you'll use in Lesson 2, "Ballet Special Bumper," when you actually create a movie.

This lesson covers the following topics:

- Identifying and organizing palettes and windows
- Identifying, color coding, and sorting source material
- Altering resolution, quality, and zoom settings
- Working with the Composition and Time Layout windows
- Navigating through time
- Playing and previewing a composition
- Identifying layer switches
- Displaying layer properties

It should take approximately 1 to 2 hours to complete this project.

Viewing the final project

Before you create any project in this book, you'll take a look at the finished movie, 01Final.mov.

To watch the QuickTime movie, you need to have the MoviePlayer application installed on your computer. You'll be using MoviePlayer to view many of the QuickTime movies you create in Adobe After Effects. See "Installing QuickTime 3.0 (or later) and MoviePlayer 2.1 (or later)" on page 4.

1 Double-click the 01Final.mov file in the 01Lesson folder to open the final QuickTime movie, and then click the Play button in the Time Controls palette or press the K key on your keyboard.

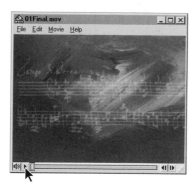

This project was created entirely from still images that were imported into After Effects and animated. The musical manuscript overlays the painted background and pans from right to left while type zooms in and rotates a quarter turn. Finally, a sequence of composer images is displayed, with a harpsichord accompaniment.

2 When you are finished, exit from the MoviePlayer application.

Video terminology

Before using After Effects, you should familiarize yourself with the following terms:

Alpha channel Color digital images often consist of three channels, one composed of red information, one of green information, and one of blue information (called RGB for short). In addition, a computer image or footage may have a fourth, invisible channel that defines transparent areas for the footage item or layer that contains the channel. With imported items, an alpha channel provides a way to store both the footage and its transparency information in a single file without disturbing the footage item's other color channels. Each After Effects layer contains one alpha channel, which can accommodate an alpha channel included with a footage item.

Footage item The source material for a movie. A footage item can be a movie, a still image, or an audio file. In After Effects, a footage item is a pointer to a file stored on a hard disk.

Frame In video, film, and digital movies, a single picture or image. In video, a frame is composed of two fields of 525 lines (NTSC) or 625 lines (PAL or SECAM), which are interlaced and displayed sequentially.

Frame rate The speed at which film or video frames are captured or displayed. The frame rate (or time base) used for video in North America is 30 fps; therefore, one second of footage contains 30 frames. (The NTSC, or National Television Standards Committee, broadcast video format is actually 29.97 fps.) Many countries use the PAL (Phase Alteration Line) or SECAM (Systéme Électronic Pour Couleur Avec Mémoire) video standard with a 25-fps frame rate. Film plays at 24 fps.

SMPTE Timecode The SMPTE (Society of Motion Picture and Television Engineers) timecode standard used to identify each frame (and the duration) of a file in terms of Hours:Minutes:Seconds:Frames. With a frame rate set to 30 frames per second, a file duration of 00:06:51:15 indicates that the footage plays for 6 minutes and 51 seconds and 15 frames (15 frames being 0.5 second).

Getting started

Every After Effects movie starts as a project—a collection of moving images, still images, and audio that you organize into *compositions*. In the compositions, the elements are organized along a timeline. The concept is similar to working with page-layout software. You import and arrange the elements of your project within the compositions that you create.

In this introductory lesson, you will open both a new project and a project that has already been constructed, and explore palettes and windows.

1 To ensure that the tools and palettes function exactly as described in this lesson, delete or deactivate (by renaming) the After Effects preferences file. See "Restoring default preferences" on page 6.

2 Start the After Effects application. An untitled Project window appears.

After Effects opens with all palettes displayed, along with the Project window in the left corner. To display a specific palette, you can select it in the Window menu or open it directly with a command key. To display or hide all palettes, press Tab.

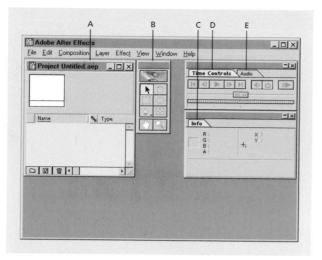

A. *Project window* B. *Toolbox* C. *Info palette*
D. *Time Controls palette* E. *Audio palette*

• The *Project* window contains links to all the elements of your project, such as moving images, still images, and audio.

• The *toolbox* contains tools for moving elements, rotating layers, magnifying images, and creating and editing masks. To open or close it, press Ctrl+1 (Windows) or Command+1 (Mac OS).

• The *Info* palette provides important feedback as to color values, pixel coordinates, in and out times, and other information. To open or close it, press Ctrl+2 (Windows) or Command+2 (Mac OS).

• The *Time Controls* palette gives tape-deck-like control over time in your projects. To open or close it, press Ctrl+3 (Windows) or Command+3 (Mac OS).

• The *Audio* palette gives fader-like control over the audio levels of a layer. To open or close it, press Ctrl+4 (Windows) or Command+4 (Mac OS).

3 Choose File > Open. Select the 01Proj.aep file in the 01Lesson folder. If you are prompted that some files have changed, click OK.

Your screen now shows some additional windows, such as the Composition window and its Time Layout window. You'll learn more about these windows later in this lesson.

You will explore this project while familiarizing yourself with the After Effects program's rich feature set. Don't be afraid of making a mess!

Arranging windows and palettes

Palettes help you monitor and modify artwork. By default, the Time Controls palette and the Audio palette are grouped. You can group other windows and palettes in this way. To show or hide a palette as you work, choose the appropriate window or palette name from the Window menu. If the window or palette name has a checkmark on the menu, choosing it conceals the entire group.

You can reorganize your work space in various ways. Try these techniques:

• To hide or display all open palettes and the toolbox, press Tab.

• To make a palette appear at the front of its group, click the palette's tab.

*Click the Audio tab to move
the palette to the front.*

• To move an entire palette group, drag its title bar.

• To rearrange or separate a palette group, drag a palette's tab. Dragging a palette outside of an existing group creates a new group.

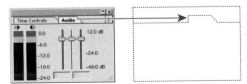

*Palettes are grouped (left). Click and drag the palette
tab to separate a palette from the group (right).*

• To move a palette to another group, drag the palette's tab to that group.

• To display a palette or window menu, position the pointer on the triangle in the upper right corner of the palette or window, and hold down the mouse button. (Not all windows and palettes have such a menu.)

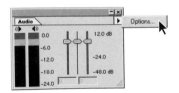

• To change the height of a palette (except the Time Controls or Info palette), drag its lower right corner.

• To collapse a group to the palette titles only, click the minimize/maximize box (Windows) or the resize box (Mac OS). Or double-click a palette's tab. You can still access the menu of a collapsed palette.

Note: If you're working with a second monitor, you may want to drag the Composition window to this additional monitor. Press Ctrl+Shift+\ (Windows) or Command+Shift+\ (Mac OS) to resize a 640 x 480 composition to fill a second monitor.

Project window

The Project window in the upper left corner of the screen contains links to all of the source material used in this project, as well as all of the compositions that have been created. Each icon indicates the type of source material—a Photoshop image, an Adobe Illustrator file, a QuickTime movie, an audio file, or a composition.

An After Effects project does not actually contain any of the source material you use to create a movie (with the exception of simple solid-color shapes). Instead, the project points to the original source material wherever it is stored. For this reason, it is important not to delete the source material after you create a project, and to be careful about moving source files.

A project contains all of the information needed to create a movie, such as how all the source material is organized over time and how it is modified by the various features After Effects offers.

When you select an item in the Project window, a thumbnail of its image is shown in the upper part of this window, and additional information, such as its size, duration, and how many times it is used in the Project, is shown to the right.

1 Resize the Project window by dragging the resize box in the lower right corner to the right, so that you can see more of the information in the window.

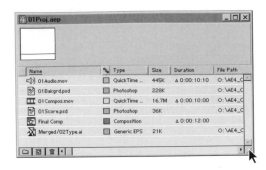

2 Single-click the Score.psd footage item, which is an Adobe Photoshop file.

Notice that a thumbnail appears, showing the item's dimensions as 490 pixels wide by 155 pixels high. It has a color depth of millions of colors. The + indicates that an alpha channel (transparency information) is included with the image. The word *premultiplied* indicates the type of alpha channel in the image. Note too that Score.psd is listed as being used one time in the project.

3 Single-click the footage item named Final Comp, which is a composition. It contains all the elements of the final movie for this project, and its Composition and Time Layout windows are currently open.

Examine the thumbnail that appears at the top of the Project window. This item is identified as having a size of 320 x 240, a duration of 0:00:12:00 (12 seconds), and a frame rate of 30 frames per second (fps).

4 Select the other footage items, and examine the thumbnail information for each one.

5 Click Type in the Project window, and notice how the Project window re-arranges itself.

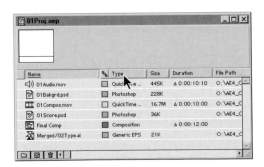

6 Also notice the colors used to quickly identify file type. Type color is a preference you can set. After Effects default colors match the default colors of Adobe Premiere. Click Name again to return the list to alphabetical order by name. You can sort source material by any category heading by clicking the category name just above your list of sources.

7 Right-click (Windows) or Control-click (Mac OS) a category name and then choose a name to show or hide it. An underline in the menu shows the current sorting method. You can also resize a column by dragging the right edge of the heading.

8 Return the Project window to its original size by using the resize box in the lower right corner of the window.

Composition window

The Composition window is where you create a composition (or comp), arranging the different footage items as layers, and animating the layers by using the myriad options that After Effects offers. Think of the composition as a stage where you assemble the actors and control their movements.

There are a number of menus, toggles, and informational displays along the bottom of the window that are of interest. You'll take a brief look at some of these controls now. More detail will be provided throughout the rest of the lessons in this book.

*A. Magnification menu **B.** Safe-zones icon **C.** Time display*
D. Resolution menu

Magnification

The Magnification menu controls the zoom level at which you are viewing the displayed composition. If you are working with a 320 x 240 project, this should be currently set to 100%.

1 Click the Magnification menu, and select 50%. The magnification of the image is reduced.

Changing the magnification changes the viewing size of the pixels in the window and does not affect the actual image data.

Notice that the entire image shrinks in size, but the Composition window itself stays the same. You now see the gray working area outside the frame of the composition. The Score.psd layer is partially positioned in the gray area outside the displayed image area. This item moves across the image area during the composition.

2 Return the magnification to its original setting (100%). You can also use the period and comma keys to zoom in and out.

3 To select the zoom tool, click the magnifying glass icon in the lower right corner of the toolbox. As you move the pointer over the image in the Composition window, it will change to a magnifying glass with a + in the middle.

4 Click anywhere in the Composition window, and notice that the image zooms by a factor of 2 and centers on the point where you clicked.

5 Hold down the Alt key (Windows) or the Option key (Mac OS). Notice that the + inside the magnifying glass turns into a − (minus sign) signifying that the tool will zoom out. Click in the window again, and notice that the image zooms out.

6 Select the selection tool in the toolbox.

To magnify the view in the Time Layout window, see "Magnifying the Time Graph" on page 82.

Time display

The Time Display shows the current time in the composition. The time is displayed in the Composition window in SMPTE timecode—hours:minutes:seconds:frames. In this case, the Time Display shows 0:00:05:00, or 5 seconds into the composition. Clicking the Time Display in any window will bring up the Go To Time dialog box, which you use to move to different points in time in the composition. For more on SMPTE timecode, see "Video terminology" on page 33.

Window snapshots

When you want to compare one view to another in any window, you can take a *snapshot* of one view and temporarily replace the window image with the snapshot.

1 Click the Take Snapshot button to take a snapshot.

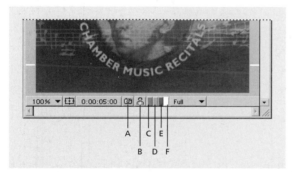

A. *Take snapshot* B. *Display snapshot* C. *Red channel*
D. *Green channel* E. *Blue channel* F. *Alpha channel*

2 Press the Home key on your keyboard to move to the beginning of the composition. The Composition window displays the footage items as they appear at that point in time.

3 Position the pointer over the Display Snapshot button and hold down the mouse button to display the snapshot in the window temporarily.

4 Choose Edit > Undo Time Change to return to the original time (05:00).

After Effects automatically names the Undo function to clarify what you are about to Undo. AfterEffects provides 99 levels of Undo. The default number is 20, but you can set the number of steps you would like to Undo by choosing File > Preferences > General.

To redo a command, select Edit > Redo or use the keyboard shortcut Ctrl+Shift+Z *(Windows) or Command+Shift+Z (Mac OS).*

Color and alpha channel display

You can preview the color channels of an image in grayscale by positioning the pointer over a button and holding down the mouse button (see the previous illustration). The white Channel Display button lets you preview the alpha channel. (In this example, there is nothing defined for the alpha channel, so it appears completely empty.) To see channel information in the appropriate color (for example, red for the red channel and so on), hold down the Alt key (Windows) or the Option key (Mac OS) as you hold down the mouse button.

Resolution

Just to the right of the channel display icons is the Resolution menu. Full is currently selected in this menu.

1 In the Resolution menu, choose Quarter.

Resolution affects the actual number of pixels being processed to display an image in the Composition window. The image now appears jagged since only every fourth pixel (both width and height) is being processed. This allows After Effects to process the composition up to 16 times faster. If screen updates are taking too long, try working with a lower resolution.

You can match the magnification to the resolution. This is especially important when you will be using RAM Preview, described later in this lesson.

2 Choose 25% from the Magnification menu to match the frame size to Quarter resolution.

3 Double-click the zoom tool in the toolbox to return the magnification to 100%.

4 In the Resolution menu, choose Full.

5 To switch back to the pointer from the zoom tool, select the selection tool in the toolbox.

As you work in After Effects, you might notice that the pointer cycles from black to white. This indicates that After Effects is processing commands and updating the display. If you see too much of the cycling arrow, reducing the resolution will help you work faster.

Note: You can still choose menu items and resize windows while the pointer cycles.

Another indication that After Effects is processing and updating your work is the panel to the right of the Resolution menu. A moving bar in this panel indicates activity.

Time Layout window

Every Composition window has an associated Time Layout window with the same name. Whereas the Composition window is used to position items in space, the Time Layout window allows you to position items in time and control the way they change over time.

If you close the Time Layout window or the Composition window, you can open either one again by clicking the Comp Family button above the right scroll bar in either window. You can also press the \ (backslash) key to do this.

If you closed both windows, you can reopen them by double-clicking the Final Comp footage item in the Project window.

1 Close the Final Comp Composition window.

2 Click the Comp Family button above the right scroll bar of the Time Layout window. The Final Comp Composition window reappears.

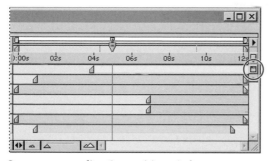 

Opens corresponding Composition window

Layers

A composition usually contains multiple items. Each item in a composition is referred to as a *layer*. A layer consists of only one item, be it a Photoshop image, a QuickTime movie, an EPS file, an audio file, or another composition.

You can identify which layers are used in this composition by reading their names along the left side of the Time Layout window. Miniatures of the icons used in the Project window identify the media type of each layer, as well as the color used to label it and the corresponding duration bar in the Time Layout window. Each layer also has a number that represents its stacking order. Number 1 is on top, and so on.

Try these basic techniques in the Time Layout window when working with layers:

• To select a layer, click the layer name.

• To deselect a layer, click another layer name or click in an open area of the window.

• To display or hide outlines of layer properties, click the triangle to the left of the layer name.

Layer ordering

Layers are stacked in the Time Layout window in the same order they are stacked in the composition, from top to bottom. This is important for arranging how layers appear in relation to other layers.

1 Resize the Time Layout window by using the resize area in the lower right corner.

2 Select the Merged/Type.ai layer (layer 2) and drag it down until a horizontal bar appears below the layer named Bakgrd.psd (layer 6).

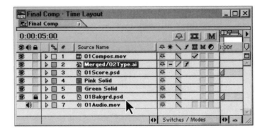

Notice how the Merged/Type.ai layer disappears in the Composition window. It is now underneath, or behind, the background layer that fills the entire composition.

3 Choose Edit > Undo Layer Reordering.

Time graph

Before examining the Layer Switches panel and the Transfer Modes panel next to the layer names, you'll collapse the panel and take a look at the layer time graph.

1 Click the double-triangle icon in the Time Layout window to collapse the Layer Switches panel.

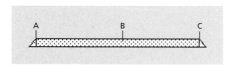

Window expansion icon

The time graph, which currently shows increments of two seconds, displays the status of the layers through time, from left to right.

In After Effects, time is displayed in SMPTE timecode, hours:minutes:seconds:frames. The blue current-time marker indicates the point in time displayed in the Composition window.

2 Notice that the current-time marker is set at 0:00:05:00 (5 seconds). The layers that you see in the Composition window represent what you see at the 5-second point in your composition. The time in the Time Layout window matches the time displayed in the Composition window.

Each layer has a *duration bar*, which represents the length of that particular layer. The left end of the duration bar is the *In point*, where the layer starts in time, and the right end of the bar is the *Out point*, where the layer ends in time. There are triangular handles at each end, but the actual In or Out point is the edge of the duration bar.

A. In point B. Duration bar C. Out point

3 Notice that the Merged/Type.ai layer's In point is at 1 second and that the Compos.mov layer's In point is at 4 seconds.

Since both the Merged/Type.ai and the Compos.mov layers fade in, you may not see them in the Composition window until a few frames after their In points.

4 Drag the blue current-time marker all the way to the left, to time 00:00. Notice how the Merged/Type.ai and Compos.mov layers disappear from the Composition window, because they do not come into the composition until later in time.

Layer switches

Now that you've had a general overview of the Time Layout window, let's take a look at some of the details.

1 Click the window expansion icon at the bottom of the Time Layout window to display the Switches panel.

After Effects provides many ways to display layers inside a composition. Most of the Switches that control these options are arranged in columns to the right of the layer names. Three additional switches are located to the left of the layer names. You'll take a brief look at the switches before moving on to the next lesson.

Switches in the Layer Switches panel

The Layer Switches panel contains seven switches that can be set for each individual layer. Above these switches are three more switches that interact with the layer switches.

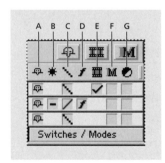

A. Shy *B. Collapse* *C. Quality*
D. Effect *E. Frame Blending*
F. Motion Blur *G. Adjustment Layer*

 Shy switch: When set, and the Hide Shy Layers button is also selected, layers will be hidden in the Time Layout window.

1 Click the Shy switch to the right of the Merged/Type.ai layer name. The icon should change to a box with a line, with no person inside. (You cannot see the little person peering over the wall.)

2 Click the Shy switch next to the Score.psd layer in the Time Layout window.

3 Now that you have selected a couple of layers to make shy, select the Hide Shy Layers button in the top section of the Switches panel in the Time Layout window. Notice that both Layers now disappear from the Time Layout window, but no change occurs in the Composition window.

4 Deselect Hide Shy Layers; notice that the layer reappears in the Time Layout window.

You use the Shy switch to cut down on clutter in your Time Layout window.

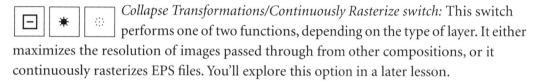

Collapse Transformations/Continuously Rasterize switch: This switch performs one of two functions, depending on the type of layer. It either maximizes the resolution of images passed through from other compositions, or it continuously rasterizes EPS files. You'll explore this option in a later lesson.

Quality switch: Layers can be represented in draft quality and best quality. These two states are represented by icons that include a dotted backslash, and a solid forward slash, respectively.

5 Try resetting the quality for some of the layers. Most of the time you will want to work in Draft mode, for faster screen redraw.

Effects switch: A box appears under this column if one or more effects have been applied to a layer.

In this example, a drop shadow effect has been applied to the Merged/Type.ai layer, so a box with an *f* appears next to the layer name. You can turn layer effects off and on for a given layer by clicking its Effects switch box.

Frame Blending switch, Motion Blur switch: These two switches provide controls for blending and blurring effects that will be discussed in future lessons.

Adjustment Layer switch: A box appears under this column if an adjustment layer has been applied to a layer. You can turn off the adjustment layer by clicking this box.

The Time Layout window has three additional buttons that interact with the layer switches:

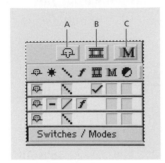

A. *Hide Shy Layers*
B. *Enable Frame Blending*
C. *Enable Motion Blur*

Hide Shy Layers: As you just saw, this button makes the layers set to Shy disappear from the Time Layout window; they will still appear in the Composition window.

Enable Frame Blending: This option calculates Frame Blending for the layers with this switch selected.

Enable Motion Blur: This button calculates Motion Blur for the layers with this switch selected.

Most of these switches may be overridden when you actually render a movie from this composition. This lets you work more quickly at lower quality and with certain effects turned off, and then automatically turn them all back on when you render the final movie.

Video, Audio, and Lock switches

The Audio, Video, and Lock switches are located in a panel to the left of the layer names.

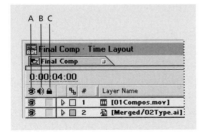

A. *Video switch* *B.* *Audio switch*
C. *Lock switch*

Video switch: If a layer has any image information (most layers do, except an audio-only source), this switch displays the layer in the Composition window (open eye) or hides it (closed eye). If no eye icon is present, the layer contains no image information.

1 Click the eye icon of the Merged/Type.ai layer. Notice that the layer disappears from the Composition window. The layer name remains in the layer list in the Time Layout window. Click the box below the eye icon to redisplay the layer.

Audio switch: If a layer contains audio or is an audio-only source, this switch turns the audio on (speaker icon inside a box) and off (empty box). If the layer has no audio, no box will appear. If a footage item contains audio, and you do not want to use it in your movie, click this switch to turn it off.

2 Click the Audio switch in the Audio.mov layer.

Lock switch: When the Lock switch is set, you cannot select or alter the properties of this layer.

3 Click the Bakgrd.psd layer and notice that the Lock switch is black and that the layer cannot be selected. To unlock the layer, simply click the Lock switch.

Layer properties

So far, you have been concentrating mainly on display and rendering-related functions. Now it's time to get to the core of After Effects—layer properties. Each image layer may have a variety of properties assigned to it, including the following: Masks, Mask Modes, Mask Feathers, Anchor Point, Position, Scale, Rotation, and Opacity. Changing these properties over the course of time is the key to creating animation in After Effects.

In the final movie you noticed that Merged/Type.ai increases in scale over time, as well as rotates a quarter turn. Several of the elements fade in, or change their opacity. All this animation was achieved by changing layer properties.

Let's take a quick look at how properties are displayed.

1 In the Time Layout window, select the layer named Score.psd. Notice the small triangular arrow to the left of the layer name; it should be pointing to the right.

2 Click that triangle to expand the outline and view the properties underneath. With the triangle pointing down, you should now see the labels *Mask, Effects,* and *Transform,* with triangles next to them.

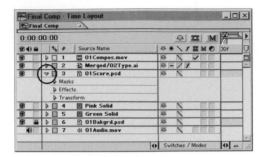

3 Click the triangle next to Transform. Notice that the remaining layer properties, Anchor Point, Position, Scale, Rotation, and Opacity, appear. Their current values are also displayed underneath the layer's switch settings. (You may need to expand your Time Layout window to see everything.)

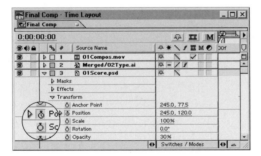

The stopwatch icon to the left of each of the properties is used for setting keyframes. When the stopwatch icon is turned on it shows watch hands on its face indicating that the layer has been animated (that it changes over time).

4 Click the triangle again to collapse the Transform outline.

5 Click the triangle next to Score.psd to collapse the layer outline.

6 Find the layer named Audio.mov, click the triangle next to it, and then click the triangle next to Audio. You'll see two properties, one named Levels and another named Waveform.

7 Click the triangle next to Audio.mov again to collapse the outline.

As you can see, displaying all of the properties for a layer can take up a lot of space on the screen. It's possible to display only specific properties for a selected layer by using the keyboard shortcuts. These shortcuts open one property at a time. To view more than one property, you can add and subtract properties by holding down the Shift key as you select their key equivalents. Subtracting a property does not remove it but only hides it from view.

8 Select the Score.psd layer, and then press the P key on the keyboard. The Position property appears.

9 Press the T key on the keyboard. The Position property disappears, and the Opacity property appears.

10 Press the Shift and P keys on the keyboard. The Position property appears in addition to the Opacity property.

See your After Effects Quick Reference Card for a complete list of the available keyboard shortcuts.

11 Experiment with other shortcuts.

You'll explore the other elements in the windows throughout the lessons in this book.

Navigating through time

After Effects provides a number of ways to move through time in your compositions.

1 Drag the blue current-time marker to a new location on the time graph. The Composition window reflects the change.

2 Click the 02s (2-second) mark in the time ruler. The current-time marker jumps to the point in time where you clicked. Once again, the Composition window reflects the change.

3 Choose View > Go to Time or press Ctrl+G (Windows) or Command+G (Mac OS). In the Go To Time dialog box, type **400** (4 seconds, 0 frames—you don't need to type the colons between the numbers), and click OK.

The current-time marker moves to 04 on the time graph, and the Composition window changes to reflect the new position in time.

Wherever you see a time display, such as the one in the Time Layout window or in the Composition window, you can click it to display the Go To Time dialog box.

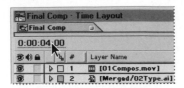

4 Click the time display in the Time Layout window, type **800**, and then click OK to move the current-time marker to 8 seconds.

5 Try navigating through time by clicking the time display in the Composition or Time Layout windows, or by moving the current-time marker.

6 Press the Home key to return to the beginning of the composition.

Setting a work area

Setting a work area is useful for limiting the amount of composition that will be previewed or rendered. The work area is defined by the markers (triangles) that are at the left and right ends of the time ruler. You will experiment with the work area now.

1 To set the start of the work area, drag the left triangle to the desired time in the Time Layout window.

2 To set the end of the work area, drag the right triangle to the desired time in the Time Layout window.

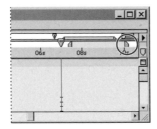

Work-area markers

You can also press the B key on your keyboard to begin the work area at the current time, and press the N key to end the work area at the current time.

Previewing the composition

After Effects provides four different methods of previewing a composition: RAM Preview, standard preview, manual preview, and wireframe preview.

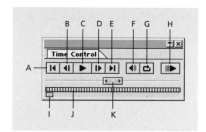

A. First Frame B. Frame Reverse C. Play
D. Frame Advance E. Last Frame F. Audio
G. Loop H. RAM Preview I. Time indicator
J. Jog control K. Shuttle control

Standard preview

This type of preview does not play the composition in real time, nor does it play any audio in the composition.

1 Click the Play button in the Time Controls palette. After Effects plays each frame of the composition.

2 Click the Pause button to stop the playback.

3 Set the resolution to Quarter using the menu at the bottom of the Composition window.

4 Click the Play button. Notice that the lower resolution allows the composition to play faster.

5 Click the Pause button, and then choose Full from the Resolution menu in the Composition window.

Depending on the speed of your system, the number of layers in the composition and the complexity of any effects applied, playback using the Time Controls palette can vary in speed. In order to preview motion in real time, you need to build a wireframe preview or a RAM Preview.

Manual preview

You can use the shuttle and jog controls to manually preview a composition.

In addition to previewing, you can use buttons in the Time Controls palette to navigate through a composition and examine individual frames. The Frame Advance, Frame Reverse, First Frame, and Last Frame buttons are all used for navigation.

1 Click the Last Frame button to move to the end of the composition.

2 Drag the Shuttle control slightly to the left to move slowly backward in the composition.

3 Now drag the Time Indicator toward the middle of the Jog control to move to that position in the composition. For finer control, drag inside the Jog control itself.

4 Click the First Frame button to go to the beginning of the composition.

> ### About RAM Preview
>
> *This option plays a preview of the frames (including audio) at the frame rate of your composition or as fast as your system allows. The number of frames previewed depends on the total number of frames requested for the preview and the number it can render. RAM Preview previews only the span of time you specify as the work area. Before you preview, check which frames are designated as the work area.*
>
> —From the Adobe After Effects User Guide, Chapter 6

RAM Preview

The only way to view your composition in real time with all the effects applied, other than *rendering* a movie, is to use RAM Preview. (Rendering processes the composition's layers, settings, and effects, turning it into a finished QuickTime movie. You'll render a movie in upcoming lessons.)

The number of frames you can preview with RAM Preview is dependent upon the amount of RAM in your system. With RAM Preview, you can also preview audio, provided the Audio button is selected and audio is enabled in the Time Layout window. For optimal results when using RAM Preview, the resolution and magnification must match. For example, use Half resolution with 50% magnification.

1 Drag the current-time marker to about 00:60, and then press the N key to set the end of the work area to that time.

2 Click the RAM Preview button in the Time Controls palette.

After Effects builds a preview of the work area, displaying a red bar at the bottom of the time ruler to show the progress. The preview plays when it's finished. By default, the Loop button is selected, which causes the preview to play continuously in a loop. Click the RAM Preview button or press any key to stop the preview.

3 Click the Loop button to deselect it, and this time press the 0 key on your keyboard's numeric keypad to start RAM Preview. The preview plays once and stops.

You can also build a preview using every other frame, which is useful if your system doesn't have enough RAM for a full preview.

4 Shift-click the RAM Preview button to build a new preview using every other frame. Notice that it takes half the time to build the preview.

5 Click the Audio button to deselect it, and then press the 0 key on the numeric keypad again. The preview plays without audio this time. Click the Audio button and the Loop button again to select them.

Wireframe preview

In a *wireframe* preview, each layer in your composition is represented by an outline of either the layer, or of an alpha channel or mask, if one is present. Because only outlines are used, this preview method is the quickest way to generate a preview of motion only.

1 Press the Home key on your keyboard to return to the beginning of the composition, and then deselect all layers.

2 To view a wireframe preview, press Alt+0 on the numeric keypad (Windows) or Option+0 on the numeric keypad (Mac OS). Watch the Info palette as After Effects prepares the preview.

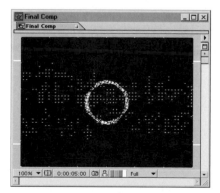

3 Press any key to stop the preview.

Rendering a movie

When you have finished assembling and editing an After Effects composition, you can create several different types of output.

You will begin rendering projects in a later lesson.

1 Choose File > Exit (Windows) or File > Quit (Mac OS).

2 Click No (Windows) or Don't Save (Mac OS) to close the file without saving changes.

Now that you have become familiar with some of the windows and palettes in After Effects, you are ready to begin creating movies with animation, video, and sound.

Ballet Special Bumper

In this lesson, you'll create a short promotional video, using more advanced settings and controls for animation.

Using video footage that comes to us courtesy of the Oakland Ballet, you will create a composition for a 10-second bumper to be used for a fictitious television special on ballet. A *bumper* is a short clip, similar to a commercial, informing TV viewers of what's coming up. They are usually shown before a commercial; the opening credits of the actual program follow the commercial.

This lesson builds on your knowledge of setting keyframes and expands on the concept of animating layers over space and time.

As you create this project, you will focus on using the Basic Text effect for creating text "on the fly," changing duration and In points and Out points of layers, and modifying a motion path.

This lesson covers the following topics:

- Trimming a layer
- Using the Basic Text effect
- Copying and pasting keyframes
- Aligning and distributing layers
- Defining spatial and temporal interpolation
- Creating and modifying a motion path
- Using roving keyframes

At the end of this lesson, you'll have a 10-second bumper for a television special.

It should take approximately 3 to 5 hours to complete this project.

Viewing the final project

Before you begin, take a look at the finished movie that you create in this lesson.

1 Double-click the 02Final.mov file in the 02Lesson folder to open the final QuickTime movie, and then click the Play button.

This movie consists of digitized video as QuickTime video footage, an audio file, and a number of animated pieces of text created within Adobe After Effects. Several different motion controls are used to get the text to swirl off the screen.

The featured dancer is Jill Taylor, of the Oakland Ballet, dancing Tchaichovsky's Sugar Plum Fairy from the Nutcracker Suite.

2 When you are finished, exit from the MoviePlayer application.

Getting started

1 To ensure that the tools and palettes function exactly as described in this lesson, delete or deactivate (by renaming) the After Effects preferences file. See "Restoring default preferences" on page 6.

2 Start the After Effects application. An untitled Project window appears.

3 Choose File > Save As, name the file **02Work.aep**, and save it in the Projects folder.

Size and memory considerations

The final goal of this project is to create a quick composition that will be used to present an idea for a bumper. For the sake of reducing disk space and memory requirements, the instructions are designed around a 320 x 240 format.

Using the footage and layer windows

You'll start by setting up the composition, importing a footage file, and examining the Footage and Layer windows.

1 Choose Composition > New Composition, and type **Ballet Bumper** for the name.

💡 *You can also create a new composition by clicking the composition icon (between the folder and the trash can icons at the bottom of the Project Window).*

2 Choose Medium, 320 x 240 from the Frame Size menu. The Lock Aspect Ratio check box indicates that a 4:3 aspect ratio will be maintained.

The aspect ratio describes the ratio of width to height in the frame dimensions. Most frame sizes for video and multimedia have a 4:3 aspect ratio. Some motion-picture frame sizes have a wider aspect ratio, such as 16:9.

3 Make sure Square Pixels is selected for Pixel Aspect Ratio.

For all the projects in this book, you will use the Square Pixels option—the standard used for computer video. Pixels with a D-1 ratio are rectangular in shape. You would use this option for proper processing of sources with nonsquare pixel ratios, such as D-1 digital video equipment. For more information, see the "Technical Information" appendix at the back of this book, or see the *Adobe After Effects 4.0 User Guide*.

4 Leave the Resolution set to Full and the Frame Rate to 30 fps.

5 Set the Duration to 11:00 (enter **1100**). Click OK.

6 Choose File > Import > Footage File, open the 02Lesson folder, select Sugar.mov, and click Open.

7 Select the Sugar.mov footage item in the Project window, and note the information to the right of the thumbnail image, which indicates that the item is 34 seconds and 8 frames in duration.

Depending on your future projects, you may be working with high-quality, uncompressed digital video. However, for this lesson, the Sugar.mov footage was captured at 15 fps using Cinepak compression to reduce disk space and memory requirements.

8 Double-click the Sugar.mov footage item in the Project window. The footage appears in a QuickTime Footage window.

9 Click the Play button in the Footage window to view the footage. You can play QuickTime movies directly within After Effects. When you are finished viewing the movie, click the Pause button, and then close the QuickTime Footage window.

10 Activate the Time Layout window by clicking its title bar, make sure that the current-time marker is set to 00:00 by pressing the Home key or dragging the blue marker, and then drag the Sugar.mov footage item into the Time Layout window.

Although you can drag a footage item into the Composition window and center it manually, dragging the item directly from the Project window into the Time Layout window automatically centers it in the Composition window.

11 Double-click the Sugar.mov layer (in either the Composition window or the Time Layout window). The Sugar.mov Layer window opens.

The Layer window lets you change attributes of an individual layer, such as duration, In and Out points, anchor point path and masks. It contains many of the same controls as you find in the Composition window and the Time Layout window, including a time display, a time ruler, and a current-time marker. Changing an attribute here affects only the instance of the item in your composition, and doesn't affect the source file.

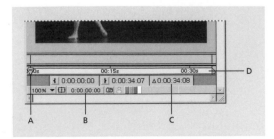

A. Current-time marker B. Time display button
C. Duration D. Time ruler

12 To preview the footage for a few seconds, press the spacebar. (Press the spacebar again to stop the playback.)

Trimming a layer

The original duration of the Sugar.mov footage item is 34 seconds, 8 frames. You need only a small section of video for your bumper, so you're going to set a new duration for the layer by *trimming* the layer in the Layer window. Trimming refers to the subtracting of frames to change a layer's duration.

Notice that the time ruler in the Layer window spans from 0 to 34 seconds, reflecting the entire duration of the source footage. Also note that just as in the Time Layout window, each end of the layer's duration bar has triangular handles indicating the layer's In and Out points.

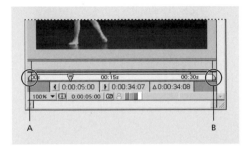

A. In point B. Out point

1 In the Layer window, set the current time to 06:12. You can set the current time by dragging the current-time marker in the Layer window as you would in the Time Layout window, or by clicking the time display button at the bottom of the Layer window.

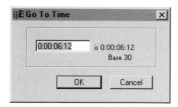

The video changes to reflect the new point in time.

2 To set the new In point to 06:12, click the In button. The layer's In point on the left moves in to the current-time marker at 06:12.

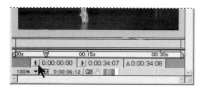

In button

3 Take a look at the Time Layout window and notice that the new In point is automatically positioned at the beginning of the composition, at frame 00:00. The first 6 seconds and 11 frames of the original source video have been subtracted from the layer and the layer has been repositioned to maintain its designated In point of 00:00 in the composition.

The Layer window and the Time Layout window reflect time in two different contexts—the Layer window shows the duration and In and Out points relative to the original footage item itself, and the Time Layout window displays them in relation to the composition.

You can also trim a layer in the Time Layout window by dragging the triangular handle at either end of the layer duration bar.

4 To experiment with trimming the layer in the Layer window, position the current-time marker in the Layer window at 14:12, and then drag the layer's Out-point handle left to the current-time marker. Watch the Info palette as you drag to see the current frame for the Out point.

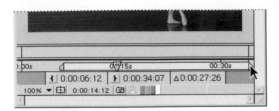

The duration of the footage item is now set to 8 seconds and 1 frame, as you can see in the Layer window's duration display. Trimming a footage item does not affect the length of the original source footage; it merely suppresses frames at the beginning or end of a layer. If you use the footage item twice in a project, you can trim the item two different ways by using each layer's individual Layer windows.

5 Take a look at the Time Layout window, and notice that the layer duration bar reflects the changes you just made. On the right side, the Out point is now positioned at 8:01. Also notice the light-shaded area beyond the right end of the layer duration bar. This shaded area indicates the suppressed frames of the layer.

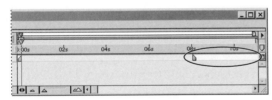

Suppressed frames

6 In the Time Layout window, drag the triangular Out-point handle at the right end of the Sugar.mov layer duration bar to the end of the composition, at 11 seconds.

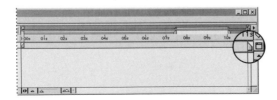

If you drag the layer duration bar and not the triangular handle, you will move the layer duration bar instead of changing the duration of the layer.

7 After you trim the layer, examine the Layer window. The changes you just made are reflected in the Layer window. The final duration of the layer is approximately 11:00.

8 Close the Layer window.

Setting a fade-out

To make this layer fade out at the end of the composition, you will set Opacity keyframes.

1 Set the current time to 09:20 by dragging the blue current-time marker in the Time Layout window, by pressing Ctrl+G (Windows) or Command+G (Mac OS), or by clicking the time display.

2 Click the triangle to the left of the Sugar.mov layer in the Time Layout window, and then click the triangle to the left of Transform to expand the outline, displaying the Transform Properties for this layer.

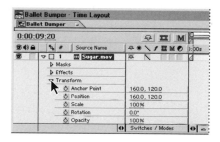

3 Click the stopwatch (👁) next to Opacity to set an Opacity keyframe. Leave the Opacity value at 100%.

4 Set the current time to 10:10, and then click the underlined Opacity value, enter **0**, and click OK.

Do not click the stopwatch again. A new keyframe is set automatically whenever you change a property value.

When you are done working with a layer's properties, it's a good idea to clean up the Time Layout window by collapsing the layer outline.

5 Click the triangle to the left of Sugar.mov to collapse the layer outline. Save the project.

Using the Basic Text effect

When you're ready to add text to your projects, you will most often create the type in another program, such as Adobe Illustrator, and import it into your project. However, you can also create simple text in After Effects by using the Basic Text effect. In this section, you will create several text elements using that effect.

1 Set the current time to 00:00 by pressing the Home key.

The text effect is applied directly to a selected layer. Since there are several different text elements to be designed, you will create a new layer with a solid image, or *solid*, for each element, and then apply the text effect to the new solid.

2 Choose Layer > New Solid, type **Sunday** for the name, set the size to **200** x **100** pixels, leave the color as the default gray, and click OK.

A gray solid layer appears in the Composition window.

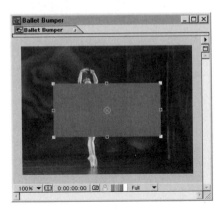

3 Make sure the solid layer is selected in the Time Layout window, and then choose Effect > Text > Basic Text from the Effect menu. The Type dialog box appears.

4 In the text entry box, type **SUNDAY** (uppercase), ensure that the Center Alignment button is selected, and choose Adobe Garamond or a similar font in the Font menu.

Note: To display text in the Basic Text dialog box using the font that you have chosen, the Show Font option in the lower left corner must be selected. Not all fonts can be displayed; if this option is unavailable, choose another font.

5 Click OK.

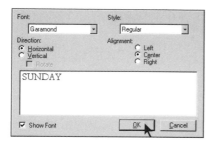

The text appears in the Composition window, in the default color red, and the Effect Controls window appears. You can set the font, size, color, position, and other type characteristics in this window. The Effect Controls window is displayed automatically whenever you apply an effect to a layer. When multiple effects are applied, a single tabbed Effect Controls window contains all controls for all applied effects. You can also display the window at any time by choosing Layer > Open Effect Controls.

6 In the Effect Controls window, click the Text Color swatch, and then use the color picker to select a light color; we used a very pale. Click OK.

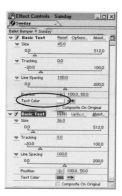

7 To set the font size, click the underlined default Size value in the Effect Controls window, enter **45** in the Slider Control dialog box, and then click OK. You can also use the Size slider.

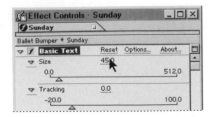

8 Leave Composite on Original display deselected.

Selecting the Composite on Original option will display the original layer to which the text has been applied. (Try selecting this option; if you do, you will see the type composited on the original gray solid layer.)

9 In the Time Layout window, click the triangle to the left of the Sunday layer name to display the layer outline. Then click the triangle next to Effects to display the properties outline. Finally, click the triangle next to the Basic Text effect to display its properties. You can change text effect values here in the Time Layout window as well as in the Effect Controls window.

💡 *To show only the effects for a layer in the Time Layout window, press the E key.*

If you need to edit the text, click Options for the Basic Text effect in the Effect Controls window or in the switches panel of the Time Layout window—to the right of Basic Text.

The text appears jagged because it is in the default Draft quality. (The Quality switch appears as a jagged backslash symbol in the switches panel of the Time Layout window.) Although you could change the quality to Best at this point by clicking the Quality switch, Best quality uses more RAM, so you may want to leave it in Draft quality while working. For more information on the Quality switch, see the After Effects User Guide.

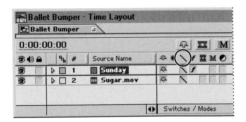

The Basic Text effect is for creating the most basic text; for greater flexibility and control in setting the type, you should import text from an illustration or imaging program, such as Adobe Illustrator or Adobe Photoshop.

10 Close the Effect Controls window and click the triangle for the Sunday layer to collapse its outline.

💡 *To open the Effect Controls window, choose Layer > Open Effect Controls.*

Viewing safe zones and grids

Television sets enlarge a video image and allow some portion of its outer edges to be cut off by the edge of the screen. This is known as overscan. *The amount of overscan is not consistent across television sets, so you should keep important parts of a video image, such as action or titles within margins known as safe zones. You can view safe zones in a Footage, Layer, or Composition window. When you arrange layers in a composition, do the following:*

• *Keep important scene elements, graphics, and actors within the* action-safe *zone.*

• *Keep titles and other text within the* title-safe *zone.*

—From the Adobe After Effects User Guide, Chapter 2

Safe zones

When preparing a composition that will be output to videotape or broadcast, you need to make sure that important elements are placed within the action-safe and title-safe zones. You can change the percentage of safe margin window area in the display preferences.

1 In the Composition window, click the safe-zones icon to the immediate right of the Magnification menu.

Safe zones overlay the composition's image.

2 Drag the text to the upper left corner of the composition, within the title-safe area.

The position point for the Basic Text effect controls is positioned directly on top of the anchor point for the solid layer. When you drag the layer, don't grab the text's position point or you might reposition the text on the solid layer.

To display the safe zones, press the apostrophe key. Pressing the apostrophe key or clicking the safe-zones icon toggles the display off and on.

Animating the text opacity

Now you will animate the text opacity, making the text fade in at the beginning of the composition, and fade out at the end of the composition.

1 Ensure that the Sunday layer is selected in the Time Layout window.

2 With the current time at 00:00, click the triangle to display Transform properties for the Sunday layer, and then click the Opacity stopwatch to set an initial Opacity keyframe. Click the underlined Opacity value (currently 100%), enter **0** in the Opacity dialog box, and click OK.

3 Move the current-time marker to 00:15, click the underlined Opacity value, enter **100**, and then click OK. You should now have two keyframes creating a 15-frame fade in of the text.

4 Move the current-time marker to 09:20, and click the keyframe navigator check box to the left of Opacity to set a keyframe that duplicates the settings of the previous keyframe. The opacity does not change between these two keyframes.

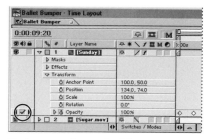

Keyframe navigator check box

5 Set the current time to 10:00, and set the Opacity to **0%**.

6 To watch the fade-in, return to the beginning of the composition; then click the Play button in the Time Controls palette (or press spacebar), and play the first second of the composition. Click Pause (or press spacebar again) when finished.

7 In the Time Layout window, click the layer triangles to collapse the layer outline, and then save the project.

Using the In and Out panels

You will use the same techniques to create and format the second piece of text, and then position it in time by using the In and Out panels.

1 Set the current time to 05:00, and then choose Layer > New Solid, type **afternoon** for the name, set the size to **200** x **100** pixels, leave the color as the default gray, and click OK.

2 Choose Effect > Text > Basic Text.

3 In the text box, type **afternoon** (lowercase), ensure that the Center Alignment button is selected, and choose a font such as Adobe Garamond or a similar font. Choose Italic for Style, and then click OK.

4 To change the color to the same color as the word *SUNDAY*, click the eyedropper in the Effect Controls window, and then click the word *SUNDAY* in the Composition window to sample the color.

5 Set the font size to 30 points. Close the Effect Controls window.

In the Time Layout window, notice that the layer begins at the current-time marker. New layers automatically start at the current-time marker. To change the In point, you will use the In and Out panels.

6 In the Time Layout window, click the Optional panel button at the bottom of the window to display the In and Out panels.

In	Out	Duration	Stretch			
0:00:05:00	0:00:15:29	0:00:11:00	100.0%			
0:00:00:00	0:00:10:29	0:00:11:00	100.0%			
0:00:00:00	0:00:10:28	0:00:10:29	100.0%			

Optional panel button with panels displayed

The In and Out panels appear. Use these panels to display and edit values for In point, Out point, time-stretch duration, and other time options in the Time Layout window.

To move the current time marker to the layer In point, make sure that the layer is selected and press the I key. To go to the layer Out point, press the O key.

7 Click the value in the In field for the Afternoon layer. Type **15** in the Layer In Time dialog box, and click OK. This moves the In point of the layer to 15 frames, without changing the duration of the layer.

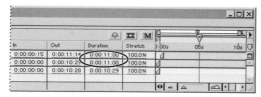

Duration remains at 11:00

8 Click the Optional panel button to collapse the In and Out panels.

9 Drag the Afternoon layer to the upper right corner of the Composition window, slightly lower than *SUNDAY,* and within the title-safe area.

10 Set the Quality to Best by clicking the Quality switch in the Time Layout window.

Animating the text scale and opacity

You'll animate the Afternoon layer to scale up from 0 to 80% at the beginning of the composition, and then to fade out in opacity at the end of the composition.

1 In the Time Layout window, set the current time to 00:15, and then click the triangle for the Afternoon layer. Click the triangle to display the Transform properties, and click the Scale stopwatch to specify an initial Scale keyframe. Set the Scale value to **0**%.

2 Move the current-time marker to 01:00, and set the Scale to **80**%. A keyframe is automatically created.

3 Move the current-time marker to 09:20, and click the Opacity stopwatch to set an Opacity keyframe, leaving the value at 100%.

4 Move the current-time marker to 10:00, and set the Opacity to **0%**. Make sure that you have four keyframes set: two each for the Scale and Opacity properties. Collapse the Afternoon layer outline.

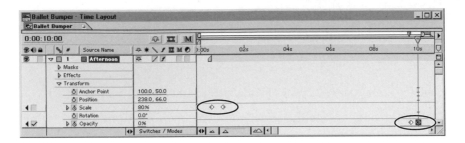

5 To watch the text scale up, return to the beginning of the composition, and then click the Play button in the Time Controls palette (or press spacebar) to play the first few seconds of the composition. Click Pause (or press spacebar again) when finished.

6 Save the project.

Creating the third piece of text

Finally, you will create and animate a third piece of text.

1 Move the current time to 02:00.

2 Choose Layer > New Solid, type **At The** for the name, set the size to **100** x **50** pixels, leave the default color as gray, and then click OK.

3 Make sure the At The layer is selected. Choose Effect > Text > Basic Text, type **at the** (lowercase) in the text entry box, select the Center Alignment button, and choose a font such as Adobe Garamond or a similar font. Click OK.

4 In the Effect Controls window for the *at the* text, use the eyedropper to choose the same color for the text as *SUNDAY* and *afternoon,* and set the font size to 30 points.

5 Position the At The layer below and slightly indented from *SUNDAY* and within the title-safe area. Set the Quality to Best.

You will set Scale and Opacity keyframes similar to those you set for the Afternoon layer.

6 Make sure the current time is set to 02:00, click the triangles for the At The layer to display the Transform properties, and then click the Scale stopwatch to set a Scale keyframe, and set the Scale value to **0**%.

7 Move the current-time marker to 02:15, and set the Scale value to **80**%.

8 Move the current-time marker to 09:15, and click the Opacity stopwatch to set an Opacity keyframe, leaving the value at 100%.

9 Move the current-time marker to 10:00, and change the Opacity value to **0**%. Make sure that you have four keyframes set: two each for the Scale and Opacity properties.

10 Return to the beginning of the composition, and then click the Play button in the Time Controls palette (or press spacebar) to play the first few seconds of the composition. Click Pause (or press spacebar again) when finished.

11 Collapse the layer outline, close the Effect Controls window, and save the project.

Duplicating and renaming layers

In this section, you will create separate solids for the letters in the word *ballet*. The letters need to be individual layers because you will be animating each letter separately. To create each letter, you start with one solid layer, and then duplicate the layer, edit the text, and rename the layer. The grid and the Align & Distribute palette will help you to align the layers.

1 Set the current-time marker to 2:00.

Since you will be concentrating on the ballet letter layers, it will be helpful to hide and lock the other layers in the Time Layout window temporarily.

2 To hide and lock the other layers in the Time Layout window, click the Shy switch and Lock switch (shown in the illustration below) for the At The, Afternoon, Sunday, and Sugar.mov layers. Then click the Hide Shy Layers button or choose Hide Shy Layers from the Time Layout window menu.

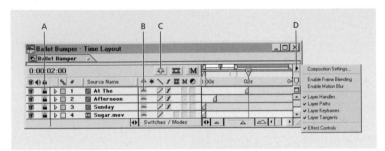

A. Lock switches B. Shy switches C. Click to hide shy layers
D. Time Layout window menu

All the shy layers disappear from the Time Layout window but remain visible in the Composition window.

3 Choose Layer > New Solid, type **B** for the name, set the size to **60** x **60** pixels, leave the default color as gray, and then click OK.

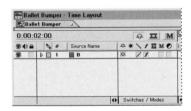

4 Choose Effect > Text > Basic Text, type **b** (lowercase) in the text entry box, select the Center Alignment button, choose a font such as Adobe Garamond or a similar font, set the style to italic, and then click OK.

5 In the Effect Controls window use the eyedropper to sample the color from any of the other pieces of text, and then set the font size to **60** points. Close the Effect Controls window.

6 In the Time Layout window, set the Quality to Best.

To help you initially position and align the letter layers, you'll display a grid in the Composition window. The default proportional grid is the well suited to this purpose because it is fairly coarse.

7 Display the proportional grid: Alt-click (Windows) or Option-click (Mac OS) the safe-zones icon, or press Alt+apostrophe (Windows) or Option+apostrophe (Mac OS).

Note: You can also display a standard grid by choosing Show Grid from the View menu or by holding down Ctrl/Command and clicking the safe-zones icon, or by using Ctrl+apostrophe (Windows) or Command+apostrophe (Mac OS). It is possible to adjust the spacing of the grids by choosing File > Preferences > Grids & Guides.

8 Position the letter *b* above the lowest horizontal line and to the right of the leftmost vertical line.

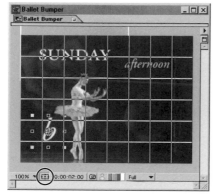

Safe-zones icon

Duplicating the layer

1 With the B layer selected in the Time Layout window, choose Edit > Duplicate. A duplicate layer appears on top of the first layer in both the Composition and Time Layout windows.

Note: When changing the name of a layer on a Mac OS system, always use the Return key, not the Enter key on the numeric keypad. Pressing Enter on a Mac OS system opens a layer window for the selected layer.

2 To rename the B layer, click the duplicated layer in the Time Layout window to activate the window, and then press Enter or Return. Type **A** for the name, and press Enter or Return again to apply the new name.

To rename any layer or footage item, you must always first press Enter or Return. You can also change the source name of a solid by choosing Layer > Solid Settings and typing a new name in the Solid Settings dialog box. Changing the name in this dialog box, however, changes only the source name, and not the layer name.

3 To edit the text, click the triangle for the A layer to expand the outline, click the triangle next to Effects to display Basic Text, and then click Options next to the Basic Text effect. The Type dialog box appears.

4 Replace the *b* in the text entry box with a lowercase *a*, and then click OK.

5 In the Composition window drag the new A layer to the right of the second vertical grid line, positioning it as shown in the illustration below. (After you click the layer, hold down the Shift key as you drag to constrain direction to horizontal movement.)

6 Click the triangle next to the A layer to collapse its outline.

7 With the A layer selected, choose Edit > Duplicate, or press Ctrl+D (Windows) or Command+D (Mac OS), and then select the new layer in the Time Layout window. Press Enter or Return, type **L** for the name, and press Enter or Return again to apply the new name.

When you duplicate a layer with a modified name in the Time Layout window, an asterisk appears next to the name of the duplicated layer.

8 Click the triangles for the L layer to expand the outline, and then click the Options button next to the Basic Text effect. Replace the *a* in the text entry box with a lowercase **l**, and then click OK.

9 With the new L layer still selected, drag it to the right of the third vertical grid line in the Composition window, constraining movement using the Shift key as before. Collapse the layer outline in the Time layout window.

10 With the L layer selected, choose Edit > Duplicate, and then position the layer. (You can delete the asterisk in the name if you'd like.)

11 With the second L layer selected, repeat steps 7 through 9 to create an E and a T layer.

Distributing layers

Although in some cases you may want to position layers manually as you just did with the letter layers, there is an easier way to accurately distribute layers. Here, you'll use the Align & Distribute Plug-in palette to evenly space the letter layers between the *b* and the *t*.

1 Choose Window > Plug-in Palettes > Align & Distribute to open the Align & Distribute palette.

2 Select all of the letter layers in the Time Layout window by choosing Edit > Select All or by pressing Ctrl+A (Windows) or Command+A (Mac OS).

3 Choose the Distribute option that is second from the right (⚏) in the Align & Distribute palette. This option distributes the selected layers evenly between the two most extreme layers (furthest left and furthest right) based upon the layers' center points.

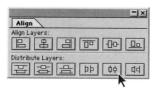

4 To align the baselines of the letters, choose the right icon in the top row (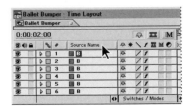) in the Align & Distribute palette.

5 Close the Align & Distribute Plug-in Palette.

Viewing layers

You can view layers two ways in the Time Layout window: by layer name or by source name.

1 Click the Layer Name heading above the stack of layers in the Time Layout window.

The heading changes to Source Name and the Source Names appear. In this case, all the solid layers reflect that the original solid is named *B*.

2 Click the Source Name heading above the stack of layers in the Time Layout window to view the layer names.

If the Source Name and Layer Name are the same, the original source file's name appears inside brackets under the Layer name heading.

Copying and pasting keyframes

In this section, you will create the effect of the *ballet* type fading in and out. Since the fade occurs at the same interval for all the layers, you can set two keyframes for one layer, and then copy and paste the keyframes in different layers, staggered every 15 frames. While you are copying and pasting, you will practice a couple of practical keyboard shortcuts.

Keep in mind that when you copy two or more keyframes and paste them, the first keyframe in the range is always pasted at the current-time marker.

1 Set the current time to 02:15, deselect all layers, select the B layer, press the T key to display just the Opacity property, and then click the stopwatch to set an Opacity keyframe. Click the underlined Opacity value, and change it to **0%**.

2 Move the current-time marker to 03:00, and set the Opacity to **100**%. A keyframe is automatically created.

3 Select both keyframes: click the first keyframe, Shift-click the second one, and then choose Edit > Copy.

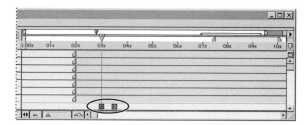

4 Select the A layer, make sure the current time is set to 03:00, and press the T key to display the Opacity property.

5 Choose Edit > Paste. The keyframes are pasted into the A layer at the current time.

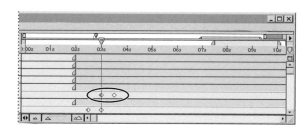

6 Select the L layer (above the A layer), move the current-time marker to 3:15, and then paste.

Even though the Opacity property is not displayed, the keyframes are pasted into the correct property.

7 Press the T key to view the Opacity keyframes.

8 Paste the keyframes for the second L layer at 4:00, the E layer at 4:15, and the T layer at 5:00.

9 To check the keyframes, select all the layers by choosing Edit > Select All or by pressing Ctrl+A (Windows) or Command+A (Mac OS). Then press the T key to view the Opacity properties for all the layers.

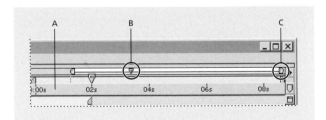

10 To collapse all the layer outlines, click any layer triangle or press the ~ (tilde) key.

11 Click in the white area below the layer stack, or press Ctrl+Shift+A (Windows) or Command+Shift+A (Mac OS) to deselect the layers, and then save the project.

Magnifying the Time Graph

So far, the time ruler has displayed the duration of the entire composition. However, there are many times when you will want to magnify a portion of the time graph so that you can get a more detailed look at the frames.

The time graph consists of two parts: the time ruler, where you have been positioning the current-time marker, and the navigator view section directly above it, which is used to magnify or shrink a part of the time ruler. On either end of the navigator view are viewing-area markers.

A. Time ruler B. Navigator view C. Viewing-area markers

1 To magnify the time ruler, drag the right viewing-area marker to the left until it's about in the middle of the navigator view.

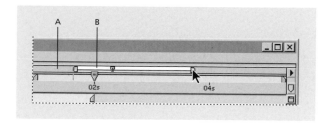

A. Gray area indicates portion you can't see **B.** *White area indicates the visible portion*

The time ruler now displays just the first 5 seconds or so of the composition. In the navigator view, the white area in between the viewing-area markers indicates the portion of the composition you are viewing. The gray area indicates the portion of the composition that you can't see.

2 Experiment with dragging the viewing-area markers in and out to magnify and shrink the time ruler.

You can also click the *zoom-in* icon to halve the amount of time displayed in the time ruler, or you can click the *zoom-out* icon to double the amount of time displayed in the time ruler. Use the Zoom slider to zoom in and out of the time graph by dragging it to the right or left.

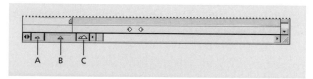

A. Zoom-out icon **B.** *Zoom slider* **C.** *Zoom-in icon*

To zoom out in the time layout window, press the = (equals sign) key above the letter keys. To zoom in, press the - (hyphen) key above the letter keys.

As you change the navigator view, notice that there is a second, smaller current-time marker positioned above the regular current-time marker. As you change the navigator view, the smaller current-time marker indicates where the regular current-time marker is in relation to the length of the composition. If the regular current-time marker is off the edge of the time graph, you can bring it back into the visible area by dragging the smaller current-time marker into the white area of the navigator view section.

3 Drag both viewing-area markers out so that you see the entire composition.

Animating the opacity

In this section, you will animate the opacity to fade the text in and out with a rippling effect. You set a few keyframes, and then copy and paste the keyframes into different layers, at different times.

1 Move the current-time marker to 6:15.

2 Make sure all the letter layers are selected.

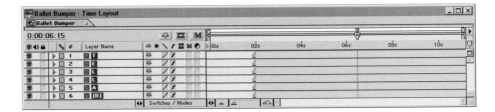

First, you'll set opacity keyframes at 6:15 and 6:20 in all letter layers, setting identical values for all the keyframes. This produces an unchanging opacity value between these two locations.

3 To set an Opacity keyframe for all the selected layers at 06:15, press Alt+Shift+T (Windows) or Option+Shift+T (Mac OS). This will create a new keyframe for all selected layers. Press the T key to display the Opacity property, click any underlined Opacity value, and then enter **0** to set all selected layers to 0% Opacity.

4 Move the current-time marker to 06:20, and then press Alt+Shift+T or Option+T again to set another Opacity keyframe with a value of **0**%.

Next, you'll set a single opacity keyframe at 100% to fade in a layer, then copy and paste it at different locations in the other layers.

5 Set the current time to 06:25, press Ctrl+Shift+A (Windows) or Command+Shift+A (Mac OS) to deselect all the layers. Then select the B layer, and set its Opacity to **100**%.

6 Make sure the keyframe is selected, and choose Edit > Copy.

7 Move the current-time marker to 07:00, select the A layer, and paste. An Opacity keyframe with a value of 100% is pasted at 07:00.

8 Paste Opacity keyframes for each letter layer as follows: 7:05 (first l), 7:10 (second l), 7:15 (e), and 7:20 (t).

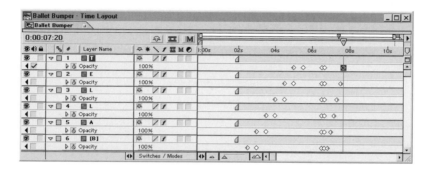

To give the letters a little more room to dance off the screen, you will scale them down slightly.

9 Set the current time to 02:00, select all the letter layers, press the S key to display the Scale property, and then press Alt+Shift+S (Windows) or Option+S (Mac OS) to set a Scale keyframe. Leave the value set to 100%.

You won't see the letters in the Composition window because the Opacity value is 0% at this point.

10 Set the current time to 07:20, make sure all the letter layers are selected in the Time Layout window, click the underlined Scale value for any layer, enter **90** for the Scale value, and then click OK. The Scale values for all the layers change to 90%.

11 Set the current time to 08:15, and then click the underlined Scale value, and set the Scale to **50**% for all the letter layers.

12 Collapse all layers and save the project.

Previewing the animation

You can preview by *scrubbing*, or dragging left or right, in the time ruler. Before you preview, you'll turn off the video for the Sugar.mov layer and turn off the grid so you can get a better picture of what is happening.

1 Click the Hide Shy Layers button to display the shy layers in the Time Layout window, and then deselect the Video switch (👁) for the Sugar.mov layer to hide the video in the Composition window.

2 Click the Hide Shy Layers button again to hide the layers in the Time Layout window.

3 Alt-click (Windows) or Option-click (Mac OS) the safe-zones icon to turn off the grid.

4 Press Ctrl+Shift+A (Windows) or Command+Shift+A (Mac OS) to deselect the layers.

To preview the opacity changes that you just set, you will *scrub* (view by dragging the current-time marker) through the composition frame by frame.

5 Set the current time to 02:00, and then press the Alt key (Windows) or Option key (Mac OS), and slowly drag the current-time marker to the right. You can use this scrubbing technique to go forward and backward through your composition.

A word on space and time

The process After Effects uses to calculate the values between keyframes is called *interpolation*. You can control *temporal* interpolation, the change between keyframe values over time, for all layer properties. Some properties, such as the Opacity and Scale values that you just set, change only through time. For properties that involve movement, such as the Position property, you can also control the spatial interpolation, the change between keyframes through space.

Controlling change through interpolation

After Effects provides several interpolation methods that affect how change occurs through and between keyframes. For example, if you are setting up motion, you can choose to make a layer change direction abruptly or through a smooth curve. After Effects interpolates values for a change using the values at the keyframes on both ends of the change.

You can control temporal interpolation (the interpolation between keyframe values over time) for all layer properties. For layer properties that involve movement, such as Position, Anchor Point, and Effect Point, you can also control spatial interpolation (the interpolation between motion-path keyframes through space).

You can make a layer property vary over time. After Effects records the resulting values of temporal interpolation in the Value graph in the Time Layout window. If the layer property includes spatial interpolation, the resulting values of spatial interpolation are displayed as a motion path in either the Composition or the Layer window, depending on the property. You can add or delete keyframes in the Value graph or motion path using the pen tool.

—From the Adobe After Effects User Guide, Chapter 7

In the next section, you will make the *ballet* letters dance off the screen by changing both the temporal and spatial interpolations of the layers using roving keyframes.

Creating a motion path

To make the letters dance off of the screen, you'll start by creating a *motion path*. You define the motion path by setting Position keyframes. After creating the initial motion path, you can edit it in the Composition window.

1 In the Time Layout window, set the current time to 07:25, and make sure all the letter layers are selected.

2 Press the P key to see the Position property for all the letters, and then press Alt+Shift+P (Windows) or Option+P (Mac OS) to set an initial Position keyframe for all the letter layers.

3 Move the current-time marker to 08:03, and press Ctrl+Shift+A (Windows) or Command+Shift+A (Mac OS) to deselect all layers. Select the T layer in the Composition window, and then drag the letter *t* slightly to the right. A second Position keyframe appears in the Time Layout window.

4 Set the current time to 08:10, and then drag the T layer slightly up and to the right. Another keyframe is created.

5 Set the current time to 08:20, and then drag the T layer down and to the right.

6 Set the current time to 09:00, and then drag the T layer off the top part of the frame.

7 To set the work area in order to preview the motion so far, move the current-time marker to 07:15, and then press the B key to set the beginning of the work area. Next, move the current-time marker to 09:10, and press the N key to set the end of the work area.

8 Preview the motion using a Wireframe preview (an outline of the alpha channels playing back motion at real time) by pressing Opt+0 (on the numeric keypad).

Because the letter was applied to a rectangular solid, you will not see the letter outline, but rather the rectangular outline of the solid layer.

9 Press any key to stop the preview.

Using the shuttle control

If you were to use the play button on the Time Controls palette (or the spacebar) to play the composition, the playback would be slow. You can use the shuttle control in the Time Controls palette to see faster playback, and to see the shapes of the letters.

1 Set the current time to 07:15.

2 In the Time Controls palette, drag the shuttle control slightly to the right.

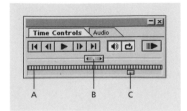

*A. Jog control **B.** Shuttle control*
C. *Time indicator*

The shuttle control *shuttles* through the composition starting from the current-time marker. The farther you drag the control from the center, the faster the content of the Composition window plays. You can play the composition both forward and backward by dragging to the right or to the left, respectively. You may have to experiment with how far to drag the control to see a helpful preview. The shuttle control does not loop the playback, so you will need to set the current-time marker to the beginning to view the frames again.

As you drag the shuttle control back and forth to preview your composition, notice the time indicator just below the jog control. The time indicator here shows which frame you are currently viewing relative to the beginning and end of the composition, and updates to reflect this as you shuttle through a composition. You can also drag the time indicator along the jog control to move quickly through the composition. To move slowly, you can drag inside the jog control.

About direction lines and direction handles

Before you draw and modify curved lines with the pen tool, it is important to know about two elements that are associated with anchor points on curves. On curved segments, each selected anchor point displays one or two direction lines *(also called* tangents*), ending in* direction handles *(also called* Bezier direction handles*). The positions of direction lines and handles determine the size and shape of a curved segment. Moving these elements reshapes the curves in a path.*

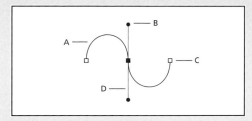

A. *Curved segment* **B.** *Direction handle* **C.** *Anchor point*
D. *Direction line or tangent*

The direction lines are always tangent to (touching) the curve at the anchor points. The slope of each direction line determines the slope of the curve, and the length of each direction line determines the height, or depth, of the curve.

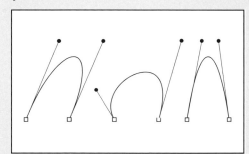

Moving direction lines changes the slope of the curve.

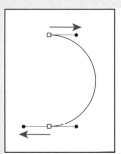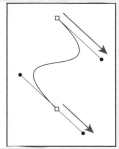

Drag in the opposite direction to create a smooth curve.
Drag in the same direction to create an "S" curve.

Editing the motion path

With the T layer still selected, you can examine the motion path for the T layer in the Composition window. Each X represents a keyframe, and each dot marks the position of the layer at each frame. The spacing of the dots indicates the speed of the layer. Notice that the dots are closer together between keyframes that are closer together in time, and farther apart where keyframes are farther apart. The closer together the dots are, the slower the layer is moving at that point. The farther apart the dots are, the faster the layer is moving.

You can edit the Position keyframes by editing the motion path.

1 In the Time Layout window, make sure the Position property is displayed for the T layer, set the current time to 8:10, and then take note of the position coordinates.

2 In the Composition window, drag the layer up and slightly to the left. The position coordinates for this keyframe change.

You don't need to move the current-time marker to edit the position keyframes.

3 In the Composition window, select the X that represents the next keyframe, and move it up and slightly to the right.

4 Select the X that is above the top of the frame, and move it to the left.

You can use the pen tool in the toolbox to edit and add keyframes to the motion path. Editing with the pen tool is similar to the way you edit paths in Adobe Illustrator.

5 Position the current-time marker at 08:20, and in the toolbox, select the pen tool. In the Composition window, position the pen over a dot on the motion path, as shown in the illustration below, so that a plus icon appears next to the pen tool icon. (This is the add control point tool.) Click the motion path. A new keyframe appears between 8:20 and 9:00.

In addition to the new keyframe symbol, two *layer tangents* or *direction handles* appear. The default spatial interpolation method is continuous Bezier interpolation. Bezier interpolation provides the most precise control over the motion path. You use the handles to control the arc of the curve, just as you do with the pen tool in Adobe Illustrator and Adobe Photoshop.

6 Select the selection tool in the toolbox, and then drag the new keyframe to the right.

Before completing your adjustments to the motion path, you will explore some of the motion path controls that you have available by selecting options in the Composition window menu in the upper right corner of the Composition window.

7 In the Composition window, choose Layer Keyframes from the Composition window menu; the keyframe symbols disappear. Choose the command again to turn the keyframes back on.

8 Choose Layer Paths from the Composition window menu; the layer path disappears. Choose the command again to turn the path back on.

The Layer Tangents option shows the direction handles of a Bezier curve. You can drag these handles to modify the path.

9 Leave the Layer Tangents command turned on (displaying a checkmark), and then click the newest keyframe that you created. Drag the direction handles to change the arc of the curve.

10 Choose Layer Handles from the Composition window menu. The handles for the selected layer disappear. Hiding the selection handles makes it easier to work with the direction handles.

11 Select each keyframe one at a time, except the first two, and use the direction handle to alter the curve until you get a path that you like. When you are finished, choose Layer Handles from the Composition window menu again to turn layer handles back on.

12 Press Alt+0 (Windows) or Option+0 (Mac OS) on your numeric keypad to preview the motion.

13 Set the current time to 07:25, and then use the jog control to see the *t* move along the motion path frame by frame. Save the project.

Setting Auto-Orient Rotation

As the letter *t* moves up the motion path that you just created, the *t* is always vertically oriented. To make the *t* to change orientation as it follows the path, you'll set Auto-Orient Rotation.

1 Make sure that the T layer is selected in the Time Layout window.

2 Choose Layer > Transform > Auto-Orient Rotation.

Auto-Orient Rotation is applied to a whole layer, not to individual keyframes, and therefore cannot be animated off and on within a single layer over time.

3 Set the current time to 07:15, and then use the shuttle control in the Time Controls palette to play a preview. Notice that the T layer now rotates as it follows along the path.

Now that the motion path is set, you'll copy and paste the motion path keyframes into the other layers.

4 In the Time Layout window, set the current time to 08:00, make sure the T layer is selected, and then click the word *Position* to select all six Position keyframes for the T layer. Then choose Edit > Copy.

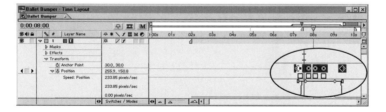

5 Select the E layer in the Time Layout window.

6 Make sure the current-time marker is set to 08:00, and paste the keyframes.

7 Move to 08:05, and paste the keyframes into the L layer under the E layer.

8 Move to 08:10, and paste the keyframes into the next L layer.

9 Move to 08:15, and paste the keyframes into the A layer.

10 Move to 08:20, and paste the keyframes into the B layer.

11 Select the E layer, and then choose Layer > Transform > Auto-Orient Rotation.

You can apply Auto-Orient Rotation to only one layer at a time.

12 Select the L layer, and then choose Layer > Transform > Auto-Orient Rotation, or press Ctrl+Alt+O (Windows) or Command+Option+O (Mac OS).

13 Repeat the previous step for each of the remaining the layers.

14 Set the current time to 07:25, and use the shuttle control in the Time Controls palette to preview your work.

Previewing with RAM Preview

You can also preview portions of the composition playing back at real-time using RAM Preview. See "RAM Preview" on page 54. If you are unable to load all of the specified frames for a RAM Preview, try decreasing the length of the work area, reducing the resolution of the composition, or allocating more RAM to After Effects. You can also preview every other frame by pressing Shift+0 on the numeric keypad.

1 Set the work area for the frames to preview to begin at 7:15 and end at 10:00.

2 Click the RAM Preview button on the Time Controls palette.

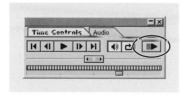

Note that After Effects replaces the jog and shuttle controls with an update showing which frames it's processing as it loads them into RAM, and when finished reports how many of those could be loaded, and the playback frame rate.

3 After a few seconds, you should see the frames within the work area playing back at real-time in the Composition window.

4 Press any key to stop the preview.

Managing the speed of layers

In this motion path, some of the dots are closer together and some are farther apart. You can change the speed of a layer by using the Speed graph in the Time Layout window.

1 In the Time Layout window, select the T layer, and then click the triangle next to the Position property to view the Speed graph.

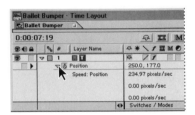

The Speed graph reflects the speed of the selected layer through time. At the left of the graph, three values represent the maximum speed (top), minimum speed (bottom), and speed at the current-time marker (middle). In the speed graph, a rising line indicates acceleration, an increase in velocity, and a falling line indicates deceleration, a decrease in velocity.

You'll work with the speed graph and explore more advanced motion controls in Lesson 6, "Station Identification."

2 Save the project.

Setting roving keyframes

One way to smooth out the speed of the layer is to set roving keyframes. Creating roving keyframes separates the *x, y (or spatial)* coordinates of the Position keyframes from their specific points in time.

1 Make sure the T layer is selected, and then zoom in the Time Layout window.

2 To create roving keyframes, deselect the tiny check boxes below the four middle keyframes. The first and last keyframes in a layer cannot rove, so they don't have check boxes.

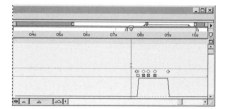

As you deselect the check boxes, the Speed graph becomes more and more flat, which indicates a constant rate of speed. Notice also that the dots in the motion path in the Composition window have become more evenly spread out.

The keyframe icons change to small circles and shift a bit, disconnecting from their original points in time.

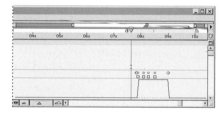

3 Click the triangle next to the T layer to collapse the layer outline.

4 Select the E layer, and then click the triangle next to Position to display the Speed graph. This time leave the first check box selected, and then deselect the last four check boxes to create roving keyframes. The keyframe at 08:00 remains non-roving so that the motion starts at a specific point in time.

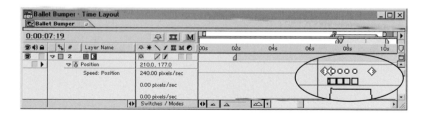

5 Select the lower L layer, and then click the triangle next to the Position property. Leave the first roving keyframe navigator check box checked, and then deselect the last four check boxes to create roving keyframes.

6 Repeat step 5 for each of the remaining layers for the word *ballet*.

Because using roving keyframes separates the spatial position coordinates from a specific point on the timeline, you would not use roving keyframes if you wanted to synchronize an animation event, such as Position, with a specific point in time, such as a key point in music.

In this exercise, however, the desired effect is to have all of the letters follow one another along a motion path while remaining evenly spaced along that path. To achieve this effect they must hit certain spatial points (position coordinates) along the path at a constant rate of motion. Because the letters have varying distances to travel from their original starting points to reach the end of the motion path, locking them to specific points in time will cause the letters with greater distances to move faster as they travel between keyframes. Those with shorter distances will move more slowly, creeping along, causing the letters to pile up on top of each other, and the type will become unreadable to the viewer.

Setting a Roving keyframe unlinks the position keyframe from its specified point in time. The first and last keyframes are now *temporal* beginning and end points, and an even rate of motion is applied as the letter travels between those end points. The letter still hits the same spatial points on the path, but no longer at the original times specified. In short, we know when we want a letter to begin moving from it's starting position (first keyframe), when we want it off screen (last keyframe), and the path that we want it to travel along (original position keyframes). We don't really care, however, when it hits those mid-points along the path as long as the letters all travel at the same constant rate of speed, remaining evenly spaced and readable.

7 Take a look at motion of the letters using RAM Preview: press the 0 key on your numeric keypad.

8 When you are finished previewing, collapse all the layer outlines, and then save the project.

Using Motion Sketch to create a motion path

The Motion Sketch plug-in is a feature within After Effects that allows you to create fluid motion paths by drawing. Rather than setting individual position keyframes, you will draw your own freehand motion path using Motion Sketch. As you draw a motion path with the mouse or pen, Motion Sketch records and sets keyframes for the position of the layer as well as the speed at which you draw. This path can be drawn anywhere within the composition window or even on the pasteboard. If you speed up, slow down, pause, and start again as you draw a path, this motion will be recorded in the keyframes that are created.

While you sketch a path with Motion Sketch, After Effects plays the audio files in the composition. (The Audio button in the Time Controls palette must be clicked to enable audio playback.) This feature is useful if you want to create a motion path that will match cues in the audio.

Here you'll use Motion Sketch to animate a snowflake that flutters in the background to the music as the type animates and dances off the screen.

Preparing the snowflake layer

Before you create the motion path, you'll import the snowflake layer, set up the work area, and then set some transform values for the layer.

1 Choose File > Import > Footage Files.

2 Select the file Snow.ai from the 02Lesson folder, and then click Open.

Note: When you import an Adobe Illustrator file as a file instead of as a composition, After Effects adds Merged/ to the filename to indicate that layers in the file have been combined, or merged.

3 Select the file Audio.mov, click Open, and then click Done.

4 Set the current-time marker to 00:00.

5 Drag Audio.mov from the Project window into the Time Layout window.

6 Resize the Composition window so you can see more of the pasteboard area around the frame. This lets you create a motion path that extends outside the composition frame.

Because you want to position the snowflake, you'll drag it into the Composition window instead of dragging it into the Time Layout window, which would center it. Regardless of whether you drag an item into the Composition window or the Time Layout window, the item appears in both windows.

7 Drag Merged/Snow.ai from the Project window into the Composition Window, placing it wherever you want it to begin. For the final movie the snowflake was placed on the paste-board (the gray area just outside of the composition frame) to flutter in from off screen.

8 In the Time Layout window, display the Scale, Rotation, Opacity, and Position properties for the snowflake layer. You can use keyboard shortcuts to display just these properties: press the S key, Shift+R, Shift+T, and Shift+P.

Next, you'll set scale and opacity values for the entire Merged/Snow.ai layer. Because these values won't change over time, you don't need to set keyframes for them.

9 Set the scale value to **75**%, and set the opacity to **80**%, but do not set keyframes. Then set an initial Rotation keyframe at 00:00 with a value of **0**.

10 Go to 7:00 and change the rotation value to **1** revolution. This will create one slow revolution over the 7 seconds during which the snowflake is on-screen.

11 Click the Quality switch icon for the snowflake layer to select Best quality, indicated by a forward solid slash.

12 Turn on motion blur for the snowflake layer by selecting the layer's Motion Blur switch.

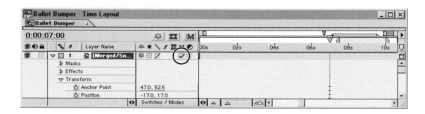

Motion blur enhances motion that you have applied to an object. In addition to turning it on for the snowflake layer, you need to enable motion blur so it is used in previewing and rendering. Motion blur can slow down previewing and rendering, but if you don't need to see it while you work, you can speed up processing by disabling motion blur. In this case, you'll enable motion blur.

13 Click the Enable Motion Blur button at the top of the Time Layout window.

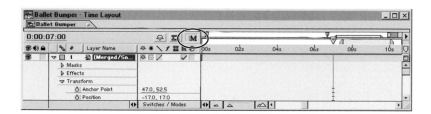

14 If the snowflake is not the top layer in the layer stack, drag it to the top position in the Time Layout window.

15 Click Switches/Modes at the bottom of the Switches panel to display the Transfer Modes panel, and then Choose Soft Light from the appropriate menu in the mode column. Click Switches/Modes again to display the Switches panel.

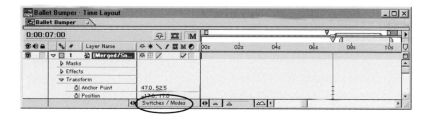

Soft Light is a transfer mode that will let various elements in the background footage and type elements show through the snowflake as it flutters over them. Transfer modes are applied to a top layer so that the color and luminance values of its pixels are affected by the pixel values of the layer(s) below it. This allows the snowflake to blend better as it interacts with the footage behind it. For more information and practice with transfer modes, see Lesson 4, "Multimedia Animation," or the After Effects User Guide.

The last step before creating the motion path is to define the start and end points for the animation. This is the time frame in which the new keyframes will be set. Motion Sketch will stop automatically when it reaches the end of the work area.

16 Set the work area to begin at 00:00 and to end at 7:00.

17 Select the snowflake layer in either the Time Layout or Composition window.

Creating the snowflake motion path

Now that you've set up the work area and modified the snowflake layer, you are ready to create the motion path using the Motion Sketch plug-in.

1 Choose Window > Plug-in Palettes > Motion Sketch to open the Motion Sketch palette.

2 Leave the Capture Speed set to 100%. The motion you draw will be captured at real-time.

Increasing this number increases the playback speed in relation to the drawing speed, giving you more time to draw the path. Decreasing this number will slow down the playback speed by the percentage you choose.

3 Leave the Show Wireframe option selected to see the outline of the layer as you draw the motion path.

4 Leave Keep Background deselected. If selected, this lets you view the background layers as you sketch.

Read through the next couple of steps before clicking Start Capture so you'll better understand how Motion Sketch records your movement.

5 Click Start Capture.

As soon as you click the mouse, After Effects begins recording its movement, setting new position keyframes for the selected snowflake layer based upon what you draw.

6 Position the pointer where you'd like to begin the motion path, and click and hold the mouse button and drag to draw the path for the snowflake.

After Effects stops recording when you release the mouse button or go beyond the end of the work area.

7 Expand the outline to display the Position property for the snowflake layer.

Notice all the new keyframes. They are very close together because there is one on each frame. To view them individually, use the zoom slider to zoom into the timeline.

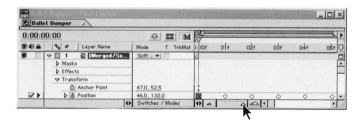

Now you'll preview the motion created using a Wireframe preview. If your system has sufficient RAM installed, you can use RAM Preview instead. See "RAM Preview" on page 54.

8 Ensure that the snowflake layer is still selected.

9 Choose Composition > Preview > Wireframe or press Alt+0 (Windows) or Option+0 (Mac OS) on the numeric keypad.

10 To revise the motion path created, delete all of the keyframes by clicking Position for the snowflake layer, press delete, and repeat steps 5 through 6 and preview again.

Smoothing motion

Because After Effects is creating a new keyframe for each frame as you draw using Motion Sketch, the resulting motion is often somewhat jerky. To create smoother motion you can apply The Smoother. The Smoother removes some of the keyframes based on a tolerance level that you choose, resulting in much more fluid motion.

1 In the Time Layout window, click Position in the snowflake layer to select all of the position keyframes.

2 Choose Window > Plug-in Palettes > The Smoother to open The Smoother control palette.

3 For Apply To, choose Spatial Path.

4 Set the Smoother tolerance to **10**, and click Apply. Notice that in both the Composition window and the Time Layout window a number of keyframes are removed, and the direction handles in the Composition window are set to create smooth curves along the motion path.

5 Preview the new motion using a Wireframe preview or RAM Preview.

6 If you are not satisfied with the way The Smoother altered the motion path, choose Edit > Undo to undo the smoothing. Select the keyframes again and choose a different tolerance value.

7 Save the project.

Creating a draft movie

To see the motion of the ballet letters, you'll create a draft movie of just the letter layers. A draft movie is especially useful if you don't have enough RAM to preview the whole composition using RAM Preview.

1 Deselect the Hide Shy Layers button (⊞), and then deselect the Video switches (👁) to hide the video for all layers except those containing the letters in the word *ballet*. For more information, see "Video, Audio, and Lock switches" on page 48.

2 Set the end of the work area to 10:10.

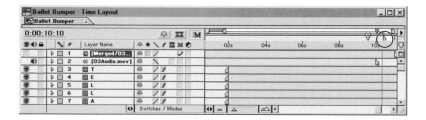

3 Choose Composition > Make Movie, type **Draft1.mov** for the name, and save the file in your Projects folder.

4 For Render Settings, choose Draft Settings.

Instead of using the MoviePlayer application to view this movie, you will import it directly into your project, and then view the movie from within After Effects.

5 For Output Module, choose Custom, and for Format, choose QuickTime Movie.

Note: QuickTime is the default format in Mac OS.

6 In Windows, the Compression Settings dialog box appears. Leave Compressor set to Animation, and then click OK. In Mac OS, leave all settings at their defaults.

7 Select Import into project when done, and then click OK.

After the draft movie is rendered, it will appear as a footage item in your Project window.

8 Click Render.

9 After the draft movie is finished rendering, close the Render Queue window, and then activate the Project window, double-click the Draft1.mov footage item, and play the movie.

Rendering the final movie

To finish the composition, you will display the video.

1 Display the video for all the layers by selecting the Video switches for the Sunday, Afternoon, At The, and Sugar.mov layers.

2 Choose Composition > Make Movie.

3 Type **Movie.mov** for the name, and save the file into your Projects folder.

The Render Queue window displays all the items that you have ever rendered for the project. The draft movie you rendered earlier appears as the first item in the Render list. Its status indicates that the movie is done. The newest item appears at the bottom of the list. Its status indicates that it is queued.

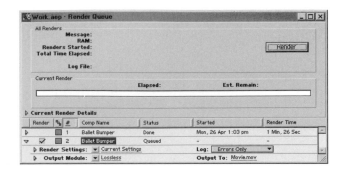

Note: After Effects saves these rendered items in the Render Queue with the project file for your reference. To delete an item from the Render Queue, select the item by clicking the composition name, and then press Delete.

4 For Render Settings, choose Best Settings. To modify the settings, click the underlined phrase *Best Settings*.

5 For Time Span, choose Length of Comp.

The default Time Span is the work area. You can select the Length of Comp, or set a custom length by clicking the Set button. Click OK.

6 For Output Module, choose Custom, and for Format, choose QuickTime Movie.

7 In Windows, the Compression Settings dialog box appears. Leave Compressor set to Animation, and then click OK. In Mac OS, leave all settings at their defaults.

8 Select Import into Project When Done.

Now you will set the audio options. Since the final goal of the project is to create a sample file to present to a client, you will select a low range of audio options.

9 Select the Audio Output option to include audio in the movie, and then choose 22.050 KHz from the left menu.

10 Choose 8-bit from the center menu. This is the standard sample depth for playback on computers. (16-bit is the standard for compact disc audio.) Choose Mono from the right menu.

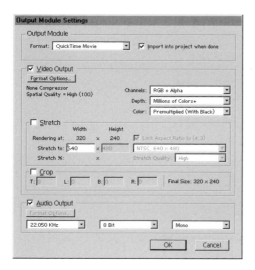

11 Leave the rest of the settings at their defaults, and then click OK.

12 Click the Render button.

13 When you are finished rendering the movie, open the footage file that appears in your Project window, play it, and then save and close the project.

14 Exit from After Effects.

Animated L-Train Logo

In this lesson, you'll explore techniques for creating transparency, including masks and a traveling matte.

In this lesson, you will create an animated logo for a fictional production company known as L-Train Productions. The project focuses on several transparency issues, including creating and animating masks and setting a traveling matte. To achieve the soft, pastel look of the final movie, you will apply a wide variety of visual effects, including tints, blurs, and a drop shadow.

You will also explore nesting compositions inside of other compositions. In the first half of the project, you're going to set up all of the motion in a single composition, and then you'll split the composition into smaller comps to which you'll apply visual effects.

This lesson covers the following topics:

- Importing Illustrator files as compositions
- Creating and editing masks, and animating mask shapes
- Animating text with the Path Text effect
- Nesting compositions
- Duplicating compositions
- Creating a track matte
- Using the Continuously Rasterize switch
- Using the Bevel Alpha, Gaussian Blur, and Channel Blur effects
- Using the Render Queue to batch render comps

At the end of this lesson you will have created an 8-second animated logo.

It should take approximately 3 to 4 hours to complete this project.

Viewing the final project

Before you begin, take a look at the finished movie that you will create in this lesson.

1 Double-click 03Final.mov in the 03Lesson folder to open the final QuickTime movie, and then click the Play button.

The movie consists of a video of a train that has been superimposed with a circular traveling matte. A variety of visual effects are applied to each layer, and the sound of a train adds the finishing touch.

2 When you are finished viewing the movie, exit from the MoviePlayer application.

Getting started

1 To ensure that the tools and palettes function exactly as described in this lesson, delete or deactivate (by renaming) the After Effects preferences file. See "Restoring default preferences" on page 6.

2 Start the After Effects application. An untitled Project window appears.

3 Choose File > Save Project As, name the file **03Work.aep**, and save it in the Projects folder.

Size and memory considerations

The final goal of this project is to create a 640 x 480 animated logo for video. However, for the sake of reducing disk space and memory requirements, the instructions are designed around a 320 x 240 format.

Setting up the project

Start the project by importing all the source files that you need to complete the logo.

1 Choose File > Import > Footage Files or press Ctrl+Alt+I (Windows) or Command+Option+I (Mac OS). Then select the Circle.ai file in the 03Lesson folder, and click Open.

2 Continue by selecting and importing the following files: Audio.mov, Logo.ai, Prod.ai, and Train.mov.

3 When you are finished importing the files, click Done.

4 Next, import the Illustrator file as a composition: choose File > Import > Illustrator As Comp, select Scr_L.ai, and click Open.

You should now have a total of seven items in the Project window, even though you imported only six items. When you imported the Scr_L.ai file as a comp, After Effects first added the source file layers in a folder, and then created the composition from the layers.

To make the composition easier to identify, rename it.

5 Select the Scr_L.ai composition in the Project window, press Enter or Return, type **Script L Comp** to rename it, and press Enter or Return again.

Animating the script letter *L*

Now that you've imported your files, you'll start the project by animating the script letter *L*. The Script L elements were prepared in Adobe Illustrator. The letter *L* was typed into an Illustrator document using the Palace Script MT font, and was then converted to artwork using the Create Outlines command.

Since the letterform overlaps itself twice, it is broken into three sections: upper, middle, and lower. An invisible box is positioned around the letter (a rectangle with no fill and no border) so that when the artwork is placed into the After Effects Composition window, all three pieces will align perfectly at the center of the screen. (You could also create crop marks from the rectangle.)

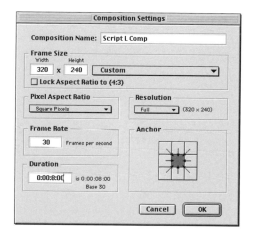

Start your work with the composition you just imported by checking the settings for the composition.

1 With Script L Comp selected in the Project window, choose Composition > Composition Settings, and make sure that the Frame Size is set to **320 x 240**, and that the Frame Rate is set to **30** frames per second. Set the Duration to **800** (8 seconds), and then click OK.

2 To open the composition in the Composition window and the Time Layout window, double-click Script L Comp in the Project window.

The three layers of Script L Comp appear in alphabetical order in the Time Layout window. All three layers are centered in the Composition window. Now you'll zoom in so you can work with individual frames when you create a mask.

3 Drag the Zoom slider at the bottom of the Time Layout window to the right until each increment in the time ruler represents one frame.

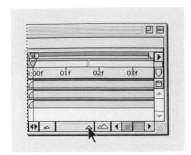

Zoom slider

Creating masks with the pen tool

To animate the script *L*, you will create three masks that progressively reveal the letter *L*, as if it were being handwritten, specifying Mask Shape keyframes as you go. You'll use the pen tool and three related mask tools available in the toolbox to create these masks. You can select these tools in a number of ways, including using keyboard shortcuts, selecting them directly from the toolbox, or using key combinations that cycle through the tools. In this part of the lesson, you'll select these tools in several ways.

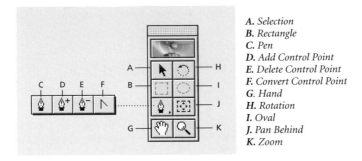

A. Selection
B. Rectangle
C. Pen
D. Add Control Point
E. Delete Control Point
F. Convert Control Point
G. Hand
H. Rotation
I. Oval
J. Pan Behind
K. Zoom

Start by hiding the layers you don't need right now, and then open the layer you'll be working on in a Layer window.

1 Press the Home key to set the current time to 00:00:00. Hide the video for the LowL.ai and MidL.ai layers by deselecting their Video switches, so that all you see is the TopL layer.

You create masks in the selected element's Layer window and preview masks in the Composition window.

2 In the Time Layout window or the Composition window, double-click the layer TopL to open the Layer window. Arrange your palettes and windows so that you can see both the Composition window and the Time Layout window.

To reveal the letter *L* one step at a time, you will draw Bezier a mask in the Layer window by using the pen tool. The first shape shows a small part of the top of the *L*; then you'll advance one frame and expand the Bezier mask to show a little more of the letter. You will set about 21 keyframes in all, revealing a little more of the *L* each time.

The pen tool works very much like the pen tool in Adobe Photoshop and Adobe Illustrator. You click to establish control points and draw straight lines; drag to create curves. The shapes you create for these masks will be straight line shapes.

3 If the toolbox is not visible, choose Window > Show tools. Select the pen tool in the toolbox, and then, in the Layer window, click near the top of the TopL layer to establish the mask's first control point.

Frame 0

4 Click three more times in a box shape to create control points around the tip of the *L*. To close the mask, either click the first point again or double-click the last point.

Frame 0   *Composition window*

Whatever is inside the mask will show in the Composition window; whatever is outside the mask will be hidden from view. The Composition window displays the progress of the mask.

5 In the Time Layout window, click the triangle next to the TopL layer to expand the layer outline, and then click the triangle for Masks to expand the properties outline. Notice that a mask has appeared, called Mask 1. Click the triangle for Mask 1 and click the stopwatch for Mask Shape to establish the first keyframe.

Editing a mask

To create the rest of the mask shapes for the top part of the *L*, you will edit the current mask by using the pen and selection tools. Because this part of the *L* has only a gentle curve, you can create the next mask shape simply by extending the existing mask. Later, you'll need to add control points to extend the mask around the curve.

1 To edit the mask for the next frame, press Page Down to go to the second frame, frame 1 (00:01) and click the selection tool in the toolbox. In the Layer window, drag each control point on the left so that the mask reveals a little more of the letter *L*. A second keyframe is created automatically.

Frame 1

To use the selection tool while you have the pen tool selected, hold down the Ctrl key (Windows) or the Command key (Mac OS).

2 Move forward one frame, either by pressing the Page Down key on your keyboard, or by pressing Ctrl+Right Arrow (Windows) or Command+Right Arrow (Mac OS).

3 To edit the mask for frame 2, select the pen tool in the toolbox, and then position the pen tool icon over the left segment of the mask. The pointer changes to the add control point tool (a pen icon with a plus sign). You can add points to the mask path by clicking the path using this tool.

Frame 2

4 Click twice to add two new points to the left segment of the mask, and then select the selection tool in the toolbox (or just hold down Ctrl/Command) and use it to drag each of the new points to the left, revealing more of the *L*. Use the selection tool to drag points, revealing more of the *L*.

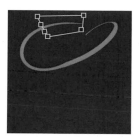 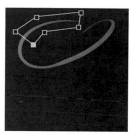

Frame 2 before and after moving the new control points.

If you position the pen tool over a control point, you will see the convert point tool, which lets you convert corner points to smooth Bezier points. In this section, you are focusing on creating straight line shapes with corner points. However, you may accidentally create a smooth point. You'll know it's a smooth point by the lines coming out of the control point. To convert a smooth point to a corner point and vice versa, click the point with the convert point tool.

Note: *You should pause for a second after clicking the mouse button to allow time for the change to register.*

5 Move forward one frame, and then use the following illustrations as guides to edit the mask for each of the next nine frames. Frame 11 will be the last frame for which you edit the mask. Don't worry about matching the mask shapes exactly.

Important: Make sure to move forward one frame before editing the mask; otherwise, you will be editing the same mask shape over and over at the same point in time, instead of changing it over time.

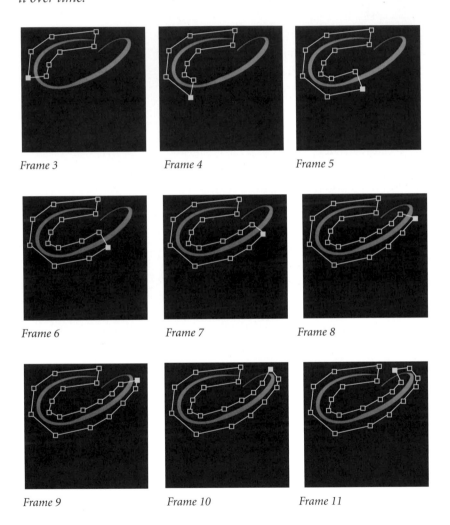

Frame 3   Frame 4   Frame 5

Frame 6   Frame 7   Frame 8

Frame 9   Frame 10   Frame 11

To show all of the script L, you could edit the mask to reveal the last portion of the artwork, but it's easier to simply reset the mask, which removes all control points.

6 In the Time Layout window, drag the blue current-time marker one frame forward to 00:12, and then choose Layer > Mask > Reset Mask to reset the mask.

You should now have keyframes set for every frame from 00:00 to 00:12. To view the mask changes, you'll move from keyframe to keyframe using the keyframe navigator, which is located in the far left panel of the Time Layout window. You'll click the right triangle to go to the next keyframe, and click the left triangle to go to the previous keyframe.

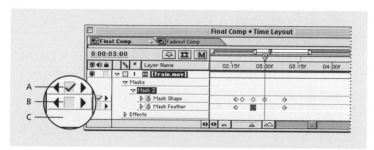

A. Keyframe at current time B. No Keyframes at current time
C. No Keyframes for layer property

7 Move the current-time marker to 00:00, and then use the keyframe navigator to move from keyframe to keyframe. (In this case, you can also press the Page Down key to move forward one frame at a time.) As you move, check your mask in the Layer window.

8 After viewing the mask, close the Layer window, and then collapse the outline for the TopL layer, and save the project.

9 Move the current time-marker to 00:00 and click the Play button to see a frame-by-frame preview.

Similar masks are needed for the MidL and LowL layers. However, since the shapes are fairly straight, they don't require as many edits to the masks.

Note: *The decision on how much of the L to reveal at each frame was based on the way people handwrite the letter L. The curves take a little more time and the long strokes go faster, so smaller advancements were made around the curves and bigger ones on the straighter lines.*

Creating another mask

After setting the In point of the MidL layer to frame 00:12, you will create and edit a mask to progressively reveal the middle section of the script *L*.

1 In the Time Layout window, select the Video switch to show the MidL.ai layer. Select the MidL layer, set the current time to 00:12 (12 frames), and then drag the layer duration bar to move the In point of the MidL layer to 00:12.

Note: When dragging a layer duration bar, drag the bar itself, not its In or Out points.

2 Hide the video for the TopL layer.

3 Double-click the MidL layer in the Time Layout window to open the Layer window.

4 Select the pen tool in the toolbox, and then create a mask to reveal a portion of the top of the middle part of the *L*.

5 Click the triangle to expand the MidL layer, and then click the Masks triangle to display Mask 2. Click the stopwatch next to Mask Shape to set the first keyframe.

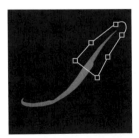

Frame 12

6 Press Page Down to go to frame 13, and then create a new mask.

Frame 13

7 Repeat for frames 14 and 15.

 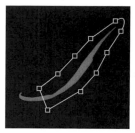

Frame 14   *Frame 15*

Just as you did with the TopL.ai layer, you'll reset the mask to reveal the last portion of the artwork.

8 Press Page Down to go to frame 16, and then choose Layer > Mask > Reset Mask to reset the mask.

9 Go to frame 00:12, and then use the keyframe navigator to check the mask at each keyframe.

10 Close the Layer window for the MidL layer and collapse its outline. Select the Video switches to display the LowL layer and hide the video for the MidL layer.

11 Save the project.

Creating the last mask

Now finish up by creating the mask for the lower part of the *L*. You will reset the mask at the final keyframe.

1 In the Time Layout window, select the LowL layer, make sure the current-time marker is positioned at frame 00:16, and then set the In point for LowL at frame 00:16 by pressing the left bracket ([) key on your keyboard.

Pressing the left bracket key preforms the same function as dragging a layer's duration bar, as you did in the previous procedure.

2 Double-click the LowL layer in the Time Layout window to open its Layer window. In the Layer window, create a small mask on the left side of the image at frame 16.

3 Press the M key to display the Mask Shape property, and then click the stopwatch next to Mask Shape to create the initial keyframe for Mask 3.

4 Move one frame forward and expand the mask at frame 17.

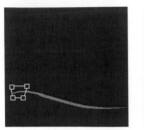

Frame 16   *Frame 17*

5 Continue to create masks at frames 18 and 19.

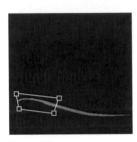
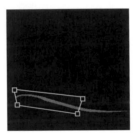

Frame 18   *Frame 19*

6 Set the current time to 00:20, and then reset the layer mask by choosing Layer > Mask >Reset Mask. Collapse the LowL.ai layer outline.

7 Return to frame 00:16, and then check each mask by stepping through the keyframes using the keyframe navigator.

8 Close the Layer window for the LowL layer and collapse its outline. In the Time Layout window, select the Video switches to display the LowL, MidL, and TopL layers.

9 Return to the beginning of the composition, and then press the spacebar to play the composition. The letter *L* should appear to write itself.

10 Close the Script L Comp Time Layout window and Composition window, and then save the project.

You will use this composition later in the lesson.

Creating a template for a composition

You're going to create a composition that contains all the animated elements in the logo. First, you'll add a composite of the logo that was created in Illustrator. After scaling and positioning the logo, you will use the logo layer as a template for aligning the rest of the elements in the animation.

1 Choose Composition > New Composition, and type **Motion Comp** for the name. All the settings should be the same as the previous composition: 320 x 240 in size, 30 frames per second, and 08:00 duration. Click OK.

2 Drag the Merged/Logo.ai footage item from the Project window to the Time Layout window.

Adding an item in this way automatically centers it in the Composition window.

Since the logo was created using black shapes, you will change the background color of the Composition window to white so that you can see the artwork.

3 Choose Composition > Background Color.

4 Click the color swatch, select white from the color picker, click OK, and then click OK again in the Background Color dialog box.

The background stays with the composition when you render a movie. When you render a movie with an alpha channel, the background becomes transparent. When you insert a composition inside another composition, the inserted composition's background becomes transparent.

5 Click the safe-zones icon in the Composition window to display the title-safe and action-safe zones.

Safe-zones icon

Next, you will scale the template layer to fit within the title-safe zone, and then set the Opacity to 20%.

6 Click the triangle for the Merged/Logo.ai layer in the Time Layout window, and then click the triangle to display the Transform properties.

7 With the layer selected in the Composition window, click a corner handle and hold down the mouse button, hold down the Shift key, and then drag until the Scale value displayed in the Info palette is 90%. Holding down the Shift key while resizing a graphic preserves its proportion.

The logo now fits inside the title-safe zone.

8 In the Time Layout window, click the underlined Opacity value, set the Opacity to **20**, and click OK.

9 To rename the Merged/Logo.ai layer in the Time Layout window, select the layer and press Enter or Return. Type **Template** for the new name of the layer, and press Enter or Return again to apply the name.

10 Click the Lock switch to lock the layer, and then collapse the layer outline.

Animating the logo

Now that the template is set up, you will begin to position and animate the logo elements, starting with the word *train*. You'll use the Basic Text effect to create and animate text on a new solid layer.

1 Choose Layer > New Solid, and name it **Train Logo**. Set the size to **320 x 240**, change the color to black, and click OK.

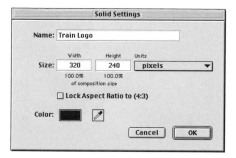

The new black layer obscures the other layers in the composition. Now you'll create the text for the logo.

2 With the Train Logo layer selected, choose Effect > Text > Path Text. Choose Gil Sans Bold or a similar font and type the word **train** in lowercase. Click OK.

The word *train* appears in the center of your screen in red. Next, you will change the settings for this text.

3 In the Effect Controls window, change the Shape Type to Line. Change the Alignment to Center. Click the color swatch and change the text color to black.

4 In the Composition window, drag the Train Logo layer so that the word *train* is directly on top of the word *train* in the template. If the words are not the same size, change the Size value in the Effect Controls window so the Train Logo layer matches the template.

5 In the Time Layout window, display the Train Logo properties, the Effects properties, and the Path Text properties. With the current time still at 0:00:00, set an initial Tracking keyframe.

6 In the Effect Controls window, use the Tracking slider to change the tracking so the word *train* spreads out across the screen.

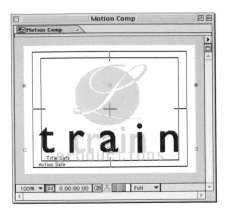

7 Move the current-time marker to four seconds (0:04:00) and change the tracking so it matches the template. Preview your motion to make sure the letters appear as if they are coming together.

Now you'll fade in the text.

8 Move the current-time marker back to 0:00:00. Press the T key to display the Opacity property. Set an initial Opacity keyframe, and change the value to **0**.

9 Move the current-time marker to 0:01:00, and change the Opacity value to **100**.

10 Close the Effect Controls window.

Positioning another element

Next, you will animate the scale and position of the word *productions* and set a fade-in.

1 In the Time Layout window, temporarily hide the video for the Train Logo layer by selecting the Video switch for the layer.

2 Set the current time to 03:24, and then drag the Merged/Prod.ai footage item from the Project window into the Time Layout window.

3 Press the S key to display the Scale property, and then click the underlined Scale value. In the Scale dialog box, deselect Preserve Frame Aspect Ratio, enter **61** for Width, leave Height at **100**, and click OK.

Deselecting Preserve Frame Aspect Ratio lets you enter different values for Width and Height, which changes the aspect ratio of the layer.

4 With the current time still at 03:24, click the stopwatch to set an initial Scale keyframe.

5 Press Shift+P to display the Position property, and then in the Composition window drag the layer so that the word *productions* is centered from left to right, and the bottom edge of the *p* aligns with the bottom of the action-safe zone (the lower of the two lines).

6 Click the stopwatch to set an initial Position keyframe.

Now you'll finish scaling the layer and then you'll return it to its original aspect ratio by selecting Preserve Frame Aspect Ratio.

7 In the Time Layout window, move the current-time marker to 05:02, and click the underlined Scale value. Then select Preserve Frame Aspect Ratio again, set the Scale to **90** for both Width and Height, and click OK.

8 In the Composition window, move the Merged/Prod.ai layer so that it matches the template. A keyframe is automatically created.

9 Set the beginning of the work area by dragging the left work area marker to approximately 03:15, and then play a wireframe preview by pressing Alt+0 (Windows) or Option+0 (Mac OS) on your numeric keypad.

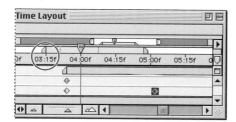

Positioning the circle

The circle starts at 320% of its original size, and then scales down to 90% over several seconds, to match the position on the template.

1 Set the current time to 00:00, and drag the Merged/Circle.ai layer from the Project window to the Time Layout window.

2 Press the S key to display the Scale property, click the underlined Scale value, enter **320**, click OK, and then set an initial Scale keyframe. The entire window is covered with the black circle.

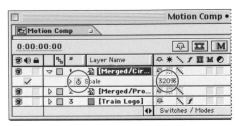

Scale keyframe value

3 Press Shift+P to display the Position property, and then set an initial Position keyframe. The value should be the center point on the composition (160, 120).

4 Set the current time to 02:15, and then set the Scale value to **90**% of the source. A keyframe is automatically created.

5 In the Composition window, position the circle so that it matches the template.

6 Set the current time to 01:00.

Continuously rasterizing

Notice how jagged the edges of the circle look. The Merged/Circle.ai file you imported is Illustrator path-based art. After Effects *rasterizes* the file, or converts it to a pixel-based image format. When you change the scale or otherwise transform a raster image, the edges can become jagged. To smooth the edges of the circle, you'll select the Continuously Rasterize switch in the Time Layout window.

1 To better see the changes continuous rasterization can make, click the Quality switch icon for the Merged/Circle.ai layer to select Best quality. See "Layer switches" on page 46.

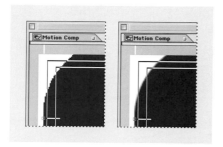

Quality set to draft (left) and Best (right) in the Time Layout window

2 With the current time still at 01:00, select the Continuously Rasterize switch for the Merged/Circle.ai layer. A star shape appears in the Switches panel.

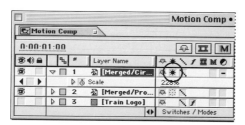

Continuously Rasterize switch selected

Notice how the jagged edges of the circle are smoothed out.

3 Move the current-time marker to 01:15. The image decreases in size, but the pixel information is recalculated so that the edges still appear smooth.

4 Try deselecting and selecting the Continuously Rasterize switch to see the effects as you move to different points in time.

The Continuously Rasterize feature is not available for Illustrator files that have visual effects or masks applied to them. Notice that in the Continuously Rasterize column for the Train Logo layer, no box is displayed. This means that you cannot continuously rasterize the layer because a mask has been applied to the layer.

If no box is displayed, continuous rasterization is unavailable

The Continuously Rasterize feature also may slow down previewing, because the image pixel information is recalculated with every editing change. To increase previewing speed, turn off the option until you are finished positioning elements.

5 Deselect the Continuously Rasterize switch to turn it off, click the Quality switch to select Draft quality, and collapse the layer outline.

Note: This switch affects a layer containing nested compositions differently than it affects a layer containing an Illustrator file. If a layer's source is a composition, selecting this switch can improve image quality and decrease viewing and rendering time. For more information, see the After Effects User Guide.

Nesting Script L Comp

Now you will nest the Script L Comp composition inside the Motion Comp. When you put a composition inside another composition, the nested composition becomes a layer in the composition that contains it. Nesting compositions helps you organize your work, apply complex changes to multiple objects, and update several compositions at once.

After positioning the Script L Comp layer, you set Scale and Position keyframes so that the layer zooms in and ends up in the middle of the circle.

1 Set the current time to 02:04, and then drag Script L Comp from the Project window into the Time Layout window.

You will be able to see only the first piece of the top part of the Script L Comp layer.

2 Display the layer outline for the Script L Comp layer, display the Transform properties, and then click the stopwatch to set an initial Position keyframe.

3 Click the stopwatch to set an initial Scale keyframe, leaving the value at 100%.

4 Move the current-time marker to 03:14, and then set the Scale value to **50% of Source**.

5 In the Composition window, move the script *L* so that it matches the template. (If necessary, hide the video for the Merged/Circle.ai layer.)

You should have two keyframes each for Scale and Position.

6 In the Time Layout window, collapse the Script L Comp layer outline.

7 To select the Video switches for all the layers, choose Layer > Switches > Show All Video.

8 Set the current time to the beginning of the composition, save the project, and then press the spacebar to play the composition.

To keep the edges of the circle smooth as you scale it, you'll use continuous rasterization.

9 Click the Continuously Rasterize switch for the Merged/Circle.ai layer to turn it on.

Splitting the comps

Now all the elements have been animated, but they are all in one composition. To set a matte from the circle and apply visual effects easily to each major element, you will separate the elements into different compositions. (Mattes are discussed later in this lesson.)

After duplicating Motion Comp three times, you will open each copy, delete some of the layers to isolate individual elements, and then rename the composition.

1 First, unlock the Template layer by deselecting the Lock switch in the Time Layout window.

2 Close the Motion Comp Time Layout and Composition windows, and select the Motion Comp composition in the Project window.

3 Choose Edit > Duplicate or press Ctrl+D (Windows) or Command+D (Mac OS).

The duplicated composition has an asterisk (*) added to the name to help you keep track of duplicated layers.

4 Choose Edit > Duplicate three more times, to create Motion Comp**, Motion Comp ***, and Motion Comp ****.

You will leave the first Motion Comp as a backup.

5 Select Motion Comp*, press Enter or Return, type **Circle Comp** to rename it, and press Enter or Return again.

6 Double-click Circle Comp to open the Time Layout window. In the Time Layout window, Ctrl-click (Windows) or Command-click (Mac OS) every item except Merged/Circle.ai to select them, and then press Delete. Close the Composition window and the Time Layout window.

7 In the Project window, select Motion Comp** and rename the new composition **Moving Script L Comp.** Double-click Moving Script L Comp to open the Time Layout window, Shift-click to select every item other than the Script L Comp layer, and then delete the selected items. Close the Composition window and the Time Layout window.

8 In the Project window, change the name of Motion Comp*** to **Production Comp,** open Production Comp, and delete everything but the Production layer. Close the Composition window and the Time Layout window.

9 In the Project window, change the name of Motion Comp**** to **Train Comp,** open Train Comp, and delete everything but Train Logo. Close the Composition window and the Time Layout window.

You should have four new compositions: Circle Comp, Moving Script L Comp, Production Comp, and Train Comp, as well as your initial Motion Comp and Script L Comp.

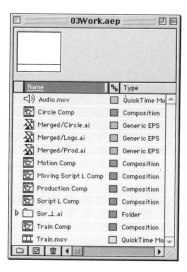

Note: *Another method that can be used to split comps is to precompose the groups of layers. For information on precomposing, see the After Effects User Guide.*

You can keep track of where a nested comp or source file is used by selecting it in the Project window, and then clicking the item name that appears at the top of the Project window.

Creating the final composition

Now you'll create a new composition in which you assemble the individual compositions that contain motion, along with the train video. Since the final composition is quite complex, and includes several visual effects, splitting the layers into different comps simplifies the creation of the final composition.

1 Make sure that all Composition windows and Time Layout windows are closed.

2 Choose Composition > New Composition, and type **Final Comp** for the name. The settings are the same as for previous compositions: 320 x 240, 30 fps, 08:00. Working with nested compositions can cause lengthy screen refresh times. To speed screen redraw, you can change the Resolution to Half. Click OK.

💡 *Press the Caps Lock key to temporarily stop screen refresh.*

Using alpha channel or luminance values for a track matte

A matte is a layer (or any of its channels) that defines the transparent areas of that layer or another layer. When you want one layer to show through a hole in another layer, set up a track matte. You'll need two layers—one to act as a matte, and another to fill the hole in the matte.

After Effects lets you define transparency in a track matte using values from either its alpha channel or the luminance of its pixels. Using luminance is useful when you want to create a track matte using a layer without an alpha channel or a layer imported from a program that can't create an alpha channel. In both alpha channel mattes and luminance mattes, pixels with higher values are more transparent. In most cases, you use a high-contrast matte so that areas are either completely transparent or completely opaque. Intermediate shades should appear only where you want partial or gradual transparency, such as along a soft edge.

—From the Adobe After Effects User Guide, Chapter 8

Creating a track matte

To begin the final composition, you'll start by creating a track matte inside of which you will see the train video footage. A *track matte* works between two layers—a layer that acts as the matte and a layer that provides the fill for the matte. In this example, the circle will be used as a stencil in which you will see the train video.

1 With the current time at 00:00, drag the Train.mov footage item from the Project window to the empty Time Layout window.

2 Drag the Circle Comp (make sure it's the composition item and not the Illustrator source file) from the Project window into the Time Layout window.

3 Make sure that the Train.mov layer is below the Circle Comp layer.

4 Move the current-time marker to 01:00 (just so that you can see what's happening).

5 In the Time Layout window, click the Switches/Modes button at the bottom of the Switches panel to display the Transfer Modes panel.

The Transfer Modes panel is where you set a variety of interactions between layers, including track mattes and layer modes like those in Photoshop.

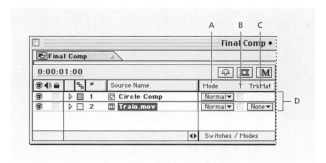

A. Mode menu B. Preserve Transparency check box
C. TrkMat menu D. Transfer Modes panel

6 Select the Train.mov layer, and choose Alpha Matte "Circle Comp" from the TrkMat menu. The train appears inside the circle. Everything outside the circle is masked.

The Alpha Matte option uses the top layer's alpha channel as the matte. In the case of the black-and-white Illustrator image, the black circular area of the illustration becomes transparent. To set a matte, you must position the matte image layer directly above the fill image layer in the stacking order.

Notice the dotted line that appears between the two layers in the Time Layout window. This indicates that a track matte has been applied. After Effects automatically turns off the video of the matte layer. The Video switch icon for the Train.mov layer also changes, reflecting an interaction between the two layers.

7 To examine the alpha channel, position the pointer over the alpha channel icon in the Composition window and hold down the mouse button.

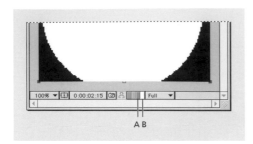

A. Blue channel icon B. Alpha channel icon

8 In the Time Layout window, click the Switches/Modes button again to display the Switches panel.

9 Press the spacebar to play the composition for a few frames, and then save the project.

Applying visual effects

Now you'll assemble the rest of the final composition and apply a variety of visual effects to the various layers, including tints, image controls, and blurs. You've already assembled the Train.mov layer and the Circle Comp composition in the final composition. To these elements you'll add another Circle Comp composition, and then the Moving Script L Comp composition, the Train Comp composition, and the Production Comp composition.

1 Set the current time to 00:00. Drag Moving Script L Comp from the Project window into the Time Layout window.

2 Drag the Train Comp from the Project window into the Time Layout window. Now reposition this new layer in the Time Layout window's layer stack by dragging it below the Moving Script L Comp layer.

3 Drag the Production Comp composition from the Project window into the Time Layout window, positioning it below the Train Comp layer.

4 Finally, drag the Audio.mov footage item from the Project window into the Time Layout window.

You've just added all the elements you'll need for the final composition. Check the order and content of this composition against the illustration below.

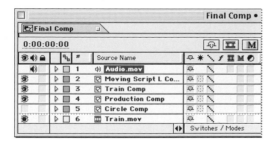

Adding a channel blur effect

You'll start by applying a channel blur to the Train.mov layer, and then modify the brightness and contrast and add a tint.

1 Set the current time to 00:00, select the Train.mov layer, and choose Effect > Blur & Sharpen > Channel Blur.

The Channel Blur effect lets you blur a layer's red, green, blue, or alpha channel individually. For information on channels, see the After Effects User Guide.

2 In the Effect Controls window, experiment with the slider for Blue Blurriness. To enter the final value, click the underlined value for Blue Blurriness, enter **20**, and then click OK.

3 To examine the blue channel, position the pointer over the blue channel icon in the Composition window and hold down the mouse button. Notice that the blue channel has become slightly blurred.

4 Choose Effect > Adjust > Brightness & Contrast. In the Effect Controls window, increase the Brightness value to 26.3 and decrease the Contrast value to -25.3. You may want to experiment with various settings to get the effect that you want.

To simplify setting tints for the elements in the rest of the project, a Photoshop file has been prepared that contains color swatches that you can sample using the Tint effect eyedropper.

5 Choose File > Import > Footage File, select Tints.psd in the 03Lesson folder, and click Open. Double-click Tints.psd in the Project window to open it in the Footage window, and then position the Footage window so that you can see both it and the Project window.

6 Activate the Final Comp Composition window, make sure the Train.mov layer is selected, and then choose Effect > Image Control > Tint. In the Effect Controls window, click the Map Black To eyedropper.

7 Click the peach color swatch in the upper left corner of the Tints.psd window to sample the color, and then set the Amount to Tint value to 53.7%.

8 If you want to modify the color, click the Map Black To color swatch in the Effect Controls window and adjust the tint using the color picker.

9 Close the Effect Controls window for the Train.mov layer.

Creating a glow effect for the circle

To create a glowing effect behind the circle and give it a slightly raised look, you'll add a second Circle Comp and apply the Fast Blur and Tint effects to it. In order to see the effect better, you'll change the background color to white.

1 Drag the Circle Comp composition from the Project window into the Final Comp Time Layout window. You now have two Circle Comp layers.

2 In the Time Layout window, select the lower Circle Comp composition.

3 Choose Composition > Background Color, and then click the eyedropper and sample white from the background in the Tints.psd Footage window. Click OK.

4 Set the current time to 02:00 so that you can see the circle.

5 In the Time Layout window, select the top Circle Comp layer and rename the layer **Glow**.

6 In the Time Layout window, drag the Glow layer beneath the Train.mov layer.

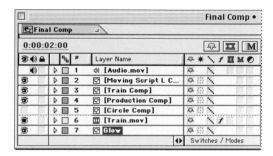

7 Move the current-time marker to 00:00, and then choose Effect > Blur & Sharpen > Fast Blur. In the Time Layout window, click the triangle for the Glow layer, click the triangle for Effects, and then click the triangle for Fast Blur. Click the stopwatch to set an initial Blurriness keyframe. Set Blurriness to **17.0**.

8 Move the current-time marker to 02:15, and change the Blurriness value to **11.4**.

9 Choose Effect > Image Control > Tint. In the Effect Controls window, click the Map Black To eyedropper, and then sample the kelly green color swatch (middle left square) in the Tints.psd Footage window. Set the Amount to Tint value to **100**.

10 Close the Effect Controls window, collapse the Glow layer outline, and save the project.

Modifying effects for the second movie clip

To get the two-toned effect for the train video, you'll duplicate the original layer, and then modify the effects in the Effect Controls window.

1 Set current time to 0:00. Select the Train.mov layer in the Time Layout window, and choose Edit > Duplicate.

2 Select the lowest Train.mov layer and change the name to **Train Background**.

3 To turn off the matte, make sure the Transfer Modes panel is displayed. Then choose No Track Matte from the TrkMat menu for the Train Background layer.

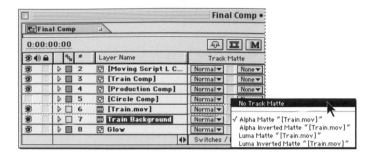

4 Drag the Train Background layer below the Glow layer.

5 Press the E key to display the Effect properties, and then double-click any effect property to open the Effect Controls window for the Train Background layer.

6 Under Channel Blur in the Effect Controls window, set the Blue Blurriness value to **0** and the Green Blurriness value to **34**.

7 Change the Brightness value to **30.5** and the Contrast value to **–15.8**.

8 To change the tint, click the Map Black To eyedropper, and then sample the lilac color swatch in the upper right corner of the Tints.psd Footage window.

9 In the Effect Controls window, set the Amount to Tint value to **63.7**.

10 Close the Effect Controls window for the Train Background layer and save the project.

Using the Bevel Alpha and Drop Shadow effects

Now you'll apply a tint, a bevel, and a drop shadow to the Moving Script L Comp layer.

1 In the Time Layout window, select the Moving Script L Comp layer.

2 Set the current time to 03:00 (so you can see the entire script *L*), and then choose Effect > Image Control > Tint. Click the Map Black To eyedropper in the Effect Controls window, and sample the dark green color swatch (middle right square) in the Tints.psd Footage window.

3 Set the Amount to Tint value to **100**%.

4 Choose Effect > Perspective > Bevel Alpha.

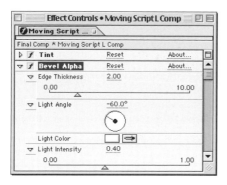

The Bevel Alpha effect gives a chiseled and lighted appearance to the alpha boundaries of an image.

5 In the Effect Controls window, experiment with the Edge Thickness and Light Angle controls, and then click Reset to use the default values.

6 Click the Light Color eyedropper, and then sample the gold color in the lower left corner of the Tints.psd Footage window.

The highlight of the beveled edge turns yellow. As a finishing touch, you'll add a drop shadow to the script L that starts blurry and far away and gets sharper and moves closer over time.

7 Choose Effect > Perspective > Drop Shadow.

8 In the Effect Controls window, set the Opacity to **30**%, the Distance to **39**, and the Softness to **10**. Leave the other settings at their default values.

9 In the Time Layout window, set the current time to 02:00, press the E key to display the Effects properties, and then click the triangle for Drop Shadow. Set initial keyframes for Opacity, Distance, and Softness.

The shadow will get closer, sharper, and darker over time.

10 Move the current-time marker to 03:13, and then set the Opacity to **50**%, the Distance to **6**, and the Softness to **15**.

11 Collapse the layer outline, close the Effect Controls window, and save the project.

Finishing the composition

To finish the composition, you will change the Opacity of the Train Comp and Production layers, and apply Tint and Gaussian Blur effects.

1 In the Time Layout window, select the Train Comp layer.

2 To sample the green from the Tints.psd Footage window, choose Effect > Image Control > Tint. In the Effect Controls window, click the Map Black To eyedropper and sample the dark green color swatch (middle right square) in the Tints.psd Footage window.

3 Set the Amount to Tint to **100**.

4 With the current time still at 03:13, press Ctrl+Shift+O (Windows) or Command+Shift+O (Mac OS) to display the Opacity dialog box without displaying the other Transform properties, enter **40** for Opacity, and then click OK. Because you didn't set any keyframes for these effects, they affect the entire Train Comp layer.

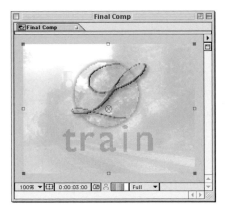

5 Close the Effect Controls window for the Train Comp layer.

Now you'll set a tint and a Gaussian blur for the Production Comp layer.

6 In the Time Layout window, select the Production Comp layer.

7 Set the current time to 03:28 and choose Effect > Image Control > Tint. In the Effect Controls window, click the Map Black To eyedropper, and then sample the dark brown color in the lower right corner of the Tints.psd Footage window. Set the Amount to Tint to **100**.

8 Choose Effect > Blur & Sharpen > Gaussian Blur. In the Effect Controls window, set the Blurriness value to **8**.

9 Press the E key to display the Effect properties, and then click the triangle for Gaussian Blur. Click the stopwatch to set an initial Blurriness keyframe.

10 Move the current-time marker to 05:09, and decrease the Blurriness value to **4.0**.

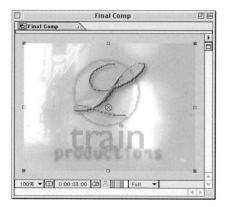

11 Close the Final Comp Time Layout and Composition windows, and close the Tints.psd Footage window and the Effect Controls window. Save the project.

Creating a fade-out composition

Now that you have completed all the motion and visual effects, you'll create one last composition in which you'll nest the Final Comp. You will set up a fade-out by using Opacity keyframes that will affect all the layers at once. Then you'll add the audio and render the movie.

1 Choose Composition > New Composition, type **Fadeout Comp** for the name, and leave the other settings as they are. Click OK.

2 Make sure the current time is set to 00:00 and drag the Final Comp from the Project window into the Time Layout window of the Fadeout Comp.

3 Move the current-time marker to 06:15 and set an initial Opacity keyframe at **100**%.

4 Move the current-time marker to 7:29, and then change the Opacity value to **0**.

5 Save the project.

Rendering the movie

If you have several versions of a composition, or several different compositions in a project, you can set them to batch render by using the Render Queue. In this section, you will use the Render Queue window to prepare a composition with two different settings—Draft and Best. You might use the Draft setting to create a movie that could be used for checking motion or for testing. You normally use the Best setting for final rendering. Selecting Best quality in the Render Queue window ensures that all compositions nested in your final composition are also set to Best Quality.

Earlier in this lesson, you turned off continuous rasterization for the Circle Comp layer to speed up previewing. Before you set up the render process, you'll turn it back on again.

1 In the Time Layout window, select the Final Comp tab, and then click the Switches/Modes button to display the Switches panel. In the Switches panel, click the Continuously Rasterize switch for the Circle Comp layer to turn this feature on.

2 Choose Composition > Make Movie, name the movie **03Movie1.mov**, and save it in your Projects folder.

3 In the Render Queue, select the Fadeout Comp item.

4 Click the underlined Current Settings to display the Render Settings dialog box. For Quality, chose Best. For Time Span, choose Length of Comp. Click OK.

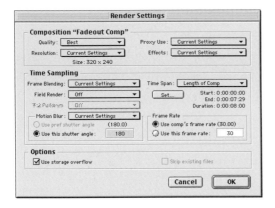

5 For Output Module, choose Custom. Then choose QuickTime Movie from the Format menu at the top of the Output Module Settings dialog box.

6 In Windows, the Compressor Settings dialog box appears. Leave the compressor set to Animation and click OK. In Mac OS, leave the settings at their defaults.

7 Select Audio Output. Choose 22.050 KHz and 8 bit, mono, and then click OK.

8 To render another version of the composition with different settings, select the item in the Render Queue window, and choose Edit > Duplicate.

9 A duplicate item appears, except the Render Queue indicates that a name has not yet been specified for the output. Click the underlined phrase Not Yet Specified next to Output To, and then rename the movie **03Movie2.mov** and click Save.

10 Choose Draft Settings from the Render Settings menu.

After Effects will render the movies in order from first to last. To change the order of the rendering list, simply drag the composition name up or down in the Render Queue.

11 Drag the 03Movie2 item up above the 03Movie1 item.

If you need to delete an item in the Render Queue, select the item, and press Delete.

12 Click Render.

The Render progress bar appears and the draft movie begins to render. When it is finished, the second movie will begin rendering.

Depending on the type of system you have, each movie can take a while to render. If you click the Stop button in the Render Queue window, a partial movie will be created.

13 When you are finished rendering the movies, close the project and view the movies using the MoviePlayer application.

You should feel that you are getting to be an experienced Adobe After Effects user by now. With the completion of this project, you have accomplished a great deal, including exploring many of the visual effects in Adobe After Effects.

Multimedia Animation

In this lesson, you'll import Photoshop files as compositions and enhance your project using a number of advanced visual effects.

In this lesson, you will create a music-video-style animation for a multimedia CD-ROM. This project focuses on using Adobe Photoshop documents with layers, and animating those layers in After Effects. The project's source files include type treatments, graphic elements, and background textures.

To complete this lesson, knowledge of and experience with Adobe Photoshop layers, layer masks, and clipping groups are extremely helpful. If you have Adobe Photoshop, you will want to have it available to open the source files.

This lesson covers the following topics:

• Importing Adobe Photoshop files as compositions and as still images

• Animating imported Adobe Photoshop adjustment layers

• Using transfer modes with imported Adobe Photoshop layers

• Using the Brightness/Contrast effect

• Using the Production Bundle Scatter and Glow effects

• Preparing a QuickTime movie for a CD-ROM

At the end of this lesson, you will have a 20-second animation with audio.

It should take approximately 2 to 3 hours to complete this project.

Viewing the final project

Before you begin, take a look at the finished movie that you'll create in this lesson.

1 Double-click 04Final.mov in the 04Lesson folder to open the final QuickTime movie, and click the Play button.

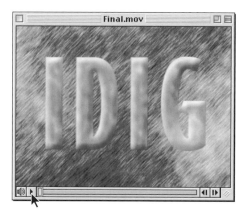

The movie consists of four different segments: I Dig, Smiley Face, You Dig?, and Dig It! After creating three of the four segments, and modifying another, you will create a fifth segment that combines the movies from all of your projects and add audio.

2 Exit from the MoviePlayer application.

Creating the You Dig? movie segment

Instead of creating the segments of the final project in the order they appear, you'll start with the third segment, *You Dig?*, because it's the easiest.

Examining the Adobe Photoshop source documents

The first step in creating the animated segments is assembling the source files in Adobe Photoshop. The third element of the sequence is the phrase *You Dig?*, which will dissolve on to the background one letter at a time. It will have a watery-looking animated background. You will find that having a text element revealed one letter at a time is quite easy when you do the proper preparation in your Adobe Photoshop source document. The source files for this project are Type.psd and Bakgrd.psd, located in the YouDig folder.

1 If you have access to Adobe Photoshop, open and examine the following files:

• Type.psd has two layers, one each for the words *You* and *Dig*. These type layers were rendered in Photoshop, in order to place a different color into each letter and to animate each word independently. Both layers have a layer mask, consisting of a horizontal black-to-white gradient; the You mask goes from white on the left to black on the right, and the Dig layer mask is black on the left and white on the right. These layer masks will serve as the basis for a gradient-style wipe, moving in a different direction for each layer.

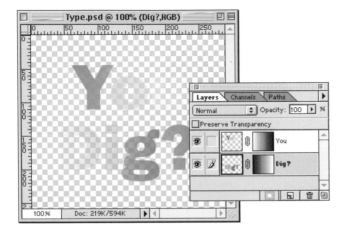

• Bakgrd.psd has three layers. Layer 1 was created by filling an empty layer with white, applying a monochromatic Add Noise filter with a setting of 100, and then using the Gaussian Blur filter with a setting of 3.

• A Hue/Saturation adjustment layer was added, with a Hue value of -30; this adjustment layer will be animated in After Effects.

• Layer 2 was also created by duplicating the bottom layer and applying the Find Edges filter to it. After desaturating the layer and increasing its contrast with Levels, we rotated it 180° and set it to the Soft Light blending mode. (After Effects 4.0 directly supports all of Photoshop's blending modes).

2 If you opened Adobe Photoshop, exit from the application.

Getting started

1 To ensure that the tools and palettes function exactly as described in this lesson, delete or deactivate (by renaming) the After Effects preferences file. See "Restoring default preferences" on page 6.

2 Start the After Effects application. An untitled Project window appears.

3 Choose File > Save As, name the file **04Work.aep**, and save it in the Projects folder.

4 To set up the project composition, choose Composition > New Composition. Name it **YouDig Comp**, set the Frame Rate to **15** frames per second, and set the Duration to **02:16** (2 seconds, 16 frames). Leave the Frame Size set to the default of **320** x **240** pixels. Click OK.

Importing the source documents into After Effects

You can import Adobe Photoshop files complete with image layers, adjustment layers, layer masks, and layer effects into your After Effects projects. This makes it possible to prearrange the composition in Adobe Photoshop; the files in this example have been set up with this in mind. In this section, you will import two Adobe Photoshop files as compositions, and then animate the layers.

1 Since you will use the You Dig composition later in the lesson, close both the Time Layout and Composition windows.

2 Choose File > Import > Photoshop as Comp, select the Type.psd file in the YouDig folder, in the 04Lesson folder, and click Open.

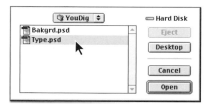

3 In the Project window, click the triangle next to the Type folder to expand the outline.

Notice that importing an Adobe Photoshop document as a composition creates a number of files in your Project window, a composition (Type.psd), and a folder of the image layers (one for each word in the phrase *You Dig?*).

4 Choose File > Import > Photoshop as Comp, select the Bakgrd.psd file, and click Open.

5 Click the triangle next to the Bakgrd.psd folder in the Project window to expand the outline.

The Bakgrd.psd composition contains three layers: the Hue/Saturation adjustment layer, Layer 1, and Layer 2. The Adobe Photoshop file was created with bigger dimensions than the final composition, to allow for the image to be vertically animated.

Animating the Type

Having imported the necessary files, you can now begin the process of animating the elements and their layers. The basic process is to edit and animate each element as a composition, allowing you to access each independent layer in each document and then assemble them in the final composition.

1 Double-click the composition named Type.psd, opening its Composition and Time Layout windows. Examine the layers in the Time Layout window. There are two layers, one for each layer in the Adobe Photoshop source file.

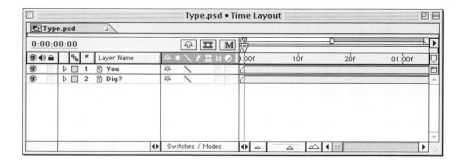

Your first step is to create the animation of the type coming onto the screen, one word at a time. You will use a combination of zooming and rotating words, decreasing blurring, and interpolating layer masks to achieve this effect.

2 In the Time Layout window, make sure the blue current-time marker is set to 00:00:00. Then click the triangle to the left of the You layer to display the layer outline. Click the triangle next to Transform to display the transform properties.

3 Set initial keyframes for Scale and Rotation by clicking their stopwatch icons. Click the underlined value next to Scale, type **0**, and click OK. This will enable the character to zoom to full view. Leave the Rotation keyframe at its default value of 0.0%.

4 Choose Effect > Channel > Alpha Levels. The Effect Controls window appears. In the Time Layout window, click the triangle to display the Effects properties and then display the Alpha Levels properties. Set two initial keyframes: one for the Input Black Level at a value of **225**, and another for the Input White Level at its default value of **255**. This will allow this layer's layer mask to change over time, revealing the layer like a wipe effect.

5 Move the current-time marker to 00:01:16, and then set Scale to **100** and Rotation to **1** revolution, **0** degrees.

6 For the Alpha Levels Effects, create two new keyframes at this same frame (00:01:16) by setting the Input Black Level to **0** and setting the Input White Level to **30**.

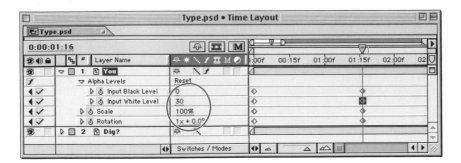

7 Preview your work so far by pressing the spacebar or by using RAM Preview.

8 Go to 00:00:00. In the Dig layer, display the Transform properties and set initial keyframes for both Scale and Rotation; don't worry about values for now.

Next, you'll make the Scale keyframes in the Dig layer match those you set earlier in the You layer.

9 In the You layer, click Scale to select all scale keyframes, and then copy them by choosing Edit > Copy. In the Dig layer, select the initial Scale keyframe and choose Edit > Paste to paste the keyframes you just copied.

10 Go to 00:01:16 and set the Dig layer's Rotation property to –1 revolution, **0** degrees. This will cause the layer to rotate in the opposite direction of the You layer.

11 With the Dig layer still selected, choose Effect > Channel > Alpha Levels. Display the Effects properties and then the Alpha Levels properties.

Now you'll copy the Alpha Level keyframes that you set earlier in the You layer and paste them into the Dig layer.

12 In the You layer, select all four keyframes for the Input Black Level and the Input White Level properties by drawing a selection marquee around them. Copy the selected keyframes.

13 Return to 00:00:00. Select the Dig layer and paste the keyframes you just copied. The You layer and the Dig layer now have identical keyframes for the Alpha Levels effect.

14 Expand all the tracks that possess keyframes; draw a marquee around all of them to select all of them. Choose Layer > Keyframe Assistant > Easy Ease. The Easy Ease function smooths out the rate of change through the keyframes, creating a smoother-looking animation.

15 Preview your motion keyframes. Return to frame 00:00:00 by pressing the Home key. Press the spacebar (or use RAM Preview) to preview the motion. When you're finished previewing, collapse the layer outlines.

16 To make the motion in this composition look smooth, select the Motion Blur option for both layers and select the Enable Motion Blur button at the top of the Switches/Modes panel. Now preview the composition again and notice the difference.

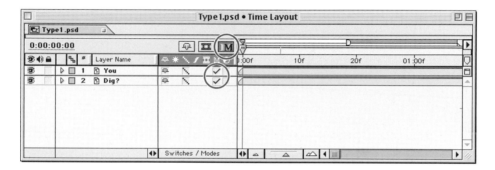

17 Close the Type.psd Composition window and the corresponding Time Layout window.

Animating the background

We also want the background to be animated, but more subtle than the foreground, and consistent with the look of the other backgrounds in the final sequence. You will simply make the two background layers crawl up the screen at different speeds and have the bottom layer do a slight color shift over time.

1 Double-click the Bakgrd.psd composition, opening its Composition and Time Layout windows.

2 In the Composition window, set the magnification to 25% so you can see the changes as you animate the background layers.

3 In the Time Layout window, display the Layer 1 outline, and display its Transform properties.

4 Make sure the current-time marker is at 00:00:00, set an initial Position keyframe, and leave X-axis set to **320** pixels and set Y-axis to **120** pixels.

5 Press the End key to go to the last frame in the composition, and leave X-axis set to **320** and set Y-axis to **480**. Collapse the Layer 1 layer outline.

 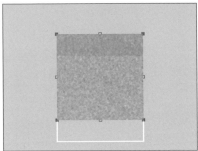

Layer 1 at first frame and last frame

6 In the Time Layout window, display the Layer 2 Transform properties, and then press the Home key to move the current-time marker to 00:00:00.

7 Set an initial Position keyframe, and leave X-axis set to **320** and set Y-axis to **360**.

8 Press the End key to go to the last frame in the composition, leave X-axis set to **320** and set Y-axis to **240**.

This layer will move at a slower rate of speed than the first layer.

9 Select both Position keyframes from Layer 2 by clicking Position in the Time Layout window. Then choose Edit > Copy. Collapse the Layer 2 layer outline.

10 Return to frame 00:00:00 by pressing the Home key, and select the Hue/Saturation adjustment layer. Press the P key to display the Position property and then paste the keyframes you copied from Layer 2.

Animating the Adjustment Layer

To create the color shift you see in the final movie, you will animate the Hue/Saturation adjustment layer that was imported from Photoshop. This effect lets you change the individual Hue, Lightness, and Saturation components of a selected layer.

Using adjustment layers from Adobe Photoshop

Adjustment layers in Adobe Photoshop versions 4.0 and later change the color and tonal qualities of an image without permanently modifying the original image. Photoshop adjustment layers affect the appearance of all layers below them. When you import an Adobe Photoshop file containing one or more adjustment layers, After Effects directly converts the Photoshop adjustment layers to After Effects adjustment layers, modifying all layers below them in the Time Layout window. You can turn off the Adjustment Layer switch in After Effects to remove the effect and display the layer as a white solid. To remove the effect and the white solid, you can either delete the adjustment layer or turn off the Video switch for the layer.

—From the Adobe After Effects User Guide, Chapter 3

1 With the Hue/Saturation adjustment layer selected, collapse the Position property. Display the Effects properties and display the Hue/Saturation properties.

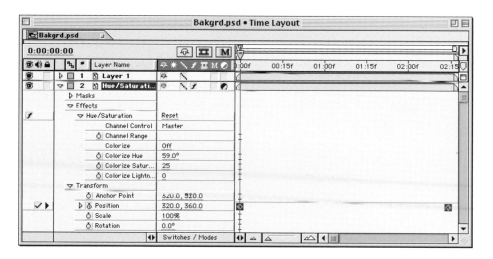

2 At 00:00:00, create an initial keyframe for the Channel Range property. While the channel range itself won't be animated, this is where the master hue, saturation, and lightness control keyframes are controlled.

3 The Effect Controls window for the Hue/Saturation adjustment layer should be open. If it isn't, double-click the effect name in the Time Layout window. The Master Hue control is set at –30°, the same setting that was specified in the original Photoshop document.

4 Go to the last frame in the composition (00:02:16) by pressing the End key. Move the Master Hue wheel 60° clockwise, to a new value of 30°. You will notice that a new keyframe is automatically created in the Time Layout window.

5 Go to frame 00:00:00 by pressing the Home key.

6 In the Composition window, set magnification to 100%. Set the Composition window to half-resolution using the menu at the bottom right of the window; this will greatly improve preview speed. Preview this composition by pressing the spacebar. You should see motion and a smooth cycling of color from yellowish-green to an aqua blue.

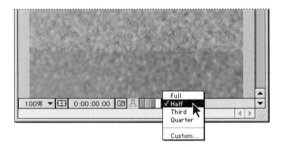

In some areas along the top and bottom of this composition, the layers do not overlap. Since the final composition will be 320 pixels wide by 240 pixels high, these areas won't be visible. The current composition is much larger, 640 pixels by 640 pixels, to allow as much movement as possible without areas of visibly empty space.

7 Close the Bakgrd.psd Composition window and Time Layout window, and the Effect Controls dialog box. Save the project.

Integrating all the elements

Now you'll place your two compositions in the YouDig composition that you created earlier. Then you'll add a drop shadow to the type layers to enhance the illusion of depth.

1 Double-click the YouDig composition in the Project window.

2 Drag the Bakgrd.psd composition from the Project window into the YouDig Time Layout window. The composition is automatically centered in the Composition window.

3 Drag the Type.psd composition from the Project window into the YouDig Time Layout window.

4 With the Type.psd layer selected, choose Effect > Perspective > Drop Shadow. Expand the Type.psd outline, display its Effects properties, and then display the Drop Shadow properties.

5 At 00:00:00 in the Time Layout window, set an initial Opacity keyframe at **100** percent, set an initial Direction keyframe at **135** degrees, set an initial Distance keyframe at **0** pixels. Set Softness to **5** without setting a keyframe. (Softness remains at this value throughout the composition, so a keyframe is not needed.)

6 Move the current-time marker to 00:01:16 and set Opacity to **50** percent, and set Distance to **10** pixels. Keyframes are automatically created for these properties.

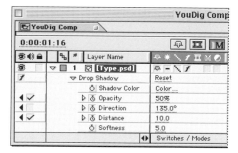

You have just created a drop shadow that moves quickly from being very strong and harsh to lighter and softer. This gives the appearance that the words are moving away from the background as they increase in size.

7 Save the project.

Rendering the YouDig movie

At the end of this lesson, you will combine four individual movie files into one project, then render the complete sequence. With a complex project such as this, you can break it down into manageable chunks, render separate movies, and then combine the movies.

Here, you'll render the YouDig movie. If your time is limited, you can simply step through the process of rendering the movie without actually starting the rendering process. The movie has already been rendered for you. It's called YouDig.mov, and it is located in the YouDig folder in the 04Lesson folder.

1 Make sure that either the YouDig Composition window or Time Layout window is active. Choose Composition > Make Movie, type **Movie1.mov** for the name, and save the file in your Projects folder.

Since the final sequence will be compressed after being integrated with the three other After Effects projects, you want to use little or no compression the first time you output a QuickTime movie.

2 For Render Settings, choose Best Settings. (If time is limited, set the Quality to Draft instead.)

3 For Output Module, choose Custom. For Format, choose QuickTime Movie.

4 In Windows, the Compression Settings dialog box appears. Leave the compressor set to Animation and click OK. In Mac OS, leave the Video Output options at their defaults. Make sure Quality is set to Best and Frames Per Second is set to 15 fps. Leave other settings at their defaults, and then click OK.

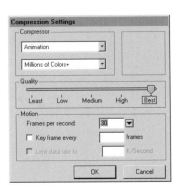
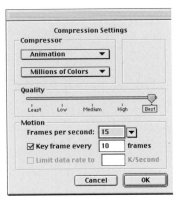

Windows   *Mac OS*

Animation is a *lossless* compression scheme that does not cause degradation in image quality.

5 Select Import into Project When Done, and click OK.

6 Click the Render button.

7 When you are finished rendering the movie, close the Render Queue window. Open the footage file that appears in your Project window, and play it.

8 After viewing the movie, save and close the Work.aep project.

Creating the IDIG movie segment

Now you will create the first segment of the sequence. This project will involve importing both Photoshop layer effects and image layers into After Effects and animating them.

Preparing the Adobe Photoshop source documents

The IDIG project is made up of two Adobe Photoshop files: Type1.psd, and Bakgrd.psd.

If you have access to Adobe Photoshop, open and examine these files:

Type1.psd has four layers.

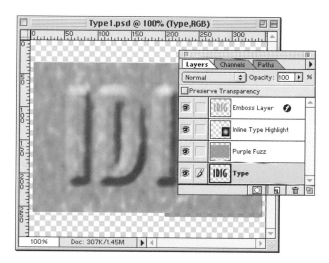

• Emboss Layer was created by loading the Type layer as a selection and filling the selection with 50% gray; this layer is set to the Overlay mode. We applied an Outer Bevel layer effect to it; the layer effect properties are mostly set to their default settings, but the shadow and highlight are both set to Normal mode (you'll see why in a little while). If applied to a 50% gray layer in Overlay mode, only the highlight and shadow are visible.

• Inline Type Highlight is a white-to-black radial gradient within a 196 x 213 pixel selection area. It is screened on top of everything to simulate a highlight from an overhead light source. Its Opacity is also set to 50%.

- Purple Fuzz contains the texture for the type. It is much larger than the type itself, to provide extra area in case it is rotated or scaled within After Effects.

- Type contains the text *IDIG*, filled with black.

This Photoshop file may look a little strange; this is because the layers are not grouped together. Rather than grouping them together in Photoshop, you'll be using After Effects' Preserve Underlying Transparency feature to clip the texture and embossing layers to the bottom *Type* layer.

The Inline Type Highlight layer will move diagonally up and left, and the properties of the Emboss layer's Outer Bevel will animate to simulate changing lighting. There is no background in this document, since we want to *composite*, or combine, it onto a background element.

Bakgrd.psd has three layers.

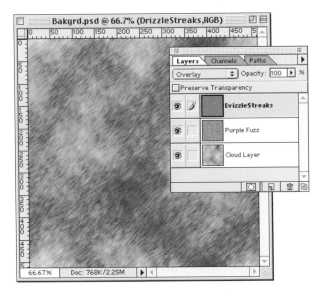

- DrizzleStreaks was created by filling the layer with black, applying the Noise > Add Noise filter with a setting of 150, and using the Blur > Motion Blur filter set to an angle of 45 with a distance of 10 pixels.

- Purple Fuzz is a duplicate of the Purple Fuzz layer from the Type1.psd file, which has been hue shifted by using the Image > Adjust > Curves command.

- Cloud Layer is a grayscale layer created by using the Filter > Render > Clouds filter.

This file will be used as the background image in After Effects, and will include a number of rotation, scaling, and filtering effects. The Type1.psd layer will be composited and animated on top of the Bakgrd.psd layer and then vaporized off the screen, through the use of filtering, color manipulation, and reduction of opacity over time.

Importing the source documents into After Effects

Now it's time to integrate these Adobe Photoshop files into After Effects.

1 In After Effects, choose File > New Project.

2 Choose File > Save As, name the file **IDIG.aep**, and save it in the Projects folder.

Note: If you want to view a completed version of this movie segment, play the IDIG.mov that is located in the IDIG folder in the 04Lesson folder.

3 Choose Composition > New Composition. Type **IDIG Comp** for the name, set the Frame Size to **320 x 240**, the Frame Rate to **15** fps, and the Duration to **03:00**. Click OK.

4 Choose File > Import > Photoshop as Comp, and select the Type1.psd file in the IDIG folder in the 04Lesson folder. Click OK.

Both a composition and a folder (which contains the individual source layers) appear in the Project window.

5 In the Project window, double-click the composition named Type1.psd to open it in the Time Layout window.

Notice that the layer effects for each layer appear as separate After Effects layers. In fact, the Outer Bevel has been expanded into two layers: one for the Shadow and one for the Highlight. Even their blending modes—Multiply and Screen, respectively—are set properly as they were in Photoshop. This will make it easy to animate each element separately.

6 Choose File > Import > Photoshop as Comp, and select the Bakgrd.psd file in the IDIG folder in the 04Lesson folder. Click OK.

7 Select the Bakgrd.psd composition in the Project window. Choose Composition > Composition Settings. Set the Frame Size to **320** x **240** pixels. Click OK.

Changing the size will crop the image to the size of the frame without actually discarding image data. The original Photoshop file is oversized to accommodate motion. You'll change the size of the Type1.psd composition as well.

8 Click the IDIG Comp tab in the Time Layout window.

9 Drag the Bakgrd.psd composition from the Project window into the IDIG Time Layout window, which automatically centers it in the IDIG composition.

10 In the Project window, select the Type1.psd composition, choose Composition > Composition Settings, and set the Frame Size to **320** x **240**. Click OK.

11 Click the Type1.psd tab in the Time Layout window.

12 In the Time Layout window, drag the right edge of the Layer Name heading to the right until you can see the full name of each layer.

13 Click the Switches/Modes button in the Time Layout window to display the Transfer Modes panel. Select the Preserve Transparency option (in the column marked "T") for every layer *except* the bottom one (named Type). This sets up the bottom layer as a mask for all the layers above it.

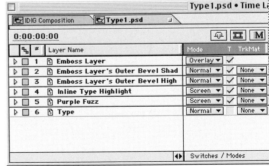

As in the YouDig composition, you will first edit and animate layers within each composition, and then assemble the compositions themselves.

If you have enough memory to have Adobe Photoshop and After Effects open at the same time, you can select any Adobe Photoshop layer in the Project window, and then press Ctrl+E (Windows) or Command+E (Mac OS) to open Adobe Photoshop.

Animating the highlight

The first layer you will animate is the Inline Type Highlight layer. It will move diagonally up and to the left, to simulate a light source moving over the type.

1 Make sure the current-time marker in the Time Layout window is set to the beginning of the Type1.psd composition (00:00:00).

2 Select the Inline Type Highlight layer, and press the P key to display the Position property. As seen in the Composition window, the layer is positioned near the lower right corner of the type.

3 Set an initial Position keyframe. Do not move the layer at this time; this is the beginning point of its move.

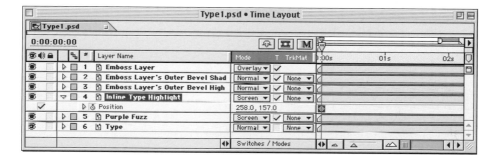

4 Move the current-time marker to the end of the composition. In the Composition window, move the Inline Type Highlight layer to the upper left corner of the composition, so that it illuminates the upper left corner of the first letter "I."

Animating the shadow

Next, you will animate the layers that make up the Outer Bevel effect applied in Photoshop. With the layer outline expanded in the Time Layout window, you can see that this layer effect has been broken into three different layers, in order to recreate this fairly complex layer effect:

• The Emboss Layer, in Overlay mode, is the original image layer to which the layer effect was applied.

• The Emboss Layer's Outer Bevel Shadow layer provides the outer soft shadow, in Normal mode.

• The Emboss Layer's Outer Bevel Highlight layer provides the outer soft highlight, in Normal mode.

These last two layers will be inverted as the highlight moves across the image. Thus, the highlight and shadow will seem to exchange places to simulate interactive lighting. The layer effect's shadow and highlight were both set to Normal mode to ensure that they would appear properly even when inverted.

1 Return the current-time marker to the beginning of the composition and select the Emboss Layer's Outer Bevel Shadow layer. Shift-click the Emboss Layer's Outer Bevel Highlight layer to select it as well.

2 Choose Effect > Channel > Invert.

3 In the Time Layout window, display the Effects properties for the Outer Bevel Shadow layer and display the Invert effect's properties.

4 Create an initial keyframe for Blend With Original at frame 00:00:00, keeping the default value of 0.

5 Go to the last frame in the composition. Change the Blend With Original value to **100** %.

6 Shift-click the two keyframes you just created to select them, and then choose Edit > Copy.

7 Move to the beginning of the composition (00:00:00), select the Outer Bevel Highlight layer, and paste the keyframes you just copied.

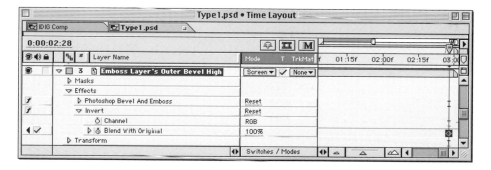

Now each embossing layer will interpolate in brightness; the shadow will become the highlight, and vice-versa.

8 Preview the composition.

9 Close the Effect Controls window, and then close the Type1.psd composition's Time Layout and Composition windows by clicking the button in the Type1.psd tab. Save the project.

Animating the Type Transition

The type will vaporize, blowing off the screen as if it were dissolving at the same time. Since the whole Type1.psd layer will be affected by this visual effect, you are going to edit the Type1.psd composition. You don't need to address each layer separately as you did with the Type1.psd composition in the previous steps.

First you will alter the type's Opacity so it fades off the screen. Then you will make the type turn white to improve visibility of the effect. Finally, you will apply a Radial Blur effect to make the type streak and blur as it fades.

1 Drag the Type1.psd composition from the Project window into the IDIG Composition's Time Layout window in order to automatically center it in the composition.

2 Display the Type1.psd layer's Transform properties.

3 Move the current time to 00:02:10 and create an initial keyframe for Opacity; this is where the vaporize effect will start. Make sure the Opacity value is set to **100**%.

4 Move the current-time marker to 00:02:28 and set the Opacity value to **0**.

5 Set the current time to 00:02:10, and then choose Effect > Adjust > Brightness & Contrast.

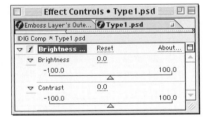

6 In the Time Layout window, display the Effect properties and display the properties for the Brightness & Contrast effect. With the current time still at 00:02:10, set two initial keyframes, one for Brightness and one for Contrast, at their default values of 0.

7 Set the current time to 00:02:28, and set both Brightness and Contrast to **100**.

8 Choose Effect > Blur & Sharpen > Radial Blur. In the Effect Controls window, choose Zoom from the Type pop-up menu. All other settings remain at their defaults. Make sure to keep the anti-aliasing option set to low; we actually want a grainy effect here. Close the Effect Controls window.

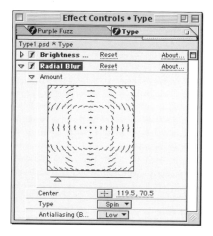

9 In the Time Layout window, go to 00:02:10, display the Radial Blur properties, and then set an initial Amount keyframe. Set the Amount value to **0**.

10 Move the current time to 00:02:28, and then set the Amount value to **300**.

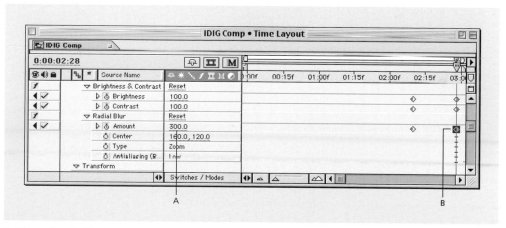

A. Blur value **B.** *Keyframe*

11 Go to 01:20, set the Resolution to Quarter in the Composition window, and preview your composition.

12 Set the resolution back to Full and save the project.

Animating the background

To make the background of the project more dynamic, you'll animate each of its layers to create a shifting, moving backdrop for the type.

1 Double-click the Bakgrd.psd composition in the Project window, opening its Composition and Time Layout windows.

The top layer, DrizzleStreaks, will be animated in a diagonal move down and to the left, at the same angle as the layer's motion-blurred noise, to generate a falling-rain effect.

2 In the Time Layout window, make sure the current-time marker is set to the beginning of the composition, at 00:00:00.

In a Composition window, press the = (equal symbol) key to zoom in, and press the , (comma) key to zoom out.

3 In the Composition window, set the magnification to 50% (press the comma key once).

4 Select the DrizzleStreaks layer in the Time Layout window and press the P key to display its Position property.

5 Set an initial Position keyframe, and set the Position coordinates to **256** for X-axis and **–16** for Y-axis.

6 Go to the end of the composition and change the Position values to **65** for X-axis and **175** for Y-axis.

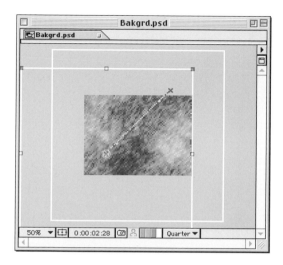

7 Collapse the layer outline.

Animating the next layer

The next layer, Purple Fuzz, is going to move in the opposite direction from DrizzleStreaks and will shift its hue over time.

1 In the Time Layout window, return the time marker to the first frame of the composition, select the Purple Fuzz layer and press the P key to display the Position property.

2 Set an initial Position keyframe and set the value to **256** for X-axis and **256** for Y-axis.

3 Go to the end of the composition, and then set the Position value to **65** for X-axis and **−15** for Y-axis.

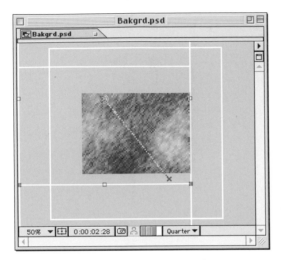

4 Return the current-time marker to the beginning of the composition.

5 Choose Effect > Image Control > Color Balance (HLS).

6 With the Purple Fuzz layer still selected, press the P key to collapse the Position property, and then press the E key to display the Effects properties and click the triangle next to Color Balance (HLS) to display its properties.

7 Set an initial Hue keyframe at the default value of 0.

8 Go to the end of the composition, click the underlined Hue value, and change the Hue to **1** revolution, or **360** degrees.

The Purple Fuzz layer will now fully shift through the color spectrum once over the course of the composition.

9 Preview the composition. When finished previewing, collapse the layer outline.

Animating the Cloud Layer

The final layer, Cloud Layer, will rotate and seem to recede in space.

1 Return the time marker to the beginning of the composition, and select Cloud Layer in the Time Layout window. Press the S key to display the Scale property and press Shift+R to display the Rotation property.

2 Set an initial Scale keyframe, and set a Scale value of **125**.

3 Set an initial Rotation keyframe, making sure that the Rotation value is set to **0**.

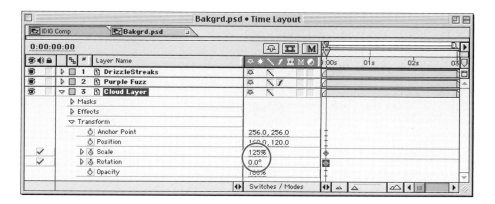

4 Go to the end of the composition, and change the Scale value to **70**%.

5 At the last frame in the composition, set the Rotation value to **1** full revolution, or **360** degrees.

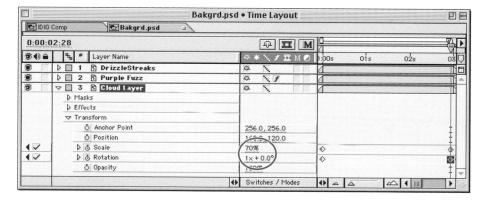

6 To play the composition, set the Resolution to Quarter, go to the beginning of the composition, and press the spacebar.

7 After playing the composition, set the Resolution back to Full and the Magnification back to 100%.

8 Save the project, and close the Bakgrd.psd Composition and Time Layout windows by clicking the button in each Bakgrd.psd tab.

9 Since the two compositions have been nested within the IDIG Composition, preview the entire IDIG Composition to see how the two work together. Do not close the IDIG windows when you are done, because you'll need them open to render the movie.

Rendering the IDIG movie

Here, you'll render the IDIG movie. If your time is limited, you can skip the process of rendering the movie, because the movie has already been rendered for you. It's called IDIG.mov, and it is located in the IDig folder in the 04Lesson folder.

1 With either the IDIG Composition window or the Time Layout window active, choose Composition > Make Movie, type **Movie2.mov** for the name, and save the file in your Projects folder.

2 For Render Settings, choose Best Settings. (If time is limited, set the Quality to Draft instead.)

3 For Output Module, choose Custom. For Format, choose QuickTime Movie.

4 In Windows, the Compression Settings dialog box appears. Leave Compressor set to Animation and click OK. In Mac OS, leave the Video Output options at their defaults.

5 Select Import into Project When Done, and click OK.

If your time is limited, you may want to render a draft movie instead.

6 Click Render.

7 When you are finished rendering the movie, close the Render Queue window, and then open the footage file that appears in your Project window, and play it.

8 After viewing the movie, save and close the project.

Creating the Dig It! movie segment

The fourth element of the IDIG sequence is an animation of the phrase *Dig It!* The text zooms forward from a distance while the background has a swirling effect. This element features heavy layering of filters to generate the final effect.

Since this segment was created by using many features that you have already tried, you will start with a partially completed project. You'll use some Transition Controls and the Spherize effect to put the finishing touches on the piece. You will also get a chance to use the Scatter and Glow effects, which are available only in the Production Bundle version of After Effects. Both the Scatter and Glow plug-ins have been included on the Classroom in a Book CD-ROM. To use the effects, make sure that you installed both plug-ins. See "Installing Production Bundle plug-ins" on page 4.

Dig It!—The Adobe Photoshop Source documents

The source files are Bakgrd.psd, Type, and Lens.psd.

Bakgrd.psd has the following layers:

• Layer 1 is a field of blurred monochromatic noise that has been motion-blurred using a distance setting of 10 pixels.

• Violet Vortex also contains blurred monochromatic noise, which has been distorted using the Zigzag filter in Adobe Photoshop.

Type is a single-layer Adobe Photoshop document with the Dig It! text.

Lens.psd is an Adobe Photoshop document in which a lens flare has been laid down on a black background.

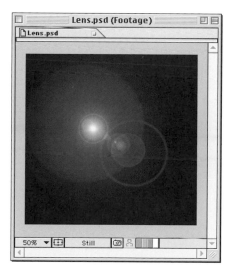

Opening the source documents in After Effects

1 If you haven't already done so, launch the After Effects application.

2 Choose File > Open, and then select and open DigBeg.aep in the DigIt folder in the 04Lesson folder.

The DigBeg.aep project contains a Bakgrd.psd footage folder and composition, which were created when the Bakgrd.psd was imported as an Adobe Photoshop comp. The Merged/Type.psd and Lens.psd items were imported as individual footage files. The project also contains the DigIt Comp, in which some of the animation and visual effects have already been set for you.

3 Choose File > Save As, name the file **DigIt.aep**, and save it in your *Projects* folder.

Note: If you want to view a completed version of this movie segment, play the DigIt.mov that is located in the DigIt folder in the 04Lesson folder.

Using transfer modes

The background item is animated to have a swirling vortex effect, starting with a hot color scheme and fading to black as the foreground type is highlighted. The layers are offset to rotate in different directions. You will apply a transfer mode to the background.

1 Double-click the Bakgrd.psd composition in the Project window to open the Composition and Time Layout windows.

Notice that this composition includes a layer named Layer 1 and a copy of that layer, which is identified by an asterisk (*) following the layer name (Layer 1*). Be sure you select the correct layer when working in this composition.

2 Make sure the current time is set to 00:00:00.

3 At the bottom of the Time Layout window, click the Switches/Modes button.

4 In the Transfer Modes panel, choose Color Dodge from the Mode menu for Layer 1*. The Color Dodge is a new transfer mode in both Photoshop 5.0 and After Effects 4.0; as you can see, the results are quite colorful.

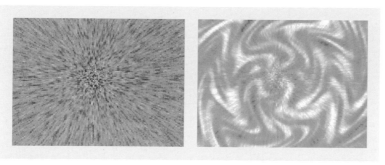

Bakgrd.psd composition before and after choosing the Color Dodge transfer mode for Layer 1.*

5 Make sure the mode of Layer 1 is set to Hard Light. (The mode for this layer was set in the original Adobe Photoshop file.)

The Hard Light mode combines colors in different ways depending on the lightness or darkness of the underlying colors. If the layer color is lighter than 50% gray, the underlying color is lightened. If the layer color is darker than 50% gray, the underlying color is darkened.

Using the Spherize effect

Now you'll apply the Spherize effect to the background image.

1 Select the Violet Vortex layer in the Time Layout window.

2 At 00:00:00, choose Effect > Distort > Spherize. In the Time Layout window, press the E key to display the Effects properties and click the triangle next to Spherize to display its properties. Set an initial Radius keyframe and change the value to **100**.

3 Go to the end of the composition and set the Radius value to **0**.

4 Save the project, and close the Effect Controls window. Then close the Composition and Time Layout windows for Bakgrd.psd by clicking the button in each Bakgrd.psd tab.

Integrating the elements

At this stage, you are going to bring the background element into the DigIt composition and apply special effects to the type. The type element swoops out of the background and becomes white-hot upon hitting the foreground, cooling off with a glow effect behind it as well as a continuing color shift. The Lens.psd layer will bolster the effect with a brief highlight.

The basic animation and some of the effects have already been applied for you.

1 In the Time Layout window for DigIt Comp, make sure the current time is set to 00:00:00.

2 Drag the Bakgrd.psd composition from the Project window into the Time Layout window, and then drag the layer to the bottom of the stack.

Using the Color Balance effect

To create the color cycling effect in the DigIt type, you will apply the Color Balance (HLS) effect and set Hue keyframes.

1 In the Time Layout window, set the current time to 00:01:22, select the top Merged/Type.psd layer, and then choose Effect > Image Control > Color Balance (HLS).

2 Press the E key to display the Effects properties, and then click the triangle next to Color Balance (HLS) to display its properties. Set an initial Hue keyframe, leaving the Hue value at **0**.

3 Move the current-time marker to the end of the composition, and then change the Hue value to **180**.

The colors in the DigIt type will cycle from 0 to 180 on the color wheel.

Using the Scatter effect

When the text swoops in, it starts with a Scatter effect, and then becomes sharper as it gets larger. The Scatter effect scatters the pixels in a layer without altering the color of each individual pixel. Scatter redistributes the pixels randomly, but in the same general area as their original positions.

1 Set the current time to 00:00:00, make sure the top Merged/Type.psd layer is still selected, and choose Effect > Stylize > Scatter.

2 Click the triangle next to Scatter to display its properties. Set an initial Scatter Amount keyframe, and set the value to **127**.

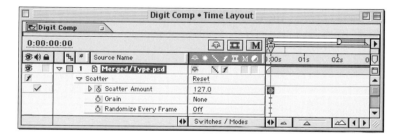

3 Move the current-time marker to 00:01:00, and then change the Scatter Amount to **0**. Set the current-time to 00:00:15 to see the Scatter effect in the Composition window.

4 Collapse the layer outline for the top Merged/Type.psd layer.

Using the Glow effect

Now you'll use the Glow effect on the second Merged/Type.psd layer to create a glow around the letters. The Glow effect picks out brighter parts of an image and diffuses those pixels to create a soft halo. Feel free to experiment with the Glow settings as you create the Glow effect.

1 In the Time Layout window, set the current time to 00:02:00, select the second Merged/Type.psd layer (layer 3), and then choose Effect > Stylize > Glow.

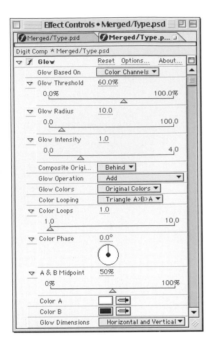

2 In the Effect Controls window, choose Alpha Channel from the Glow Based On menu. Using the Alpha Channel limits the type of colors you can use, so click OK if you get a warning dialog box.

The Based On option determines whether the Glow effect will select the bright parts of the color channels or the solid parts of the alpha channel. The Alpha Channel option is the best choice for applying glow to text.

3 For Glow Colors, choose A & B Colors. This option lets you specify any two colors using the Color A and Color B eyedroppers. Leave the eyedroppers (at the bottom of the window) set to the defaults of white and black.

4 Set Glow Threshold to **0**%. Pixel values less than this setting will be ignored in the glow operation.

5 Set Glow Radius to **20** pixels. This option specifies the maximum distance over which the glow is distributed. The larger the value, the more diffuse the glow.

6 Make sure that Color Loops is set to **1**. This setting determines the number of times the glow will pulsate.

7 Make sure the Color Phase is set to **0**. This cycles between the A & B colors that you have selected, in this case, between white and black.

8 In the Time Layout window, display the Glow effect properties, and set an initial keyframe for Color Loops at 00:02:00.

9 Set an initial Color Phase keyframe.

10 Go to 00:03:20. Set the Color Loops value to **5**, and set the Color Phase to **90** degrees.

11 Select all four of the Glow keyframes, and choose Layer > Keyframe Interpolation, and choose Auto Bezier for Temporal Interpolation. Click OK.

The keyframe icons change from diamonds to circles. The default temporal interpolation for a keyframe is *linear* interpolation, which creates a uniform rate of change between keyframes. Auto Bezier interpolation creates a smooth rate of change through a keyframe. You'll explore this option again in Lessons 6 and 7.

12 Collapse the layer outline, close the Effect Controls window, and save the project.

Rendering a movie

1 With either the DigIt Composition window or Time Layout window active, choose Composition > Make Movie, type **Movie3.mov** for the name, and save the file in your Projects folder.

2 For Render Settings, choose Best Settings. (If time is limited, set the Quality to Draft instead.)

3 For Output Module, choose Custom. For Format, choose QuickTime Movie.

4 In Windows, the Compression Settings dialog box appears. Leave Compressor set to Animation and click OK. In Mac OS, leave the Video Output options at their defaults.

5 Select Import into Project When Done, and click OK.

6 Click Render.

7 When you are finished rendering the movie, close the Render Queue window, and then open the footage file that appears in your Project window, and play it. Save and close the project.

Assembling the final project

The final project with all four segments will yield a QuickTime movie that will play at 15 frames per second smoothly off a double-speed CD-ROM.

You'll start by creating a new project, and then importing the three movies that you made during this lesson. If you were not able to render complete movies, each individual project folder contains a completed movie; you can import those instead.

1 Choose File > New Project, create a new composition named **Compiled Comp** that is **320 x 240** and **15** fps, with a Duration of **15:02**.

2 Choose File > Import > Footage Files, and do one of the following:

• If you rendered the movies, navigate to the Projects folder, and import the three movies that you created.

• If you didn't render the previous projects, navigate to the IDIG folder and import the IDIG.mov file, open the YouDig folder and import the YouDig.mov file, and then open the DigIt folder and import the DigIt.mov file.

3 Finally, open the Smiley folder, and select Smiley.mov. Click Done to close the dialog box.

4 Drag all four QuickTime movies from the Project window into the center of the Composition window. Stack them in the Time Layout window in the following order from top to bottom: Movie2.mov (or IDIG.mov), Smiley.mov, Movie1.mov (or YouDig.mov), and Movie3.mov (or DigIt.mov).

5 In the Time Layout window, display the In and Out panels by clicking the Optional panel button to the right of the Switches/Modes button.

6 Use the In and Out panels to set the In point for Movie2.mov at 00:00:00, the In point for Smiley.mov at 00:02:24, the In point for Movie1.mov at 00:08:18, and the In point for Movie3.mov at 00:10:26.

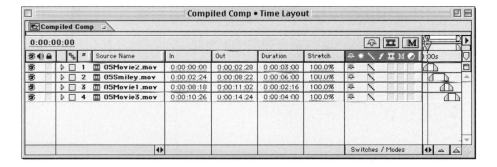

7 Close the In and Out panels by clicking the Optional panel button again.

8 Choose File >Import > Footage File, select Audio.mov in your 04Lesson folder, and click Open.

The music for the project was composed by Chris Meyer of CyberMotion.

9 Set the current time to 00:00:00, and drag the audio footage item from the Project window into the Time Layout window.

10 Choose File > Save Project As, type **Compil.aep** for the name, and save it in your Projects folder.

Rendering a movie for CD playback

Now you're ready to render the final movie sequence.

1 Choose Composition > Make Movie.

2 Type **IDIGSeq.mov** for the name, and save the movie in your Projects folder.

3 For Render Settings, choose Custom.

The Render Settings window should be checked for the following settings: Best Quality, Full Resolution (320 pixels by 240 pixels), Use No Proxies, and Effects All On.

4 For Time Span, choose Length of Comp. Under Frame Rate, select Use Comp's Frame Rate (15.00). The remainder of the default settings are acceptable. Click OK.

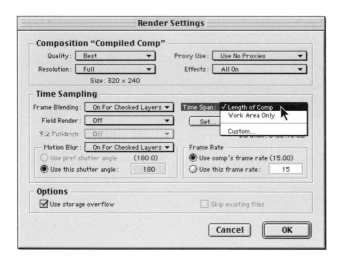

5 For Output Module, choose Custom.

6 For Format, choose QuickTime Movie.

7 Set the compression to Cinepak in one of the following ways:

• In Windows, the Compression Settings dialog box appears. Set Compressor to Cinepak.

• In Mac OS, click the Format Options button, and set Compressor to Cinepak.

You use the Cinepak compressor when compressing 8-bit and 24-bit video for playback from CD-ROM discs or for desktop presentations. For best results, you should use the Cinepak compressor on raw source data that has not been previously compressed.

8 Leave Quality set to Best, select Keyframe Every and enter **15**, and select Limit Data Rate To and enter **300**. Click OK to close the Compression Settings dialog box.

9 In the Output Module Settings dialog box, select Audio Output. Choose 22.050 KHz from the left menu. This is the standard sample rate for movies played on computers. 44.100 KHz is the standard sample rate for compact disc audio.

10 Choose 8-bit from the center menu. This is the standard sample depth for Windows or Mac OS playback. (16-bit is the standard for compact disc audio.)

11 Click OK to close the Output Module Settings dialog box.

12 Click Render.

When rendering is complete, get some popcorn and watch your movie.

Horror Festival Ad

In this lesson, you'll use a number of techniques to control timing and sychronization of video and sound.

The project in this lesson uses original art, animation, and classic movie footage to advertise a fictional horror movie festival at an equally fictional theater. The lesson builds on the knowledge of After Effects that you have gained so far: animating Photoshop comps, animating layer properties, and using visual effects. You will also focus on timing issues, including synchronizing animation with audio, time stretching, and time remapping.

This lesson covers the following topics:

• Using a luma matte

• Time stretching

• Time remapping

• Animating and feathering multiple masks

• Using markers

• Synchronizing animation with audio

• Using a project that serves as a library of keyframes

• Using various effects

• Animating an image sequence

At the end of this lesson you will have created a 30-second TV commercial advertising a horror film festival.

It should take approximately 2 to 3 hours to complete this lesson.

Viewing the final project

Before you begin, take a look at the finished movie that you'll create in this lesson.

1 Double-click the Final.mov file in the 05Lesson folder to open the final QuickTime movie, and then click the Play button.

This project uses a variety of media, including captured film, video, a Photoshop comp, animated masks, and a Photoshop sequence.

2 After watching the movie, exit from the MoviePlayer application.

Examining the Photoshop source document

To create the dramatic effect of clouds moving across a full moon, a Photoshop file with five layers was painted from scratch.

1 If you have access to Photoshop, open and examine the Moon.psd file.

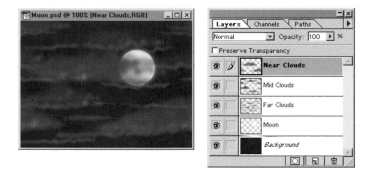

The image consists of the following layers:

• *Background* (dark blue to black gradient with hue-specific noise to minimize banding)

• *Moon* (with a little glow created using a blurred copy of the moon pasted on top of itself)

• A dense layer of little clouds

• A less dense layer of bigger clouds

• A sparse layer of even larger clouds

We created the clouds with the airbrush tool, using dark blue for the body of the clouds and white for the highlights. The Offset filter in Photoshop helped us examine the edges of the cloud layers and ensure that they wrap seamlessly right to left.

2 If necessary, exit from Photoshop, and return to After Effects.

Getting started

1 To ensure that the tools and palettes function exactly as described in this lesson, delete or deactivate (by renaming) the After Effects preferences file. See "Restoring default preferences" on page 6.

2 Start the After Effects application. An untitled Project window appears.

3 Choose File > Save As, name the file **05Work.aep**, and save it in the Projects folder.

Using context menus

Context menus make it easy to access commands specific to the current window. You'll use it now to import a file.

1 Right-click (Windows) or Control-click (Mac OS) in an open area of the Project window and choose Import > Photoshop As Comp. Open the 05Lesson folder, and select Moon.psd. Click Open.

The item appears as a composition in the Project window, along with a folder of individual layer images.

2 Double-click the Moon.psd composition in the Project window to open the Time Layout and Composition window, and notice that it consists of five layers.

Since several clips were originally shot on film (rather than video), you'll set the frame rate of this composition to 24 fps (the frame rate of film). Matching the frame rate of the original footage makes it easier to synchronize effects.

3 Activate the Time Layout window, right-click (Windows) or Control-click (Mac OS) in an open area in the Time Layout window and choose Composition Settings from the context menu. Change the Frame Rate to **24** fps and the Duration to **30:00** (30 seconds), and then click OK.

To display the time in the ruler at 24 fps, you can change the Time preference.

4 Choose File > Preferences > Time. The Time Preferences dialog box appears.

5 Under Display Style, choose 24 fps for the Timecode Base, and then click OK.

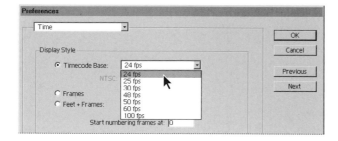

This setting affects only how the time is displayed and entered. It does not affect the frame rate of any composition.

Increasing the duration of still images

When you increased the duration of your composition, the duration of the layers did not change. You can increase the duration of still images by trimming the layer in the Layer or the Time Layout window.

1 Click the zoom-out icon in the Time Layout window until you can see the full duration of the composition.

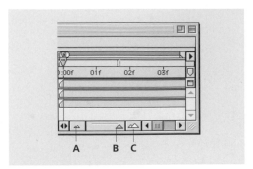

A. *Zoom-out icon* **B.** *Zoom slider* **C.** *Zoom-in icon*

2 Double-click the Far Clouds layer to open the Layer window. In the Layer window, drag the Out point triangle handle to the right end of the composition to increase the duration of the still image to 30 seconds.

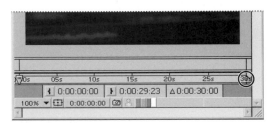

Out point triangle

3 Close the Layer window.

You can also change duration in the Time Layout window by using the mouse or a keyboard shortcut.

Note: You can lengthen a still-image as long as you want, but you can lengthen video footage only to its original duration. Here you'll lengthen all the still image layers to match the duration of the Far Clouds layer, which you just lengthened.

4 Move the blue current-time marker to the end of the composition either by dragging it there, or by pressing the End key on your keyboard. Click the first layer and Shift-click the last layer to select all the layers in the Time Layout window. Press Alt+] (Windows) or Option+] (Mac OS) to trim the length of the layer duration bars to the current-time marker.

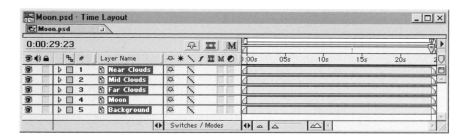

Important: Make sure you use the Alt (Windows) or Option (Mac OS) key to trim the layer. *If you accidentally use the Ctrl (Windows) or Command (Mac OS) key, you will time-stretch the layer instead. If you forget and don't use any modifier key at all, the layer's Out point will snap to the last frame, but the duration of the layer will not change, meaning that the In point will move as well. These are all very useful shortcuts, but learn them well if you want to use them effectively.*

Using the Offset effect

Now you'll animate the different cloud layers by using the Offset effect. This effect creates off-screen copies of the specified layer and lines them up edge to edge, repeating them as needed to create an infinitely large virtual layer that extends in two directions outside the composition. When you specify an offset, this huge virtual layer moves behind the real one, using the real layer as a sort of window through to the larger, tiled image.

The Offset effect is particularly useful with a layer that has been designed so that it can cleanly wrap at its edges. (This effect can be used to create a continuously moving background in cartoons, for example.)

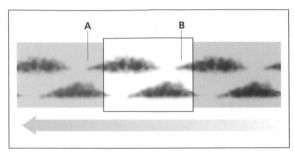

*The cloud layer was designed so that as you pan from **A** to **B**,
the movement of clouds appears smooth and continuous.*

In your project, you'll use the Offset effect to create the illusion of cloud movement.

1 Set the current time to 00:00, deselect all the layers, and then Shift-click to select the Near Clouds, Mid Clouds, and Far Clouds layers.

2 Activate the Composition window, right-click (Windows) or Control-click (Mac OS) the layer in the Composition window and choose Effect > Distort > Offset from the context menu. The Offset effect is applied to all three layers. The Effect Controls window appears with three tabs along the top, one for each layer. You may need to resize the Effect Controls window to see all three tabs.

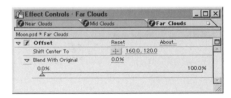

Tabbed Effect Controls window.

3 In the Effect Controls window, Alt-click (Windows) or Option-click (Mac OS) Shift Center To. This option is highlighted briefly, indicating that you have set a keyframe for this property. Using this keyboard shortcut sets a keyframe for all three layers automatically. Leave the default values, which are the current position coordinates for the layers.

4 Press the U key to display the animated properties in the Time Layout window; you should now see the Offset effect and the Shift Center To property displayed under each cloud layer in the Time Layout window.

To give the illusion of depth, you will offset the three cloud layers different amounts to create motion at different speeds. Distant objects appear to move more slowly, relative to closer objects.

5 In the Time Layout window, move the current-time marker to the end of the composition and Ctrl-click (Windows) or Command-click (Mac OS) the Near Clouds and Mid Clouds layers to deselect them, leaving only the Far Clouds layer selected.

6 Hide the Near Clouds and Mid Clouds layers by deselecting their Video switches (⊛) in the Time Layout window.

To wrap the clouds across the composition once during the course of the project, you will move the center point to the left so that the distance between the anchor point and the shifted center point is equal to the width of the composition.

7 In either the Effect Controls window or the Time Layout window, click the underlined Shift Center To value for the Far Clouds layer and then select % of Composition from the Units menu.

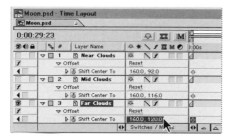

The values in the X-axis and Y-axis text boxes reflect the current center point (50%, 50%).

8 To shift the center point to the left, enter **–50** for X-axis. (Make sure the Y-axis value remains at 50%.) Click OK.

Note: The center point of the composition is 50%, 50% of Source; to move one full layer to the left, subtract 100% from the X-axis value, leaving you with a center point position of -50%, 50%.

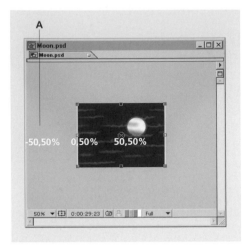

A. *Center point*

The Shift Center To value freezes the anchor point and creates an additional center point, around which the large virtual layer pans. Negative X-axis values shift the center point to the left; positive X-axis values shift the center point to the right. Negative Y-axis values shift the center point up; positive Y-axis values shift the center point down.

9 In the Time Layout window, click the Video switches (▢) for both the Near Clouds and Mid Clouds layers to turn on their video.

10 Make sure the current-time marker is positioned at the end of the composition, select the Mid Clouds layer, click the underlined Shift Center To value, and offset it twice the width of the layer by changing the X-axis value to **–150**% of the layer (50% minus 200%). Leave the Y-axis value as is. Click OK. This layer wraps across the composition twice, making it appear twice as fast as the Far Clouds layer.

11 Select the Near Clouds layer, and offset it three times the width of the composition by changing the Shift Center To X-axis value to **–250** of the composition (50% minus 300%), and then click OK. This layer wraps across the composition three times, thus appearing three times as fast as the Far Clouds layer.

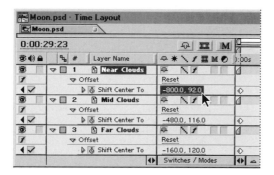

12 Set the work area markers (see "Setting a work area" on page 52) to include about 5 seconds of the offset clouds anywhere in the composition, and then click the RAM Preview button in the Time Controls palette to preview the motion you have created. The front clouds now appear to rush by, while the distant clouds creep by.

13 You're finished making changes to this composition, so close the Time Layout, Composition, and Effect Control windows and save the project.

Setting a luma matte

After setting up the composition that will serve as the final composition, you will import a half-second of a spooky-looking house that will overlay the Moon.psd layer. You will then use a luma matte to drop out the background of the movie footage using the luminance values of the matte file.

1 In the Project window, click the New Composition button (▣) type **Final Comp** for the name, and retain the previous settings (frame size 320 x 240, 24 fps, 30 seconds duration). Click OK.

2 Right-click (Windows) or Control-click (Mac OS) in an open area of the Project window and choose Import > Footage File. Select House.mov in the 05Lesson folder and click Open.

3 In the Project window, drag the Moon.psd composition on top of the Final Comp composition, and then do the same with the House.mov footage item. This is a quick way to add footage, automatically aligning it to the center of a composition.

The sky in House.mov needs to be masked out, so that the animated Photoshop comp background can show behind the house. A Bezier mask would work, but too much detail in an edge can make a Bezier mask impractical. An alternative method to creating a mask in After Effects is to generate a black-and-white image in Photoshop, import the file into After Effects, and use the image as a track matte.

4 Right-click (Windows) or Control-click (Mac OS) in the Project window and choose Import > Footage File, select HMatte.psd from the 05Lesson folder, and click Open.

The Photoshop image was created by exporting a frame of the house video as a Photoshop image using the Composition > Save Frame As command in After Effects. The exported still was used as a template in Photoshop to create a high-contrast image, in which white fills the area of the house and black fills the area of the sky.

5 Drag HMatte.psd on top of the Final Comp icon in the Project window, to add it, centered, at the top of the stack.

6 At the bottom of the Time Layout window, click the Switches/Modes button to display the Transfer Modes panel.

7 From the TrkMat menu for the House.mov layer, select Luma Matte HMatte.psd. After Effects automatically turns off the video of the top layer (HMatte.psd), and a dotted line appears between the top two layers, indicating that one layer is used as a matte for the other.

Using a luma matte lets you create a track matte from a layer that doesn't contain an alpha channel. After Effects uses the luminance values of the layer to create transparency. The lighter the pixel, the more opaque the corresponding pixel on the underlying layer appears. The white areas of the HMatte.psd image allow the underlying image (the House.mov layer) to appear completely opaque. The black areas of the HMatte.psd image allow the underlying image to appear completely transparent, so you can see the moon image beneath. Luma mattes work best with high-contrast files like the HMatte.psd image.

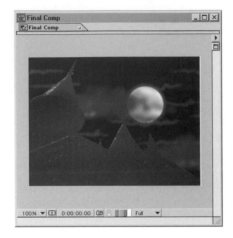

Note: If an alpha channel had been saved with the Photoshop file, the alpha matte setting could have been used instead.

Using the Time Stretch command

After viewing the House.mov footage, you will increase the duration by employing the Time Stretch command. *Time stretching* a layer slows it down or speeds it up.

1 Double-click the House.mov footage item in the Project window, and play the movie.

The footage looks a little too flickery—a little variation in the house layer is desirable, but not this much. To slow down the flicker, you will time stretch the House.mov 300% and apply frame blending to keep the results from being too jerky.

2 Close the QuickTime Footage window.

3 Select the House.mov layer in the Time Layout window, and then choose Layer > Time Stretch.

4 In the Time Stretch dialog box, enter **300** for the Stretch Factor.

This increases the duration of the layer by 300% and redistributes the original frames along the new duration, interpolating the in-between frames. If you rendered a movie now, you would notice the flicker slowing by a factor of 3.

5 Make sure Hold In Place is set to Layer In-point, and then click OK.

The layer increases in duration from the In point. Notice the new Out point for the layer duration bar in the Time Layout window.

6 Display the In and Out panels by clicking the Optional panel button to the right of the Switches/Modes button, and verify that the value in the Time Stretch box is 300%. Close the In and Out panels.

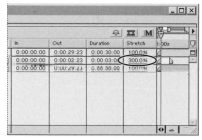

Time Stretch box

7 Display the Layer Switches panel again by clicking on the Switches/Modes button again.

8 Smooth out the interpolated motion: in the Layer Switches panel inside the Time Layout window, select the Frame Blending option for the House.mov layer. You won't see the effect of this smoothing until you enable frame blending later in this lesson.

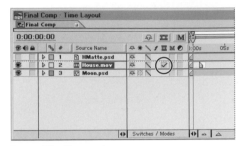

Frame Blending option

Frame blending generates cross-fades between original frames to create smoother playback of time-stretched or time-remapped frames.

The layer is still not quite long enough. You will set it to loop 2 times using the Interpret Footage dialog box.

9 Activate the Project window, right-click (Windows) or Control-click (Mac OS) the House.mov footage item, and then choose Interpret Footage > Main. Under Looping, enter **2** to make the footage loop twice, and click OK.

10 To increase the duration of the layer, drag the Out point at the right end of the House.mov layer duration bar in the Time Layout window to 04:00 on the time ruler. Watch the Info palette to confirm the time position of the Out point.

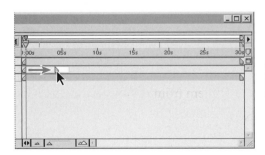

Importing footage with an alpha channel

Now you will import a QuickTime movie with audio of an actress asking, "What are you trying to do, scare us half to death?" The footage is one of four old horror clips superimposed over the background.

After scaling the layer, you will apply several different effects to fade the layer in and out, and to give it a sepia tone.

1 Activate the Project window, right-click (Windows) or Control-click (Mac OS) in an open area of the window, and select Import > Footage File. Select the Scary.mov file. Click Open.

2 Double-click the footage item to open the Footage window, and then press the Play button to play the footage.

3 With the item still selected in the Project window, look at the footage thumbnail.

A mask for the original footage was prepared in After Effects using the pen tool, and then a traveling matte was created. To save time, the file was masked, cropped, and prerendered for you. The resulting footage is a 24-fps QuickTime movie with an alpha mask.

4 Close the QuickTime Footage window. In the Time Layout window, set the current time to 01:00, and drag the Scary.mov footage item from the Project window into the Time Layout window so it is centered in the Composition window.

5 In the Time Layout window, click the Switches/Modes button to display the Transfer Modes panel, and set the mode for the Scary.mov layer to Hard Light.

The Hard Light mode changes the resulting brightness, depending on the original layer's brightness. If the color in the top layer is lighter than 50% gray, the underlying layer lightens. If the color in the top layer is darker than 50% gray, the underlying layer darkens.

You will apply the Brightness & Contrast effect to bring out more of the detail that was lost with the Hard Light mode.

6 In the Time Layout window, right-click (Windows) or Control-click (Mac OS) the Scary.mov layer. Choose Effect > Adjust > Brightness & Contrast; experiment with the settings to get a result that you find pleasant. We set the Brightness to 18 and the Contrast to -10.

To make the image look more sepia in tone, you will use the Tint effect.

7 In the Time Layout window, right-click (Windows) or Control-click (Mac OS) the Scary.mov layer. Choose Effect > Image Control > Tint. Set the Amount To Tint slider to about 50%, click the Map Black To color swatch, and select a dark brown color. Click OK. Change the Map White To value to a pale tan, and click OK.

8 Close the Effects Control window.

Working with the audio waveform

The image needs to fade in as the character starts talking, and then fade out again at the end of the question. To fade the image in and out, you'll set Opacity keyframes cued to the audio waveform.

1 In the Time Layout window, press the L key to display the Audio Levels property for the Scary.mov layer, and then click the triangle to display the waveform.

2 In the Time Layout window, drag the right viewing-area marker until the audio waveform fills most of the time graph, as shown in the illustration.

3 Press Shift-T to add Opacity to the properties displayed in the Time Layout window. Make sure the current time is set to 01:00, set an initial Opacity keyframe by clicking the stopwatch, and change the Opacity value to **10**.

4 Move the current time to the beginning of the audio waveform at approximately frame 01:10, and then set the Opacity to **100**.

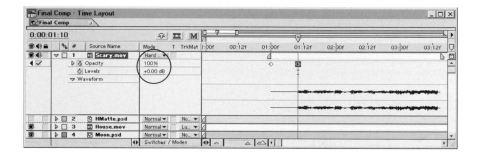

5 Move the current time to 03:00, and then click the keyframe navigator check box (to the left of the stopwatch icon) to set an Opacity keyframe with the same value as the previous Opacity keyframe.

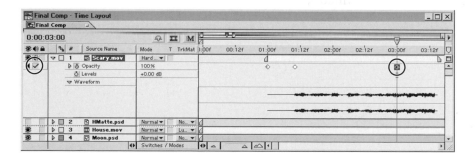

6 Move the current time to the end of the waveform (03:14), and set the Opacity to **10**. While you're working on this clip, you'll want to increase the volume of the audio.

7 In the Time Controls palette, click the Audio tab to display the Audio palette.

8 Drag the center slider up to an Audio Level of +7.00 dB. You'll probably need to increase the vertical size of the palette to be able to select exactly +7.00 dB by dragging; as an alternative you can click in each dB box and enter the value directly, but you'll have to do it separately for each channel.

9 In the Time Layout window, click the triangle to the left of the Scary.mov layer name to collapse the layer, and then drag the layer down between the House.mov layer and the Moon.psd layer.

10 In the Composition window, set the current time to 2:12, and with Scary.mov still selected, use the arrow keys to position the layer so that the woman's facial features are approximately centered in the moon.

11 Save the project.

Rendering a draft

You might want to render a draft movie to save a preview of your work. You can always render a RAM preview, of course, but sometimes you might want to save a record of your progress, and some of you might not have enough RAM to render a longer preview. If you want to render a draft movie to check your work, you can speed up rendering time by turning off some video layers, setting a work area, and choosing draft settings.

1 Drag the right viewing-area marker to the end of the composition so that the work-area marker is visible.

2 Drag the work-area markers to set the work area to begin at 01:00 and end at 03:12.

3 Select Final Comp in the Project window. Choose Composition > Make Movie, or press Ctrl+M (Windows) or Command+M (Mac OS). Name the movie **05Draft1.mov** and save it to your Projects folder.

4 Choose Draft Settings from the Render Settings menu.

5 Choose Custom from the Output Module menu. In the Output Module Settings dialog box, choose QuickTime Movie from the Format menu.

6 In Windows, the Compression Settings dialog box appears. Leave Compressor set to Animation, and then click OK. In Mac OS, leave the settings at their defaults.

7 Select Audio Output and choose the following settings:

• Choose 22.050 KHz from the first pop-up menu.

• Choose 16-bit from the second pop-up menu.

• Choose Stereo from the third pop-up menu. Click OK.

8 Click Render.

9 After the movie is rendered, choose File > Import > Footage File, and then double-click the movie in the Project window. Click the Play button.

10 Close the window when you are finished viewing the movie.

About 3:2 pulldown

When you transfer 24-fps film to 29.97-fps (NTSC) video, you use a process called 3:2 pulldown, in which the film frames are distributed across video fields in a repeating 3:2 pattern. The first frame of film is copied to fields 1 and 2 of the first frame of video, and also to field 1 of second video frame. The second frame of film is then spread across the next two fields of video—field 2 of the second video frame and field 1 of the third frame of video. This 3:2 pattern is repeated until four frames of film are spread over five frames of video, and is then repeated.

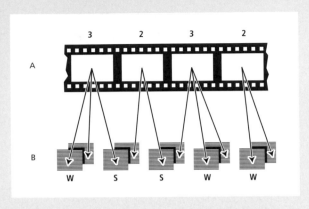

*When you apply 3:2 pulldown to footage, one frame of film (**A**) is separated into two or three interlaced video fields (**B**), which are grouped into video frames containing two fields each.*

The 3:2 pulldown process results in whole frames (represented by a W) and split-field frames (represented by an S). The three whole video frames contain two fields from the same film frame. The remaining two split-field frames contain a video frame from two different film frames. The two split-field frames are always adjacent to each other. The phase of 3:2 pulldown refers to the point at which the two split-field frames fall within the first five frames of the footage.

Phase occurs as a result of two conversions that happen during 3:2 pulldown: 24-fps film is redistributed through 30-fps video, so each of four frames of 24-fps film is spread out over five frames of 30(29.97)-fps video. First the film is slowed down 0.1% to match the speed difference between 29.97 fps and 30 fps. Next, each film frame is repeated in a special pattern and mated to fields of video.

—From the Adobe After Effects User Guide, Chapter 3

Preparing video transferred from film

At about 4 seconds, the house fades away and a funeral scene takes its place against the sky. In this section, you will import film footage that has been transferred to video, and explore how to prepare the footage.

Because the film was transferred to videotape, 24-fps film footage was converted to 30-fps videotape by using a process called *3:2 pulldown*, which compensates for the discrepancy between the frame rate of film (24 fps) and the frame rate of video (approximately 30 fps). For more information on 3:2 pulldown, see the After Effects User Guide.

It is important to remove 3:2 pulldown from video footage that was created by transferring film to video via the telecine process so that effects created in After Effects will synchronize with the original frame rate of the film. If you don't remove the pulldown, unwanted artifacts can appear in your output.

1 Activate the Project window, right-click (Windows) or Control-click (Mac OS) in an open area of the window, and choose Import > Footage File. Then import Funrl.mov.

This footage item is 640 x 480 in size.

2 Double-click the footage item, and examine it in the Footage window. Note the horizontal, spiked lines that distort the outline of the man in the center of the frame. Pause playback and while moving forward one frame at a time, note that the lines do not appear in all frames. Observing fields that appear and disappear is the surest way to identify 3:2 pulldown. Close the window.

3 Right-click (Windows) or Control-click (Mac OS) the Funrl.mov footage in the Project window, then choose Interpret Footage > Main. In the Interpret Footage dialog box, click the Guess 3:2 Pulldown button under Fields and Pulldown.

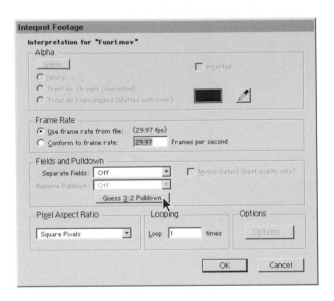

Depending on the type of computer that you are using, and the number of frames that you are working with, it can take anywhere from a few seconds to several minutes for After Effects to analyze the footage. For this particular footage, "Upper Field First" appears in the Separate Fields menu, and "SWWWS" appears in the Remove Pulldown menu. The effective frame rate has been changed to approximately 23.976. Different footage might yield different results.

An NTSC video frame is *interlaced*, which means it consists of two *fields*, one containing the upper scan lines and one containing the lower scan lines. NTSC video with a frame size of 640 x 480 will usually yield the Upper Field First setting as the Funrl.mov footage did.

The Remove Pulldown menu reflects the *phase* of 3:2 pulldown—in this case, SWWWS. Phase is based on the sequence of whole frames and split-field frames in the footage. When the film footage was transferred to video, the 24 frames per second were redistributed to 30 frames per second, and the non-interlaced footage was converted to interlaced frames. These two conversions create a repeating pattern of five video frames, three of which are whole frames (W), and two of which are split-field frames (S). These were the frames you observed when you examined the footage before.

4 Click OK to close the Interpret Footage dialog box.

5 Alt-double-click (Windows) or Option-double-click (Mac OS) the footage in the Project window to open it in an After Effects window (rather than a MoviePlayer window, which shows the original, non-interpreted footage). Examine the frames again, one at a time, and note that the interlacing artifacts are gone. Close the Footage window.

The final medium for this project is video at 29.97 fps, so when you render this movie, you'll reintroduce 3:2 pulldown. This step ensures that effects created in After Effects synchronize with the original frame rate of the film. If you were rendering this to film at 24 fps, you would not reintroduce 3:2 pulldown.

Positioning the footage

Now you'll position and scale the Funrl.mov footage.

1 In the Time Layout window, set the current time to 03:13, and then add the Funrl.mov footage item to the Final Comp Time Layout window. Position it between the House.mov and Scary.mov layers.

Since this footage is in 640 x 480 format, you will scale it down. To scale the footage to fit the Composition window, you would scale it 50%. However, you will make the footage slightly larger than that to hide the black area at the top of the footage.

2 In the Time Layout window, press the S key to display the scale property for Funrl.mov, and click the underlined scale value. Type **65** to scale it to 65% and click OK.

3 Position the layer in the Composition window so that the lower right corner aligns with the lower right corner of the composition. Use comma and period keys to zoom in and out of the Composition window, if necessary.

4 In the Transfer Modes panel inside the Time Layout window, set the mode for the Funrl.mov layer to Soft Light.

The Soft Light mode darkens or lightens resulting colors, depending on the colors in the underlying layers. If the color in the underlying layers is lighter than 50% gray, the layer is lightened. If the color in the underlying layers is darker than 50% gray, the layer is darkened. In this case, the Soft Light mode works to drop out the white areas of the black-and-white film.

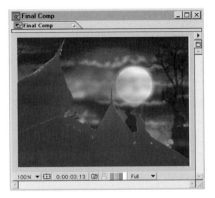

Time stretching the layer

To lengthen the layer and make the mourners march in slow motion, you will time stretch the layer to 300% and use frame blending to keep the motion smooth.

1 Make sure the Funrl.mov layer is selected in the Time Layout window. Choose Layer > Time Stretch, enter **300** for the Stretch Factor, leave the other settings at their defaults, and click OK.

2 In the Time Layout window, click the Switches/Modes button to display the Layer Switches panel, and then click the Frame Blending switch for the Funrl.mov layer.

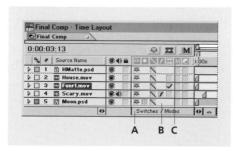

A. Switches/Modes button **B.** *Layer Switches panel* **C.** *Frame Blending switch*

3 Save the project.

Creating a transition between layers

To create a cross-dissolve between the House.mov and Funrl.mov layers, you will fade out the opacity of the House.mov layer and fade in the opacity of the Funrl.mov layer.

1 Make sure the current time is set to 03:13, press the T key to display the Opacity property, set an initial Opacity keyframe for the Funrl.mov layer, and change the Opacity value to **0**.

2 Select the House.mov layer, press the T key, and set an initial Opacity keyframe, leaving the value at **100**%.

3 Set the current time to 04:00, and then set the Opacity for the House.mov layer to **0**%. Set the Opacity for the Funrl.mov layer to **100**%.

4 Close the Final Comp Time Layout and Composition windows and save the project.

Creating the ghost by using solids and masks

It's at this point in the animation that the main narration comes in. It consists of audio from a classic movie trailer, *The Haunted Palace*, with spooky music followed by a melodramatic speech, more spooky music, and a scream. A fairly simple animated ghost will deliver the narration.

To create the ghost, you create a new composition, and then use solids and masks for the ghost's body, mouth, and eyes. You'll animate the masks to create motion, matching the sounds to the moving mouth.

1 In the Project window, click the New Composition button (▣), type **Ghost Comp** for the name, set the Frame Size to **320 x 240**, the Frame Rate to **24** fps, and the Duration to **15:00** (15 seconds). Click OK.

2 To create a white solid that will become the ghost's body, activate the Time Layout window, right-click (Windows) or Control-click (Mac OS) in an open area of the Time Layout window and choose New Solid. Name it **Ghost** and set the size to **320 x 240** pixels. Click the Color swatch, click the white swatch, and click OK to choose white for the color. Click OK to close the Solid Settings dialog box.

You will use Bezier masks to define the shape of the ghost's body, eyes, and mouth. Don't worry too much about exactly re-creating the sample movie; a ghost is pretty ethereal, so there is a lot of room here for creativity and personal expression.

3 Double-click the Ghost layer in the Time Layout window to open it in its Layer window. Position your Layer and Composition windows so that you can see both.

4 If the toolbox is not already open, open it by pressing Ctrl+1 (Windows) or Command+1 on the main keyboard. Select the pen tool (✦). You'll use it to draw the first ghost shape as in the following illustration. Feel free to be creative.

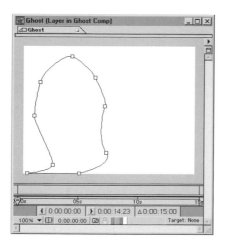

Note: To create curved lines, hold down the mouse button after you have clicked to make a control point, and then drag to lengthen the direction line and adjust the direction handles. Once you've adjusted the curve, release the mouse button, and then click again to create the next control point. See "About direction lines and direction handles" on page 91.

5 Working in the Layer window, click the pen tool to create control points along the outline of the ghost. Close the path by clicking with the pen tool on the first control point. Use the selection tool to adjust the Bezier handles and the arc of your curves.

💡 *If you can't get your mask to close using the pen tool, choose Layer > Mask > Closed.*

6 After completing the Ghost mask shape, select the Ghost layer in the Time Layout window, and display the Mask properties. To rename the mask, select the property name Mask 1, press Enter (Windows) or Return (Mac OS), type **Ghost Body**, and press Enter or Return again to change the name.

7 Press the F key to display the Mask Feather property, enter a value of about 15, and click OK. The Mask Feather value will remain constant throughout the composition.

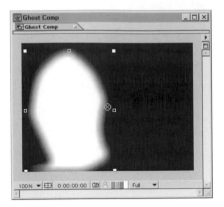

Now you'll use the same technique to create one eye shape and the initial mouth shape in the same layer. Feel free to be creative when designing the eyes and the mouth.

8 In the Layer window, use the pen tool to draw another mask. Create something vaguely resembling a left eye. Again, feel free to experiment and customize the shape.

9 Note that the name Mask 2 has appeared under the Mask properties in the Time Layout window. Rename it as before, this time calling it **Left Eye**.

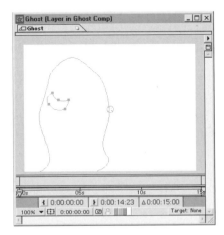

10 Once you get the eye the way you want it, click the mask name, Left Eye, in the Time Layout window. This selects all of the points that make up the mask shape. Press Ctrl-C (Windows) or Command-C (Mac OS) to copy the mask.

11 Click anywhere in the layer window to deselect everything, and then press Ctrl/Command-V to paste the mask. (If you don't deselect first, the new shape will paste in over the old one, and nothing will change.)

A new mask (Mask 3) appears in the Time Layout window, although you won't see it in the Layer window because it's exactly on top of the left eye.

12 Rename the new mask **Right Eye**.

To keep the ghost's eyes symmetrical, you'll now flip the duplicated eye.

13 With the Right Eye mask still selected in the Time Layout window, activate the Layer window, and then press Ctrl/Command-T to enable Free Transform points for the selected mask points.

Your eye mask is now surrounded by eight small squares, or transformation handles, with an anchor point for the transformation in the center.

14 Drag the anchor point to the approximate position of your ghost's nose, and then drag one of the left transformation handles over to the right. This will scale the eye down and then back up again, reversed. You should now have two mirror-images of your ghost's eye. Double-click in the Layer window to exit Free Transform mode.

15 Select the pen tool and draw another mask, this time located where the ghost's mouth would be. Name it **Mouth**.

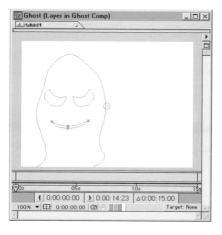

You may have noticed that the eyes and the mouth, although visible in the layer window, have had no effect on the mask in the Composition window. That's because the mask modes for these elements are still set to Add.

16 In the Transfer Modes panel, choose the Subtract mode for the Left Eye, Right Eye, and Mouth masks and they will punch holes in the layer. Close the layer window.

17 Save the project.

Animating masks

To create the effect of the ghost changing shape, you will animate the masks by setting Mask Shape keyframes and Position keyframes. The intent here is to change the shape of the ghost slightly, not to move it around on the screen. To save time, a library of keyframes has been provided. You can experiment on your own or use the keyframes from the library.

1 In the Time Layout window, make sure the current time is set to 00:00, select the Ghost layer, press the M key to display the Mask Shape properties, and then set an initial Mask Shape keyframe for the Ghost Body mask.

2 Set the current time to 01:00, and double-click the Ghost layer to open it in a Layer window. Now modify the Bezier mask to change the ghost's shape: click outside the mask to deselect all control points, click the mask outline to select it, and then click a specific control point to select it and drag it slightly in or out to change the shape of the mask.

A new Mask Shape keyframe is automatically created. After Effects will interpolate the movement between keyframes, creating ghostly motion.

3 Set the current time to 02:00, and then adjust some control points to create a new shape for the mask in the Ghost Body layer. Adjust control points again to create another shape at 03:00.

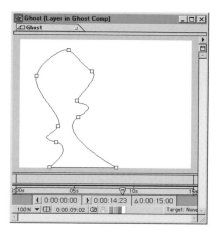

4 Close the Layer window, and then preview the animation by clicking the RAM Preview button, or press the 0 key on your numeric keypad.

You will change the mask shape several more times, at one second intervals, until you have about ten seconds of wafting motion. Although you can continue to create mask shapes on your own, you can speed things up by copying and pasting keyframes you have already completed, *or* you can use the library of Mask Shape keyframes described next. If you choose to create your own shapes, skip ahead to step 9 of the next section when you are done.

Using a library to store keyframes

When designing complex animations, it can be helpful to create a library of keyframes. For the ghost animation, a library of mask shapes for the ghost's body, and mouth has been saved as a separate project, which you will import into your current project.

1 Choose File > Import > Project, and then select the 05Lib.aep file in the 05Lesson folder. Click Open.

2 Since you have changed some files in this project, After Effects displays a message telling you that. Click OK.

The project appears as a folder in the Project window.

3 In the Project window, click the triangle next to the 05Lib folder to expand the outline of its contents. Then double-click the Ghost Library composition to open it.

The Ghost Library composition contains a Ghost Body layer with several Mask Shape keyframes, the GAud.mov layer, and the Mouth layer. The GAud.mov layer displays several markers, which will be covered later in this lesson when you'll use them to prepare the audio layer.

To finish the ghost body, you will choose a few keyframes to copy into your Ghost composition.

4 Select the Ghost Body layer in the Ghost Library Time Layout window, press the M key to display the Mask Shape property, and then use the keyframe navigator icons (to the left of the stopwatch icon) to move from keyframe to keyframe while you examine each mask shape. (You can also press the J key to move back one keyframe, or press the K key to move forward one keyframe.)

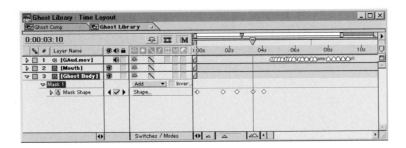

5 Shift-click several Mask Shape keyframes with shapes that you prefer, and then choose Edit > Copy.

6 Click the tab for the Ghost Comp Time Layout to activate the Ghost Comp, set the current time to 4:00, click the mask name Ghost Body, and paste.

7 Click in an open area of the Time Layout window to deselect all keyframes, and then drag the position of the keyframes so that each of them aligns on a second, for example, 5:00, 6:00 and so on.

8 Preview the animation by clicking the RAM Preview button in the Time Controls palette, or press the 0 key on your numeric keypad.

9 When you are finished previewing, click Mask Shape under the Ghost Body mask in the Time Layout window to select all the keyframes for that mask, and then right-click (Windows) or Control-click (Mac OS) any one of the highlighted keyframes and choose Keyframe Assistant > Easy Ease.

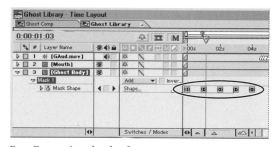

Easy Ease assigned to keyframes

The Easy Ease function smooths out the rate of change through the keyframes.

10 Collapse the layer outlines and save the project. Set the work area, and then preview the composition by pressing the 0 key on your numeric keypad to see the results of the Easy Ease function.

Preparing the audio for an animation

To give the impression that the ghost is speaking, you'll animate the ghost's mouth. The first step in this process is to mark the dialog in the audio track. For this example, the audio has been prepared for you. The audio was imported into an audio-editing program, in this case Adobe Premiere, and timecodes were noted where important syllables or consonants occur. This results in a map of audio events.

You	04:14	se	06:10
are	04:17	where	06:16
in-	04:20	hor-	07:00
vi-	05:01	ror	07:05
ted	05:05	will	08:00
to	05:11	be	08:08
an	05:13	your	08:14
o-	05:17	hos	08:21
pen	05:23	t	09:04
hou	06:06		

Setting these markers is time-consuming, but it makes the process of synchronizing audio very accurate. At the end of this lesson, you will learn how to map the audio directly in After Effects.

Marking the Audio layer

Once you have created an audio map, you can mark the Audio layer by using *layer-time markers*. Layer-time markers will help you position the Mouth layer mask shapes later. Once again, you can use the library if your time is limited.

1 Activate Ghost Comp, make sure the current time is set to 00:00, and then drag the GAud.mov footage item from the Project window into the Ghost Comp Time Layout window.

2 Preview the audio you just imported: choose Composition > Preview > Audio Preview, or press the period key on the numeric keypad.

3 Set the current time to 04:14, where the narrative comes in and the ghost begins speaking (the first item in the audio map table).

4 To add a layer-time marker to the GAud.mov layer at the current time, press the asterisk key on your numeric keypad. A white layer marker appears on the layer duration bar.

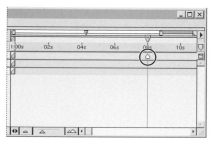

Layer marker

5 Double-click the white layer marker, type **You** for the name, and then click OK. This is the point in the audio where the narrator says the word *You*.

6 Set the current time to 04:17 (the next time in the audio map table), and then press the asterisk key on your numeric keypad. Double-click the layer-time marker, type **are** for the name, and click OK.

7 Drag the Zoom slider in the Time Layout window all the way to the right to see the frames.

8 If necessary, drag the viewing area markers out until you can see both of the markers.

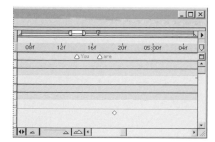

💡 *If you make a mistake and need to delete a layer-time marker, press the Ctrl key (Windows) or the Command key (Mac OS), and click the layer-time marker to delete it.*

9 Set the current time to 04:20, and then press the asterisk key on your numeric keypad. Double-click the layer-time marker, and type **In-** for the name. Click OK.

10 Continue setting layer-time markers according to the audio map table on page 224.

If time is limited, follow the next three steps to copy the Audio layer with preset markers from the Ghost library to your Ghost composition.

11 Click the tab for the Ghost Library's Time Layout, and then select the GAud.mov layer, and choose Edit > Copy.

12 Click the tab for the Ghost Comp's Time Layout, and then paste the GAud.mov layer into your Ghost Comp Time Layout window.

You can copy and paste a layer from one composition to another, but you cannot copy layers by dragging them from one composition to another.

13 Delete your first GAud.mov layer. It is the second one from the top.

Now the GAud.mov layer is marked according to the audio map. You can use the markers to help align the Mask Shape keyframes for the ghost's mouth.

In addition to layer-time markers, you can set *composition-time* markers by dragging triangular shaped markers from the icon located at the end of the time ruler in the Time Layout window. Composition-time markers are numbered and are useful for quickly marking a limited number of points. If you need to mark more than ten points or you want to add text labels, use layer-time markers.

Matching the ghost mouth to the audio

You will set Mask Shape keyframes for the Mouth layer to match the audio narration. Shapes have been created for the different syllable and vowel sounds, and you'll apply each of these shapes to the Mouth layer at the appropriate time. For example, an *O* shape will be used whenever the ghost makes an *O* sound. After Effects interpolates all of the intermediate keyframes, and the results can be very effective.

You can get a lot of practice here by setting all the mouth shape keyframes, or you can again use the keyframes available in the Ghost library. If you choose to create your own shapes, complete this section. If time is limited and you'd like to use the library of shapes, skip to the first step of the next section, "Using the library of Mask Shape keyframes" on page 228.

1 Set the current time to 00:00 and select the Ghost layer.

2 Press M to display the mask properties. Set an initial Mask Shape keyframe for the Mouth mask.

3 Move the current-time marker to 04:00 and click the keyframe navigator check box to set another Mask Shape keyframe with the same value as the previous one.

4 Drag the current-time marker near the layer-time marker for the word *You*, and press the Shift key to snap it to the layer-time marker.

5 Double-click the Ghost layer to open its Layer window.

6 Use the selection tool to reshape the mask into a small oval shape for the sound of the word *You*. A third Mask Shape keyframe is added to the layer.

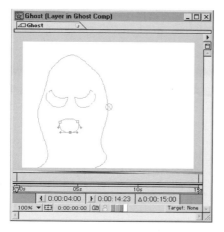

7 Move to the next layer-time marker, and then modify the shape of the mask for the word *are*.

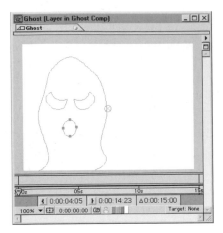

8 Continue moving forward, modifying mask shapes as you reach layer-time markers.

9 When you have modified the mask at each marker, skip to step 5 of the next section.

Using the library of Mask Shape keyframes

If time is limited, perform the following steps to copy Mask Shape keyframes from the Ghost library composition to Ghost Comp.

1 In the Time Layout window, click the Ghost Library tab, and then display the Mask Shape property for the Mouth layer (not the audio layer).

2 Use the layer-time markers to locate the first Mask Shape keyframe that you want to copy, and then drag a selection marquee to select the mask shape (or shapes) that you want. Choose Edit > Copy.

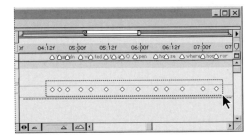

3 To paste the Mask Shape keyframes into your Ghost Comp composition, click the Ghost Comp tab in the Time Layout window, select the Mouth mask in the Ghost layer, set the current time to the appropriate layer-time marker, and then paste the keyframes.

4 Align the keyframes with the layer-time markers: hold down the mouse button and then hold down the Shift key while dragging the keyframes to snap them into place at the layer-time markers.

5 Using the keyframe navigator to move from keyframe to keyframe, ensure that the appropriate shape is aligned with each layer-time marker. (You can also press the J key to move back one keyframe, or press the K key to move forward one keyframe.)

Now you'll use Easy Ease to smooth out speed changes between keyframes.

6 Click the Mask Shape property for the Mouth layer to select all the Mask Shape keyframes, and then choose Layer > Keyframe Assistant > Easy Ease.

7 Set the beginning of the work area to 04:00 and the end of the work area to 10:00. Click the RAM Preview button to see a motion preview with audio.

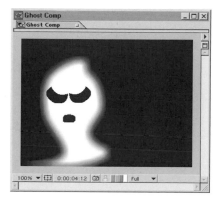

8 After making any necessary adjustments to the keyframes and to the positions of the mouth and eyes, close the Ghost Library Composition window and its Time Layout window.

9 Close the Ghost Comp Layer windows, and save the project.

Using the Wave Warp effect

After adding Ghost Comp to the Final Comp, you will set Opacity keyframes to fade the ghost in and out. Then you will add to the ghostly appearance by applying the Wave Warp effect.

The Wave Warp effect is included in the Production Bundle version of After Effects, but is not available in the standard version. However, it has been included for you on the After Effects Classroom in a Book CD-ROM. To use the Wave Warp effect, make sure that you have installed the Wave Warp plug-in according to the instructions in the "Getting Started" chapter at the beginning of this book.

1 Open Final Comp and set the current time to 03:00.

2 In the Project window, drag Ghost Comp onto the icon for Final Comp. This will center the Ghost composition on the top of the stack in Final Comp.

3 In the Time Layout window, set the Opacity of the Ghost composition to **0**, and then set an initial Opacity keyframe.

4 Move the current time to 07:01, and then change the Opacity value to **80**.

5 Move the current time to 12:18, and then click the keyframe navigator check box to set a duplicate keyframe.

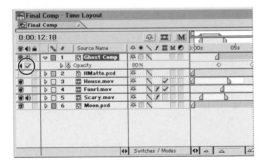

6 Move the current time to 15:04 and then set the Opacity to **0**.

To scroll the list of layers so that the selected layer appears at the top of the Time Layout window, press the X key.

Now you're ready to apply Wave Warp, which produces the effect of a wave traveling through your image.

7 Set the current time to 03:00. With the Ghost Comp layer still selected, right-click (Windows) or Control-click (Mac OS) the layer and choose Effect > Distort > Wave Warp.

You'll set keyframes so that the Wave Warp effect will start large, fade to almost nothing during the duration of the ghost's speech, and then come on strong again during the fade-out.

8 Press the E key, and then display the Wave Warp parameters in the Time Layout window.

9 Set initial keyframes for Wave Height and Wave Width. Set both the height and width values to **50**. (To see the effect, move the current-time marker to 05:00.)

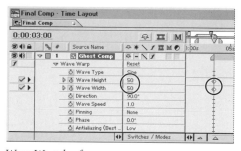

Wave Warp keyframes

10 Set the direction to **0**. Since this value will remain constant, there is no need to set a keyframe.

11 Set the current time to 05:23, and then change the Wave Height to **3** and the Wave Width to **5**. Larger numbers produce bigger waves.

12 Set the current time to 12:18 and click the keyframe navigator check box to set duplicate keyframes for both Wave Height and Wave Width.

13 Move the current-time marker to 15:04, and then set the Wave Height to **150** and the Wave Width to **150**.

Adding the Fast Blur effect

As a finishing touch, you'll add the Fast Blur effect at the beginning of the Wave Warp effect.

1 Set the current time to 03:00, and use the context-sensitive menu to choose Effect > Blur & Sharpen > Fast Blur.

2 In the Time Layout window, click the triangle for Fast Blur, and then set an initial Blurriness keyframe. Set the Blurriness amount to **40**.

3 Move the current time to 05:12 and set the Blurriness amount to **8**. Close the Effect Controls window, collapse the layer outline, and save the project.

Rendering a draft movie

Unless your computer has lots of RAM, the project is getting too long to view entirely in RAM. Both the Wave Warp and Fast Blur effects take significant time to render. There are several strategies you can use to render a draft movie to check the Ghost image.

1 Start by turning off the video for all the layers except the Ghost Comp layer. Set the beginning of the work area at 03:00 and set the end of the work area at 14:12.

2 Select Final Comp in the Project window. Choose Composition > Make Movie, name the movie **05Draft2.mov**, and save the file in your Projects folder.

3 For Render Settings, choose Draft Settings. Click the underlined phrase Draft Settings to customize the settings. In the Render Settings dialog box, select Use This Frame Rate, and enter **12**. Click OK.

4 For Output Module, choose Custom. For Format, choose QuickTime Movie.

5 In Windows, the Compression Settings dialog box appears. Leave Compressor set to Animation, and then click OK. In Mac OS, leave the settings at their defaults.

6 Select Import into Project When Done. Select Audio Output to render the audio. Click OK.

7 Render and view the movie.

Adding the lightning footage

You'll continue to assemble elements in the composition. After importing the lightning footage, you'll adjust the image with a few effects.

1 Turn on the video for all the layers except HMatte.psd. Right-click (Windows) or Control-click (Mac OS) in the Project window, choose Import > Footage File, select Litng.mov, and click Open.

2 Set the current time to 15:00 and center Litng.mov in the Composition window by dragging it from the Project window into the Time Layout window.

Now you'll increase the contrast of the image, and then use the Lighten mode to drop out the black background.

3 Press the Page Down key twice to move forward a couple of frames so that you can see the lightning image.

4 With the Litng.mov layer selected in the Time Layout window, right-click (Windows) or Control-click (Mac OS) Litng.mov and choose Effect > Adjust > Brightness & Contrast. Set the Brightness to **20** and the Contrast to **61**.

5 Display the Transfer Modes panel, and then set the mode to Lighten.

6 Close the Effect Controls window.

Fine-tuning the audio

After adding several audio clips to your project, you'll adjust them by using the Audio palette and then you'll add a cross-fade.

1 Activate the Project window, right-click (Windows) or Control-click (Mac OS) in the Project window, and choose Import > Footage Files. Select Bass.mov and click Open. Select ScrAud.mov, click Open, and then click Done.

2 Set the current time to 00:00, Ctrl/Command-click ScrAud.mov to deselect it, and then drag Bass.mov from the Project window into the Final Comp's Time Layout window.

This audio gives a nice, foreboding bass growl to introduce the piece. To prevent distortion in the mix, you'll adjust the level of Bass.mov down to about -2.50 decibels (dB).

3 Click the tab for the Audio palette, make sure the Bass.mov layer is selected, and then drag the middle slider down to -2.50 decibels (dB). You may have to expand the window vertically to drag more precisely.

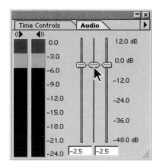

4 Now that you're done working with the Bass.mov layer, move it out of the way by dragging it down to the bottom of the layer stack in the Time Layout window.

5 Next, set the current time to 13:03, and drag ScrAud.mov into the Time Layout window. Adjust the volume of the audio down to about -4.00 dB.

Creating an audio fade

The audio for the Scary.mov layer is set to +7.0 dB so you can hear it better, but when the GAud.mov layer overlaps the Scary.mov layer, the audio level gets a little too high, or *hot*. To fix this, you'll cross-fade the audio in the overlap section (03:00 to 03:15).

First, you should listen to the audio you are about to modify.

1 Set the current time to 00:00:00 and choose Composition > Preview > Audio Preview. Listen to the audio for the composition and watch the level on the VU meter in the Audio palette. Press the spacebar to stop the preview.

2 Set the current time to 03:00.

3 Double-click Ghost Comp in the Project window to open it in the Composition window and the Time Layout window.

4 Click the tab for the Ghost Comp composition (where the GAud.mov is placed) and drag the tab out of the Time Layout window so you can work with both time lines simultaneously. Position the two Time Layout windows so that one is directly above the other.

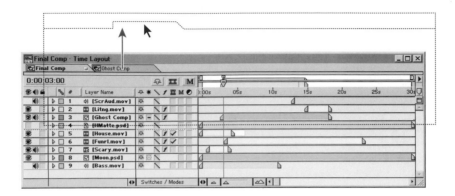

5 Choose File > Preferences > Display, and then make sure that Synchronize Time of All Related Items is selected, and click OK. The current-time marker will display the related time in both Time Layout windows.

6 Select the Scary.mov layer in the Final Comp Time Layout window, press the L key to display the Audio Levels property, and then set an initial Audio Levels keyframe at the current value of +7.00 dB.

7 Move the current-time marker to 03:14, and use the Audio palette to lower the levels to +0.00dB.

8 With the current time still at 03:14, select the GAud.mov layer in the Ghost Comp Time Layout window, and then set an initial Audio Levels keyframe with a value of +0.00 dB.

9 Move the current-time marker to 00:00. In the Audio palette, set the Levels to –96.00 dB by entering **–96** in each level value box.

10 Save the project, and then close the Ghost Comp Time Layout window and Composition window.

Importing an image sequence

One of the last elements of the advertisement is the title-card animation. A poster for a fictional film festival was created in Adobe Illustrator. The Roughen filter was applied to three versions, resulting in three different sets of edges for the card. All the files were then opened in Photoshop, sized to 320 x 240 (so they'd line up in After Effects), and saved as Photoshop files.

1 Activate the Project window, right-click (Windows) or Control-click (Mac OS) in the Project window, choose Import > Footage File, and then open the Title folder in the 05Lesson folder. Select the Title1.psd file, select Photoshop Sequence, and click Open.

2 Click the Guess button in the Interpret Footage dialog box to guess the type of alpha channel, and then click OK.

The three files are consolidated and appear in the Project window as a sequence. You'll now use the looping function to lengthen the sequence. You want a duration of about 2.5 seconds, so you'll loop the sequence 23 times (23 x 3 images = 69 frames, or about 2.5 seconds).

3 In the Project window, right-click (Windows) or Control-click (Mac OS) the Title sequence, and choose Interpret Footage > Main. Enter **23** in the Loop entry box, and click OK.

4 Set the current time to 15:00. In the Project window, drag the Title sequence icon onto the Final Comp icon.

5 Activate the Time Layout window. With the Title layer still selected, choose Layer > Time Stretch, and then enter **400** for the Stretch Factor. (This time you want the image to flicker, so you'll leave frame blending alone.) Click OK.

You'll use Position, Scale, Rotation, and Opacity keyframes to spin the poster quickly in from the moon. You'll then use the Difference mode to drop out the black while making the poster look creepier.

6 Set the current time to 15:21 (where the title card will end up), and display the Transform properties for the Title layer (press the P key, Shift+S, Shift+R, and Shift+T). Then set Position, Scale, Rotation, and Opacity keyframes without changing their values.

7 Return the current time to 15:00, and set the Opacity value to **0**.

8 Drag the Title layer so that its center anchor point is in the center of the moon.

9 Change the Scale value to **0** and the Rotation value to **2** revolutions.

10 Set the beginning of the work area to 15:00 and the end to 16:00, and then preview the motion using RAM Preview.

11 In the Layer Switches panel, select the Motion Blur switch for the Title layer and click the Enable Motion Blur button. Preview the motion again and notice how motion blur makes it look more realistic.

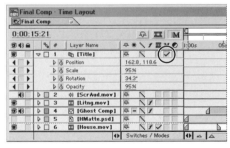

Motion Blur switch

12 Set the current time to 15:21, and display the Transfer Modes panel, and then choose Difference from the Mode menu for the Title layer. This will drop out the black and blend the colors of the poster with the background.

The Difference mode subtracts the channel values of the layer and underlying colors and displays the absolute value of the result.

13 Save the project.

Creating a gradient wipe

To finish the project, dripping blood obscures the screen and a woman fades in and screams. To make the blood seem to drip, you'll use the Gradient Wipe effect and a gradient layer image to modify a red solid color layer. The gradient layer image, Blend.ai, was created in Illustrator.

1 Right-click (Windows) or Control-click (Mac OS) in the Project window, choose Import > Footage File, and then select the Blend.psd file in the 05Lesson folder. Click Open, and then click Done.

Because the Blend layer is being used to modify the red solid layer, it must be in the Time Layout window, but you don't need to see it. You can use the Send Layer to Back command to move the layer to the bottom of the layer stack in the Time Layout window.

2 Set the current time to 22:04, drag Blend.psd from the Project window into the Time Layout window, and choose Layer > Send Layer to Back.

3 Choose Layer > New Solid, type **Red** for the name, set the size to **320 x 240**, click the color swatch to change the solid color to a blood red, and then click OK. Click OK again to close the Solid Settings dialog box.

4 With the Red solid layer selected in the Time Layout window, choose Effect > Transition > Gradient Wipe.

The Gradient Wipe effect creates a transition based on the luminance values of a second layer, called the *gradient layer*. The luminance of a pixel in the gradient determines the time at which the corresponding pixel in the first layer will become transparent. Lighter areas of the gradient layer represent those areas that will become solid first, followed by darker areas.

5 In the Time Layout window, press the E key to display the Effect properties, and display the Gradient Wipe effect properties. Then create an initial Transition Complete keyframe at 22:04, and set the value to **100**.

6 In the Gradient Wipe effect in Effect Controls window, choose the Blend.psd image from the Gradient Layer menu. The other defaults remain the same.

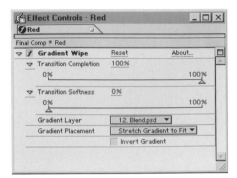

7 Move the current time to 23:15, and change the Transition Complete value to **0**.

8 Set the time to 22:20, and then preview the effect using the Jog control at the bottom of the Time Controls palette.

9 Collapse the layer outlines and close the Effect Controls window.

Time remapping

As a finishing touch, footage of a screaming woman is added to the end of the movie. You will use time remapping to change the duration and speed of the layer to match audio that was acquired from a different source.

Preparing the audio and video layers

1 Choose File > Preferences > General, set the Audio Preview duration to 16:00, and then click OK.

2 In the Time Layout window, display the Audio property for the ScrAud.mov layer, and then click the waveform triangle to display the Audio waveform.

3 Set the current time to 23:00, and then press the Period key on your numeric keypad to preview the audio.

The ScrAud.mov footage has four screams at the end—one long one followed by three shorter ones. You will set markers at the beginning of the first scream, in between the other screams, and at the end of the last scream, framing the screams with markers.

4 Preview the audio again, this time pressing the asterisk key on the numeric keypad at the beginning of each scream and at the end of the last scream.

This creates layer-time markers at the points where the screams start. (You won't be able to see the markers until the preview is finished.) You can adjust the markers by dragging them along the layer duration bar. The spikes in the waveforms will help you place them. For this exercise, it is not necessary to be precise.

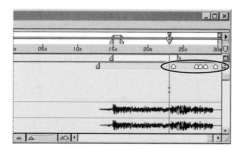

Layer-time markers

Enabling Time Remapping

1 Import the ScrVid.mov file from the 05Lesson folder.

2 Double-click the ScrVid.mov item in the Project window, and press Play to view the footage.

The footage item is a 2-second clip of an actress screaming once, but none of the audio clips of screams is exactly 2 seconds long, so you need to enable Time Remapping to make her action fit the audio.

3 Set the current time to 23:06 (which should be near the first layer-time marker in the ScrAud.mov layer), and then drag the ScrVid.mov item from the Project window into the Time Layout window.

4 With the ScrVid.mov layer selected, choose Layer > Enable Time Remapping.

Notice that the Time Layout window now shows that this layer is trimmed. (There is now a white bar extending from the end of the layer to the end of the composition.)

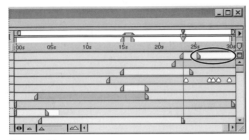

Trimmed layer

5 Grab the right triangular handle of the layer, and drag it to the end of the composition.

6 Display the layer outline for the ScrVid.mov layer.

Notice that two keyframes have been added: one set at the In point of the layer and one at 2 seconds into the layer, which is the last frame of the original footage. You can now change the duration of the layer by dragging the end keyframe wherever you want it.

7 Display the properties for Time Remap. Drag the second keyframe to align it with the second layer-time marker of the ScrAud.mov layer (approximately 26:16). Now the actress' scream is exactly the length of the first scream in the audio.

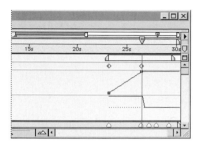

Time Remapping works as a dynamic scrub technique, similar to using the scrub wheel on the front of a professional video deck. When you set keyframes, you are setting the video to play forward and backward.

8 With the current-time marker at the first keyframe (23:06), press the asterisk key on your numeric keypad to create a layer-time marker. Double-click the layer-time marker, and name it **A**.

9 Move the current-time marker to the second keyframe, create a second layer-time marker, and name it **B**.

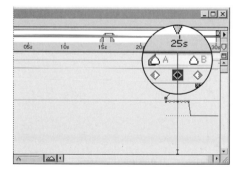

At this point, you could just copy the first keyframe and paste it in at the third reference marker to get her to "scream backward" and just seesaw back and forth to the end. But her mouth is open at the beginning of the footage, and she should close it between screams, so instead you will create a new keyframe at the midpoint of the scream (which is a wide-open-mouth position).

10 Position the current-time marker between keyframes A and B where the mouth is wide open, and then click the keyframe navigator check box next to the Time Remap property to set a keyframe.

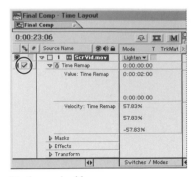

Keyframe checkbox

11 Create a layer-time marker for this keyframe, and name it **C**.

You now have three keyframes to play with: A, partially open; B, closed; and C, wide open.

12 Copy keyframe B and paste it at both the third and fourth layer-time markers in the ScrAud.mov layer (at approximately 27:07 and 28:04).

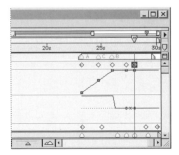

13 Now copy keyframe C and paste it between the second and third ScrAud.mov layer-time markers and between the third and fourth layer-time markers.

14 At the end of the last, longer scream (at approximately 29:07), copy and paste keyframe A.

15 Click the Time Remap property to select all the Time Remap keyframes, right-click (Windows) or Control-click (Mac OS) the layer and choose Keyframe Assistant > Easy Ease.

16 Generate a RAM preview to check the results. Then collapse the layer outline.

Creating a fade

Now all that remains is to fade the ScrVid.mov layer in and out and to set the mode to Lighten so the layer shows up nicely on the blood layer.

1 In the Transfer Modes panel, choose Lighten from the Mode menu for the ScrVid.mov layer to drop out the black.

2 Set the current-time marker to 23:06, and then set an initial Opacity keyframe with a value of **0** for the ScrVid.mov layer.

3 Move the current-time marker to 25:00, and then set the Opacity value to **100**. Move the current-time marker to 29:00, and click the keyframe navigator check box to set a duplicate keyframe.

4 Go to the last frame in the composition, and set the Opacity value to **0**. Save the project.

Rendering the movie

When you render this movie, you will take a look at reintroducing 3:2 pulldown since you removed it when you imported the Funrl.mov movie.

1 Choose Composition > Make Movie, type **Movie.mov** for the name, and save it into your Projects folder.

2 In the Render Queue window, choose Best Settings for Render Settings, and then click the phrase Best Settings to display the Render Settings dialog box.

Note: *Depending on the type of system that you have, this movie can take an hour or more to render. If your time is limited, you may want to create a draft movie or a half-size movie.*

3 For Frame Blending, select On For Checked Layers. This option renders frame blending for layers selected in the Switches panel, regardless of the composition's Enable Frame Blending setting.

4 For Motion Blur, select On For Checked Layers. This option renders motion blur for layers selected in the switches panel, regardless of the composition's Enable Motion Blur setting.

Since you removed 3:2 pulldown when you imported the Funrl.mov footage and you are preparing the final QuickTime movie for video, you will reintroduce 3:2 pulldown before rendering the movie.

In this example, you will reintroduce 3:2 pulldown with the same phase as when it was removed. However, this is not always the case. See the After Effects User Guide for more information.

5 For Field Render, choose Upper Field First. For 3:2 Pulldown, choose SWWWS.

6 Change the Time Span option to Length of Comp.

7 Click the Use This Frame Rate button, enter **29.97**, and click OK.

The movie will be rendered with the standard frame rate for video 29.97.

8 For Output Module, choose Custom. For Format, choose QuickTime Movie.

9 In Windows, the Compressor Settings dialog box appears. Leave Compressor set to Animation, and then click OK. In Mac OS, leave the settings at their defaults.

10 Select Import into project when done, and then click OK.

11 Select Audio Output. Choose 22.050 KHz from the left pop-up menu, 16-bit from the center pop-up menu, and Stereo from the right pop-up menu. Click OK.

12 Click Render.

13 When you are finished rendering the movie, open the footage file that appears in your Project window, and play the movie.

14 After viewing the movie, exit from After Effects.

Congratulations! Not only have you created a very complex movie, you've also learned a great deal about a wide range of visual effects and animation techniques.

Station Identification

In this lesson, you'll look at techniques for creating more sophisticated animation, such as changing interpolations and adjusting velocity.

In this lesson, you will create a 15-second station identification for a children's network on television. The focus of this lesson is on motion. Your challenge is to create realistic motion for the bouncing pogo stick. You'll use a variety of motion controls to create up-and-down movement, side-to-side swing, and a squash effect at the bounce, and you'll see how to set the velocity to reflect the sharp acceleration at the bounce and the deceleration at the top of the bounce.

This lesson covers the following topics:

- Controlling temporal and spatial interpolation
- Creating squash, bounce, and peak effects
- Controlling velocity by using the speed graph
- Using folders to organize footage items
- Replacing artwork
- Nesting compositions
- Moving an anchor point
- Removing unused footage items

At the end of this lesson, you will have created a 15-second cartoon animation complete with sound.

It should take approximately 3 hours to complete this project.

Viewing the final project

Before you begin, take a look at the finished movie that you'll create in this lesson.

1 Double-click the 06Final.mov file in the 06Lesson folder to open the final QuickTime movie, and then click the Play button.

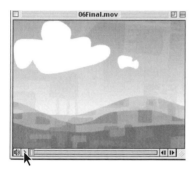

Most of the artwork that you see was drawn in Adobe Illustrator, and then imported and scaled in Adobe After Effects.

All of the cats on pogo sticks were actually created by using one animated composition with a variety of up, down, and side-to-side motions applied. The composition is duplicated, the artwork is replaced with the individual lettered cats, and the In points are staggered in the timeline.

2 When you are finished viewing, exit from the MoviePlayer application.

Getting started

1 To ensure that the tools and palettes function exactly as described in this lesson, delete or deactivate (by renaming) the After Effects preferences file. See "Restoring default preferences" on page 6.

2 Start the After Effects application. An untitled Project window appears.

3 Choose File > Save Project As, name the file **06Work.aep**, and save it in the Projects folder.

Designing and producing animation is a challenging and often time-consuming endeavor. It can take hours or days to produce just a few minutes. This lesson has been set up to give you a taste of cel animation, but it provides several shortcuts to help speed up the process.

Size and memory considerations

The final goal of this project is to create a full-screen video clip for television. However, for the sake of reducing disk space and memory requirements, the instructions are designed around a 320 x 240 format, at 30 frames per second.

Animating the background

After importing the artwork, you'll start the project by creating the background scene of the final composition.

1 Use the context-sensitive menu to import two files: right-click (Windows) or Control-click (Mac OS) in the Project window and choose Import > Footage Files. Open the 06Lesson folder, select Bakgrd.psd, and click Open. Then select Clouds.ai, and click Open. Click Done when you are finished importing the footage.

2 Create a new composition: click the new composition icon (⊠) in the Project window, name it **Final Comp**, and then make sure that the Frame Size is set to **320 x 240**. Set the Frame Rate to **30** fps and the Duration to **15:00** (15 seconds). Click OK.

3 Drag the Bakgrd.psd footage item from the Project window into the Time Layout window. As you recall from other lessons, doing this automatically centers the item in the Composition window.

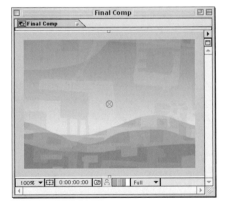

The background art was created in Illustrator, and then modified in Adobe Photoshop.

4 Select the Lock switch in the Time Layout window to lock the layer.

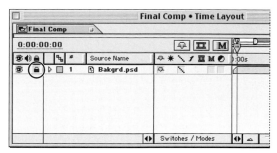

Lock switch

Animating the clouds

Now you'll animate the clouds by using simple horizontal motion.

1 Resize the Composition window so you can see the gray pasteboard area around the composition stage.

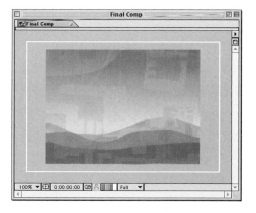

2 In the Time Layout window, make sure the blue current-time marker is set to 00:00. Drag the Merged/Clouds.ai art from the Project window into the Composition window, and position it anywhere.

3 In the Time Layout window, click the triangle next to the name of the Merged/Clouds.ai layer to display the layer outline. Then click the triangle next to Transform to display the properties outline. Click the underlined Scale value, type **50**, and press Enter or Return.

4 In the Composition window, position the clouds in the top left corner of the composition, aligning the left and top edges of the Cloud layer with the left and top edges of the frame. Set an initial Position keyframe by clicking the stopwatch in the Time Layout window.

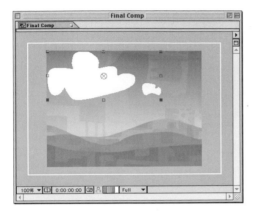

5 In the Composition window, set the current time to 07:16, and drag the clouds off the right edge of the frame, pressing the Shift key while dragging to constrain the movement. This creates a new keyframe. In the Time Layout window, collapse the layer outline by clicking the triangle next to the layer name.

6 Set the current time to 09:11, and then drag Merged/Clouds.ai from the Project window into the Composition window a second time, position it anywhere. In the Time Layout window, set the Scale value for this new layer to **15**.

7 In the Composition window, drag the clouds artwork outside the composition to the left, about one-third of the way down the composition. Then return to the Time Layout window and set an initial Position keyframe.

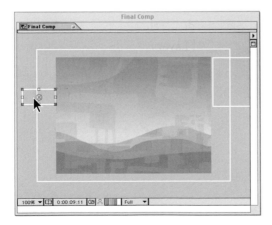

8 Go to the last frame of the composition by pressing the End key. In the Composition window, drag the clouds to the right side of the frame so that the right edge of the Cloud layer aligns with the left edge of the frame. Press Shift while dragging to constrain the movement.

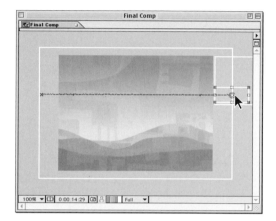

9 In the Time Layout window, collapse the layer outline by clicking the triangle next to the layer name, and save the project.

10 Deselect all the layers, and preview the motion by pressing 0 on your numeric keypad.

11 Lock both Cloud layers.

Animating a masked solid

Masks applied to solids can be used to create quick elements for animation, like the eyes for the first cat on a pogo stick that jumps into the frame at the beginning. You will design a separate composition that contains the eye animation.

1 Double-click in an open area of the Project window, select the CatPogo.ai file, and click Open. In the CatPogo.ai dialog box, leave Merged Layers selected and click OK.

2 Select the Merged/CatPogo.ai footage item in the Project window. As you can see by looking at the information beside the item's thumbnail, the item is 393 x 692 pixels in size. You will create a composition that is slightly larger than the artwork.

3 Create a new composition, name it **Moving Eyes**, set the Frame Size to **400 x 700**, set the Frame Rate to **30** fps, and set the Duration to **7:00** (7 seconds).

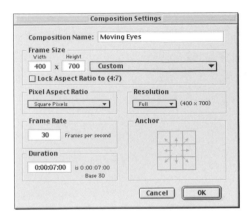

4 Drag the Merged/CatPogo.ai item from the Project window into the center of the Moving Eyes Composition window. Resize the Composition window so that you can see just the top half. If necessary to speed up screen redraw, choose Half from the Resolution menu at the bottom of the Composition window.

To animate the cat character's eyes, you will create a solid black rectangle, and then construct an oval mask that will function as the pupil for the right eye (the right eye as you are looking at the cat). After setting Position keyframes, you will duplicate the layer for the left eye.

5 Choose Layer > New Solid, type **Right Eye** for the name, set the size to **100 x 100** pixels, use the eyedropper to sample black for the color, and then click OK.

6 Scroll down to the center of the composition, locate the new solid, and then drag the solid over the eye on the right.

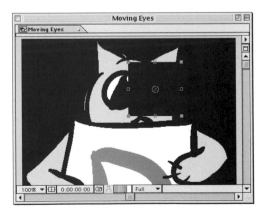

7 Open the Right Eye Layer window by double-clicking the solid. Drag the Layer window as close as you can to the Composition window.

8 Make sure the Layer window is active, and click the oval tool in the toolbox.

9 Use the oval tool to draw a mask in the center of the Layer window. The mask allows you to turn a rectangular solid into an oval-shaped solid.

Once you create the initial shape, you can see the cat image beneath the solid in the Composition window. Use the Layer window to make adjustments to the mask. Don't worry about the exact size. The style of the illustration requires only a rough oval shape.

Note: Be careful to resize the mask in the Layer window and not in the Composition window. If you resize the mask in the Composition window, you are actually changing the scale of the solid, instead of setting its initial size.

10 Position the oval in the Composition window so that it is on the right eye and the cat appears to be looking to your right.

11 Close the Layer window.

12 In the Time Layout window, set the current time to 00:10, press the P key to display the Position property, and then set an initial Position keyframe for the Right Eye layer.

13 Set the current time to 00:13. In the Composition window, reposition the eye oval so that it is still on the right eye but the cat now appears to be looking to the left.

Since the mask is not changing in size, but only in position, you do not need to set Mask Shape keyframes.

Copying and pasting keyframes

To create the look of the cat glancing left and right, you will copy and paste the two keyframes that you just created along various points in the time ruler. You can copy and paste property keyframes only one layer at a time.

Your first step is to copy the first keyframe of the Right Eye layer, where the right eye is looking to the right.

1 Select the Right Eye layer and click the first Position keyframe in the time ruler. (The eye is looking right.)

2 Choose Edit > Copy, move the current-time marker to 00:20, and choose Edit > Paste.

3 To see more space between keyframes, magnify your view of the time ruler by dragging the right viewing-area marker to the left until the time ruler is displayed in 10-frame increments.

Right viewing-area marker

4 Set the current time to 01:15, and paste again. Paste one last keyframe at 01:20.

5 To keep track of keyframes, choose Use Keyframe Indices from the Time Layout window menu in the upper right corner. The keyframes are displayed with numbers in sequential order.

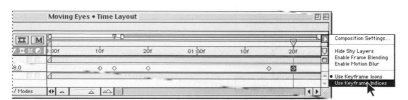

Time Layout window menu

Sequential keyframes

Next, you'll copy the second keyframe of the Right Eye layer (the right eye is looking to the left) and position it at points in between the other keyframes. (When you are finished editing, the pattern will be right-left-left-right, left-right-right-left.)

6 Set the current time to 00:13, select the second Position keyframe (the eye is looking left), and choose Edit > Copy.

7 Set the current time to 00:18, and paste. Then move the current-time marker to 01:12, and paste. Move the current-time marker to 01:22, and paste again.

You should have a total of eight keyframes.

8 Position the current-time marker at 02:00, and set the end of the work area by pressing the N key. Make sure the Right Eye layer is selected, and then press Alt+0 (Windows) or Option+0 (Mac OS) on your numeric keypad to see an alpha motion (wireframe) preview. When you are finished, press any key to stop the preview.

Changing Spatial Interpolation

Notice that the eye motion drifts slightly. To get crisp motion when the eyes change direction, you will change the spatial interpolation method to linear. Linear interpolation creates a straight motion path between keyframes.

1 To select all the keyframes for the Right Eye layer, click the word *Position* in the Time Layout window.

2 Choose Layer > Keyframe Interpolation. The Keyframe Interpolation dialog box appears.

3 Choose Linear from the Spatial Interpolation menu, and then click OK.

4 Press Alt+0 (Windows) or Option+0 (Mac OS) on your numeric keypad to see a wireframe preview.

Duplicating the layer and keyframes

To create parallel movement for the left eye, all you need to do is duplicate the Right Eye layer, and then adjust the position of the masked solids.

1 In the Time Layout window, select the Right Eye layer, and then choose Edit > Duplicate. A new layer appears at the top of the stack in the Time Layout window.

2 With the new layer still selected, press Enter (Windows) or Return (Mac OS), rename the layer **Left Eye**, and press Enter or Return again to apply the name.

3 With the Left Eye layer still selected, press the P key to display the Position property. The layer and all keyframes have been duplicated.

4 Set the current time to 00:10.

5 Click the word *Position* to select all the keyframes, and then drag the duplicated oval solid in the Composition window until the mask is positioned over the left eye. The left eye should be looking to your right.

Note: *It is critical that you select all the keyframes before you adjust the position.*

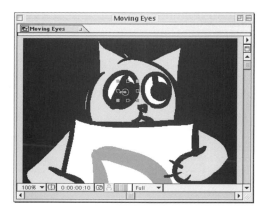

6 Deselect all layers by clicking in an open area of the Time Layout window, and then press Alt+0 (Windows) or Option+0 (Mac OS) on your numeric keypad to preview the motion.

If you need to make any adjustments, make sure to select all the keyframes again.

7 If necessary, set the Resolution back to Full in the Composition window. Save the project.

You might be curious as to how a designer knows where to position keyframes. Individual designers have different strategies, but to most it is simply a matter of trial and error, plus experience. They use motion previews and draft movies, making adjustments until they are satisfied.

Many designers use a stopwatch, and count out the motion or snap their fingers to get an idea of approximate timing.

Animating the moving eyes composition

Now that you've completed the movement of the eyes, you're going to add the Moving Eyes composition to the Final Comp and create the effect of the cat bouncing into the frame of the Composition window. Putting one composition inside another is called *nesting*. For more information on nesting, see the After Effects User Guide.

1 At the top of the Time Layout window, click the Final Comp tab to display the composition. Set the current time to 01:10, and then drag the Moving Eyes composition from the Project window into the Final Comp, aligning the left edge of the graphic with the left edge of the frame.

2 In the Composition window, set the Magnification to 50%.

3 Start dragging the Moving Eyes layer down, hold down the Shift key to constrain the movement vertically, and then continue dragging until the Moving Eyes layer is down below the visible area.

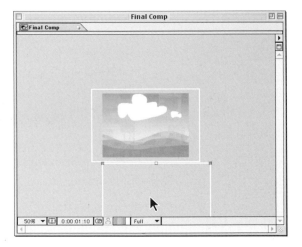

4 In the Time Layout window, set the current time to 01:14, press the P key to display the Position property, and set an initial Position keyframe.

5 Move the current-time marker to 01:20, and then in the Composition window, drag the Moving Eyes layer up until just the eyes show above the bottom edge of the frame.

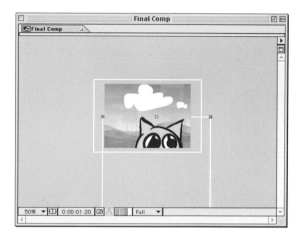

6 To hold the layer in this position for a few frames, move to 02:00, and then in the Time Layout window, select the keyframe navigator check box. This duplicates the position coordinates from the previous keyframe.

7 Move to 02:08, and in the Composition window, drag the Moving Eyes layer down (while pressing the Shift key) until the cat is out of the frame.

8 In the Time Layout window, move to 02:12, and select the keyframe navigator check box to set a duplicate keyframe.

9 In the Composition window, move to 02:22, and drag the cat up a little higher so that you can see the eyes and part of the sign.

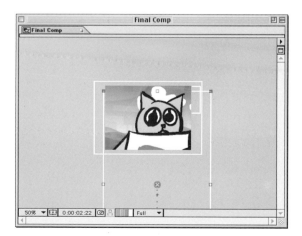

10 In the Time Layout window, move the current-time marker to 03:02, and then click the keyframe navigator check box to set a duplicate keyframe.

11 In the Composition window, move to 03:16, and drag the Moving Eyes layer down off the lower part of the frame.

12 In the Time Layout window, move the current-time marker to 04:16, and then click the keyframe navigator check box to set a duplicate keyframe.

13 Finally, move to 04:22, and in the Composition window, drag the Moving Eyes layer off the top of the frame. You may need to drag in several steps to get the layer all the way out of the composition.

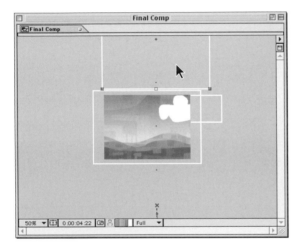

14 In the Composition window, set the Magnification back to 100%.

15 In the Time Layout window, collapse the Moving Eyes layer outline. Save the project, press the Home key to return to the beginning of the composition, and then preview the motion by using the Jog control in the Time Controls palette.

16 Close the Composition window and the Time Layout window.

Now you're ready to animate the rest of the cats.

Creating the pogo stick motion

In this section, you'll create a new composition in which you set the pogo stick motion for the rest of the cats. You are going to create up-and-down motion, squash the layer dimensions to simulate bouncing, and change the velocity.

1 Create a new composition, type **Bounce Comp** for the name, and then set the Frame Size to **320** x **240**, the Frame Rate to **30** frames per second, and the Duration to **10:00** (10 seconds). Click OK.

2 Drag the Merged/CatPogo.ai art from the Project window into the Time Layout window, and then display the Transform properties for the layer.

Moving the anchor point

Whenever you set a Position keyframe, the position is based on the anchor point of the layer. For this animation you're going to move the anchor point to the bottom of the pogo stick.

1 Double-click the Merged/CatPogo.ai image in either the Composition window or the Time Layout window to open the Layer window. In the Composition window, set the magnification to 50% so you can see more of the cat.

2 To see the anchor point, choose Anchor Point Path from the Layer window menu located in the upper right corner. The anchor point's default position is the center of the layer.

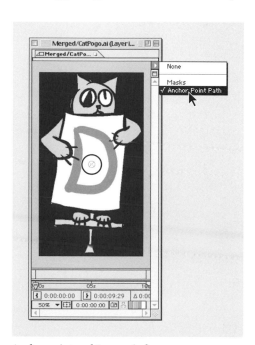

Anchor point and Layer window menu

3 Drag the anchor point to the bottom of the pogo stick, and then close the Layer window. Notice how the position of the layer has changed in the Composition window.

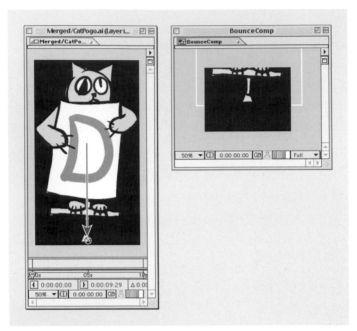

Dragging the Anchor point changes the position of the footage in the Composition window.

You can move the anchor point from the center of a layer to any other position, even outside of the layer.

Note: It is important to change the anchor point position before you set other motion properties. If you don't, you may get surprising results, since changes in Scale, Position, and Rotation are based on the anchor point position.

Creating a squash effect

To make the character bounce twice a second, you will specify up or down motion every seven frames. You'll modify the dimensions of the Merged/CatPogo.ai layer so that it changes from a normal scale ratio of 1:1 in the up position to a squashed ratio of 1:2 in the down position. Over time, the dimensions gradually change back toward 1:1 and the motion decreases, reflecting a shorter and slower bounce.

You'll set a full scaled keyframe one frame before impact so the squash doesn't occur before the actual bounce.

1 Make sure the current time is set to 00:00. Set the magnification to 100% in the Composition window, and resize the window so you can see as much of the Merged/CatPogo.ai layer as possible.

Since you are using the same Merged/CatPogo.ai artwork that you used for the first animation, you'll need to scale it down.

2 In the Time Layout window, set the Scale to **20**% for both width and height, and set an initial Scale keyframe.

3 In the Composition window, start dragging the layer up and then press and hold Shift. Keep dragging until the top of the cat is even with the top of the screen. Then set an initial Position keyframe in the Time Layout window.

Note: You don't need to worry about keeping the image within the action-safe zone because you will be nesting this composition inside another composition.

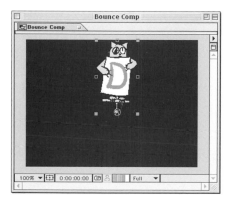

4 Press the U key to display all animating properties, and verify that you have both a Scale and Position keyframe set at 00:00.

5 In the Time Layout window, set the current time to 00:07. Click the Scale value. In the Scale dialog box, deselect Preserve Frame Aspect Ratio, leave width set to **20**, enter **9** for height, and click OK.

As you move the Merged/CatPogo.ai layer up and down, you'll want to avoid moving it from side to side. You'll use a keyboard shortcut to constrain the movement to the vertical axis.

6 In the Composition window, start dragging the layer down and then hold down Shift. Keep dragging until the bottom of the pogo stick is at the bottom of the screen.

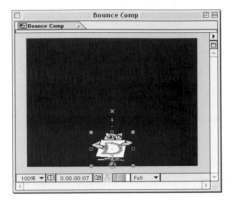

7 In the Time Layout window, set the current time to 00:15, and then set the Scale for both width and height to **20**%. (Because width and scale are set to the same value, Preserve Frame Aspect Ratio is automatically selected when you click OK in the Scale dialog box.)

8 In the Composition window, start dragging the layer up and then hold down Shift, dragging the layer so that the cat's ears touch the top edge of the screen.

9 In the Time Layout window, move to 00:22, and in the Scale dialog box deselect Preserve Frame Aspect Ratio, leave the width at **20** and set the height to **9**. In the Composition window, start dragging down, hold down Shift, and then drag the artwork down so that the bottom of the pogo stick is even with the bottom of the screen.

10 Return to the beginning of the composition, and then press the 0 key on the numeric keypad to view what you have so far.

Now you will create a full-scale keyframe one frame before impact so the squash occurs only at the bounce, and not on the way down.

11 In the Time Layout window, move the current-time marker to 00:06. The height at this frame is 11%. Set the Scale value to **20**%, **20**%.

12 Copy the keyframe you just set, move to 00:21, and paste the keyframe. Now return to the beginning of the composition and play the composition again.

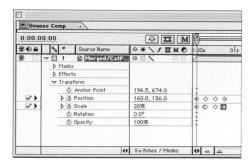

To have a few more keyframes to play with in the next section, you will copy and paste a second set of keyframes.

13 Position the pointer to the left and above the first Position keyframe, drag a selection marquee around all of the Position and Scale keyframes you have set so far, and then choose Edit > Copy.

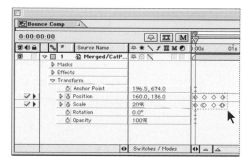

14 Set the current time to 01:00, and paste. All the keyframes are duplicated and positioned starting at the current-time marker.

15 Set the work area from 00:00 on the left to 2:00 on the right, and then press 0 on your numeric keypad to preview motion. Save the project.

Setting the interpolation and velocity

When creating certain types of motion, like the characters on the pogo sticks, you do not want the animation to progress at a constant rate of speed. The motion should reflect the bounce and peak of the pogo stick character. There should be acceleration on the descent, deceleration on the ascent, and a hold on the apex. To create these effects, you will change the interpolation and the velocity of the animation.

1 In the Time Layout window, click the triangle next to the Position property. The Speed graph appears. Yours may look slightly different than the one shown below.

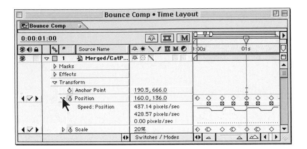

When you create keyframes for any property, like the Position keyframes at 00:07 and 00:15, After Effects interpolates the positions of the layers in the frames between the two keyframes. The default temporal interpolation style is linear. With linear interpolation, the speed of the change between keyframes is uniform and constant and can result in sudden changes at the keyframe. Linear interpolation can give a mechanical and unnatural look to your animation. With Bezier interpolation, the velocity can be set to create a smooth rate of change through keyframes.

2 Drag the right viewing-area marker to the left until the time ruler is displayed in five-frame increments. If the speed graph is not visible, press the Home key to move to the beginning of the composition.

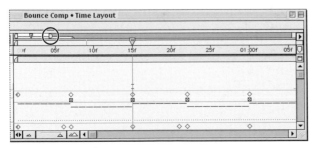

Viewing-area marker

As you can see from the graph, the segments mapping the change between keyframes are straight.

3 Press 0 on your numeric keypad to preview the motion with linear interpolation again.

The speed is constant in between keyframes, but changes abruptly when a keyframe is reached. Now you'll change the interpolation method to Continuous Bezier.

4 Click the word *Position* in the Time Layout window; all the Position keyframes are selected.

5 Choose Layer > Keyframe Interpolation. Choose Continuous Bezier from the Temporal Interpolation menu, and click OK.

Notice that the keyframe icon has changed from a diamond, which represents linear interpolation, to the Bezier interpolation icon. Bezier interpolation automatically creates a smooth rate of change through a keyframe. Notice that the graph curve has smoothed out.

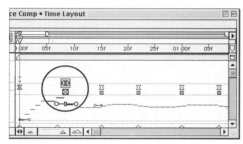

Continuous Bezier

6 Preview the motion by pressing 0 on the numeric keypad.

The motion should appear somewhat smoother than it did with the linear setting, especially at the top and bottom of the bounce.

The handles that appear on the graph are known as *ease handles* and allow you to fine-tune the velocity. You will see a pair of ease handles only for keyframes that are currently selected.

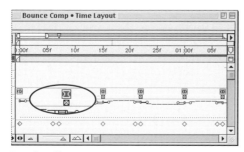

Ease handles

Factors affecting speed

After you create your keyframes and motion paths, you may want to make more precise adjustments to the way the spatial coordinates or speed of a moving layer changes through keyframes. You can fine-tune nearly all changes over time using the Speed graph or Velocity graph in the Time Layout window. The Speed graph provides complete information about and control of the value and rate of change for all spatial values, such as Position, at any frame in a composition. The Velocity graph provides complete information about and control of the value and rate of change for all non-spatial values, such as Rotation, at any frame in a composition.

The change of value or speed over time is affected by the following factors:

Time difference   The time difference between keyframes in the Time Layout window. The shorter the time interval between keyframes, the more quickly the layer has to change before reaching the next keyframe value. If the interval is longer, the layer changes more slowly, since it must make the change over a longer period of time. You can use distance to adjust speed by moving keyframes forward or backward along the timeline.

Value difference   The difference between the values of adjacent keyframes. A large difference between keyframe values, such as the difference between 75% and 20% opacity, creates a faster rate of change than a smaller difference, such as the difference between 30% and 20% opacity. You can use value differences to adjust the rate of change by increasing or decreasing the value of a layer property at a keyframe.

Interpolation type   The type of interpolation applied for a keyframe. For example, it is difficult to make a value change smoothly through a keyframe when the keyframe is set to Linear interpolation; but at any time, you can switch to Bezier interpolation, which supports a smooth change through a keyframe. If you use Bezier interpolation, you can adjust the rate of change even more precisely using ease handles.

Editing the speed graph

To enhance the bounce effect of the pogo stick, you want a quick change at the bounce point, where the character is near the bottom of the screen, and you want a slower, smoother change at the top of the jump.

In the speed graph, a rising line indicates acceleration, an increase in velocity; a falling line indicates deceleration, a decrease in velocity. To change the speed for the pogo stick animation, you want a graph that peaks at the keyframes where the pogo stick is at its lowest point and bottoms out where the pogo stick is at its highest point.

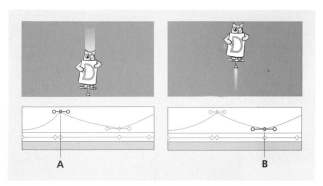

A. The graph peaks at the keyframe where the pogo stick is at its lowest point and B. bottoms out where the pogo stick is at its highest point.

The Speed graph reflects the maximum speed of the entire layer at the top of the graph and the minimum speed of the layer at the bottom of the graph. The middle value displayed in the Switches panel reflects the speed at the current-time marker.

1 In the Time Layout window, deselect all the keyframes, and set the current time to 00:00.

Note: When selecting a keyframe, be sure to click the keyframe icon, not the roving keyframe option directly below it. If you accidentally click the roving keyframe option, choose Edit > Undo to turn the roving keyframe option back off again.

2 Select the Position keyframe at 00:00, when the character is at its highest position, and then drag the small round ease handle down so that the handle is near the bottom of the graph. (Be sure to grab the handle, which is on the right, and not the control point.) Try not to move the handle in or out.

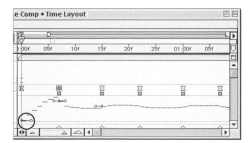

Ease handle for the first keyframe

The current speed, which is displayed in the middle of the Switches panel, should be between 10 and 50 pixels per second.

3 Select the keyframe at 00:07, and drag one of the ease handles up to just under the top of the graph. Note that if you move the handle left or right, the shape of the curve changes. This is called *influence*, and it will be covered in the next part of the lesson.

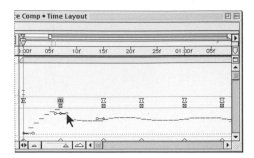

4 Select the third keyframe, and drag the handle down near the bottom of the graph.

Where the Merged/CatPogo.ai layer is at its lowest point, the graph is at its peak speed; the graph is at its lowest speed when the Merged/CatPogo.ai layer is at its highest point.

5 Select the fourth keyframe, and then drag a handle slightly past the top line. Dragging past the top of the graph changes the range of the graph.

Notice how the graph resets itself. The maximum speed reflects the new range.

6 Press 0 on your numeric keypad to preview the motion.

Changing the influence

Not only can you change the acceleration and deceleration by dragging up and down, you can also drag the ease handles left and right to change the *influence* of a keyframe. The influence determines how quickly the speed at the keyframe is reached.

1 To create a sharper change at the peak of the graph, select the keyframe at 00:07, and drag the ease handles in, one at a time.

The graph reflects the sharp change of speed at the bounce of the character.

2 To create a more gradual change in speed, select the keyframe at 00:15, and then drag the ease handles out, smoothing the curve at the bottom of the graph, as shown below.

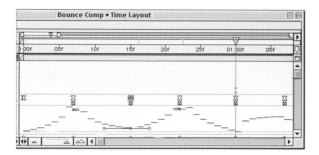

The ease handles represent the incoming and outgoing speeds.

3 Use ease handles to smooth out the bottom curve of the graph and to create a sharp peak at the top.

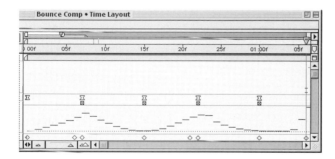

4 Continue selecting keyframes and changing the Speed graph to reflect the increase in speed as the character bounces up, and the decrease in speed as the character descends from the peak of the bounce.

Don't worry about getting the graph exactly the same as the illustration. The important thing is to get a feel for working with the ease handles.

Make sure to select the keyframe to control the ease handles on both sides.

5 Preview the motion by pressing 0 on your numeric keypad.

Changing the velocity values

You can change the velocity by entering precise speeds in a dialog box.

1 Select the keyframe at 00:07, and then choose Layer > Keyframe Velocity. Enter a speed of **1150** pixels per second for the incoming velocity.

If the Continuous (Bezier) option is selected, both incoming and outgoing velocities stay the same.

You can also set a percentage of influence. The range of influence between keyframes is one-half the distance to the next keyframe. The higher the percentage of influence, the smoother the acceleration or deceleration. The lower the percentage of influence, the more abrupt the change in speed.

Set the Influence to **15** for both incoming and outgoing, and then click OK.

Adjust the ease handles for the keyframes at 00:22 and 01:07 so that they are near the top of the graph, and make any final adjustments to the other keyframes.

2 Drag the viewing-area markers out to display the entire time ruler.

3 Click the triangle next to Position to collapse the Speed graph.

Copying and pasting multiple keyframes

To repeat the bounce motion for the rest of the composition, you'll copy and paste multiple keyframes and edit the keyframes.

1 Drag a marquee to select all the Position and Scale keyframes that you have set so far, and then choose Edit > Copy.

2 Set the current time to 02:00, and paste.

3 Set the current time to 04:00, and paste.

4 Adjust the work area, and press 0 on the numeric keypad to preview the motion.

Editing the keyframes

To create the effect of bouncing less and less, change the squash amount and position of some of the keyframes.

1 Double-click the Scale keyframe at 04:07 to display the Scale dialog box, and then set the height of the Scale value to **13**, and click OK.

2 Use the following table to set the Height values for the rest of the Scale keyframes.

04:22	15
05:07	17
05:22	18

As a finishing touch, you will drag the Merged/CatPogo.ai layer down slightly so that the cat doesn't jump as high at the end of the composition.

3 Select the Position keyframe at 05:00, where the cat is at the top of the bounce.

You may need to adjust the viewing-area markers to see the area of the time ruler that you want to see.

> *To quickly find a keyframe at a specific time, move the current-time marker to that time; the marker will then be on top of the keyframe.*

4 Shift-drag the layer down to about the middle of the frame so that the cat is bouncing only half as high.

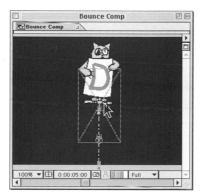

5 Set the current time to 05:15, and then drag the layer down to the middle of the frame.

Later, you'll adjust the top speed so it gets slower and slower.

6 Select the Position keyframe at 04:22, and choose Layer > Keyframe Velocity. Set the speed for Incoming Velocity to **700** pixels per second. Leave the Influence as is, and click OK.

7 Select the Position keyframe at 05:07, choose Layer > Keyframe Velocity, and set the speed for Incoming Velocity to **400**. Leave the Influence as is, and click OK.

8 Finally, select the Position keyframe at 05:22, choose Layer > Keyframe Velocity, and set the speed for Incoming Velocity to **200**. Click OK.

Finishing the Bounce Comp

In the final 4 seconds of the composition, the cat character is just slightly bouncing. You'll copy and paste the keyframes that start at 05:00.

1 To fill the rest of the composition with Position and Scale keyframes, select the four Position and six Scale keyframes starting at 05:00, and choose Edit > Copy.

2 Paste these keyframes at 06:00, 07:00, 08:00, and 09:00.

3 In the Switches panel, select the Motion Blur switch (under M) for the Merged/CatPogo.ai layer. You'll enable and set up Motion Blur later in this lesson.

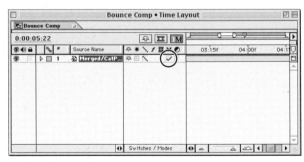

Motion Blur switch

4 Return to the beginning of the composition, set the work area, preview the composition one last time. Collapse the outline for the Merged/CatPogo.ai layer and then save the project.

Replacing the artwork

As you have seen so far, creating this type of animation can be very time-consuming. It would take hours to create a separate animation for each of the letter cats. Luckily, you can use the Bounce composition motion for the rest of the cats by swapping out the Merged/CatPogo.ai artwork.

After duplicating the Bounce Comp four times, you'll replace the original illustration that was used in the Bounce composition with a new illustration for each letter in the word *Kids*. The animation for the word *Network* has already been prepared for you.

But first, you'll organize your Project window.

1 Click the create folder icon (▭) at the bottom of the Project window. Select the untitled folder, press Enter or Return, name the folder **Letter Artwork**, and then press Enter or Return again.

2 Right-click (Windows) or Control-click (Mac OS) in the Project window and choose Import > Footage Files.

3 Open the LetrCats folder in the 06Lesson folder, and then select and open the following files: Merged/CatPogoK.ai, Merged/CatPogoI.ai, and Merged/CatPogoS.ai. As a dialog box opens for each layer, click OK to choose Merged Layers. Click Done.

4 Drag all the new files into the Letter Artwork folder in the Project window. Close the LetrCats folder.

5 In the Project window, click the create folder icon (▭), press Enter or Return, name the new folder **Bounce Comps**, and press Enter or Return again.

6 Drag the Bounce Comp composition into the Bounce Comps folder.

7 Click the triangle next to the Bounce Comps folder to open it.

8 Select Bounce Comp in the Bounce Comps folder in the Project window, choose Edit > Duplicate, and then duplicate the Bounce composition two more times, for a total of four compositions.

9 Select any one of the Bounce Comp items, press Enter or Return, name the new composition **D/Bounce**, and press Enter or Return again.

10 Select each Bounce Comp and name each by using one of the following letters: K, I, or S, resulting in four compositions—K/Bounce, I/Bounce, D/Bounce, and S/Bounce.

You now have four identical compositions with new names.

Switching out the artwork

Next, you'll replace the original Merged/CatPogo.ai artwork with new letter illustrations.

1 In the Project window, double-click the K/Bounce composition to open its Time Layout window and Composition window, and then select the Merged/CatPogo.ai layer.

Because you'll be using some long filenames, you'll need to expand the Name field in the Project window and the Source Name in the Time Layout window.

2 In the Project window, drag the right edge of the Name heading to the right so that none of the filenames below it are cut off.

3 In the same way, expand the Source Name heading in the Time Layout window.

4 In the Project window, open the Letter Artwork folder and select Merged/CatPogoK.ai.

5 Hold down the Alt key (Windows) or Option key (Mac OS) and drag the Merged/CatPogoK.ai item into the Composition window (or Time Layout window).

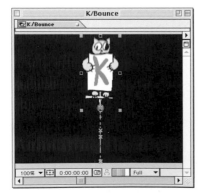

The new art replaces the original, but all the properties and motion remain the same.

Note: If you do not select the layer in the Time Layout window before dragging the footage item from the Project window, you will add the layer into the composition, instead of replacing the original file.

6 Press Alt (Windows) or Option (Mac OS) and click the close box of the current Time Layout window or Composition window to close all the windows associated with the K/Bounce composition.

7 Double-click the I/Bounce composition to open its Time Layout window, and then select the Merged/CatPogo.ai layer.

8 Activate the Project window, and select Merged/CatPogoI.ai.

9 Alt-drag (Windows) or Option-drag (Mac OS) the Merged/CatPogoI.ai item into the Composition window (or Time Layout window).

10 Close all the windows associated with the I/Bounce composition.

11 Repeat steps 7 through 10 for the S/Bounce composition. (The D/Bounce composition already contains the D letter cat.) Save the project.

Enabling Motion Blur

Motion Blur allows layer motion to appear smoother and more realistic. When you view one frame of film or video, motion in the frame is often blurred. This is because a frame represents a sample of time, and in that time, a moving object is traveling across the frame so it cannot be shown as a sharp still object. The speed of a moving object affects how blurred it appears in each frame. Another factor in the degree of blur is the shutter angle of a motion-picture or video camera, which determines the effective exposure time of each frame. Without Motion Blur, a layer animation may produce a strobe-like effect of distinct steps. For more information on Motion Blur, see the After Effects User Guide.

1 Open any one of the letter comps, and select the Enable Motion Blur button.

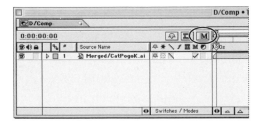

2 Click the Play button on the Time Controls palette to preview the effect of the Motion Blur.

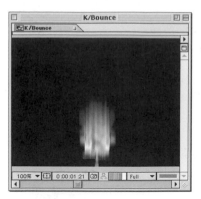

You can adjust the intensity of Motion Blur by setting the Shutter Angle preference.

3 Choose File > Preferences > General, set Shutter Angle to **90**, and then click OK.

The shutter angle is measured in degrees, simulating the exposure of a rotating shutter.

4 Play a few seconds of the composition. Notice that the Motion Blur effect is reduced with a smaller shutter angle setting.

5 Before going on with the lesson, deselect the Enable Motion Blur button, because Motion Blur can slow down screen redraw and affect performance. You can enable Motion Blur in the Render Queue when you are ready to render the movie.

6 Save the project.

Creating side-to-side motion

To add more interest and movement to the pogo stick animation, you will nest one of the Bounce compositions inside a new composition set with side-to-side motion. This motion is created by using the Rotate and Position properties.

1 Create a new composition, type **Sideways Comp** for the name, set the Frame Size to **400** x **340**, the Frame Rate to **30** fps, and the Duration to **15:00**.

2 Drag the D/Bounce composition from the Project window into the Time Layout window.

You will set Position keyframes and animate the left-right motion so it moves a larger distance at first and gradually moves back and forth less and less until it stops at 3 seconds. You'll set keyframes every 15 frames, which ensures that each keyframe corresponds to when the pogo stick is in the down position.

First, you'll display a proportional grid in the Composition window as an aid in positioning the layer.

3 Press Alt (Windows) or Option (Mac OS) and click the safe-zones icon at the bottom of the Composition window.

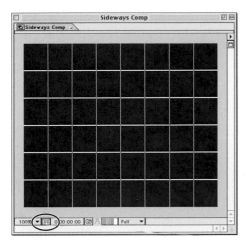

4 Set the current time to 00:07, and position the cat illustration centered at the third vertical grid line and aligned with the bottom of the screen. (The position coordinates for the layer, displayed at the bottom of the Info palette, are approximately 150, 220.)

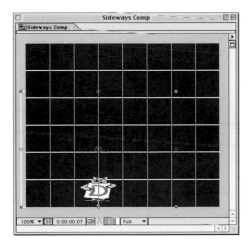

5 In the Time Layout window, set an initial Position keyframe.

You will now position the layer left or right of the center position, without changing the vertical position. To make this easier, you'll use a keyboard shortcut again to constrain movement, this time to the horizontal axis.

6 Move the current-time marker to 00:22. Start dragging horizontally, press and hold Shift, and then drag the illustration to the right between the fifth and sixth vertical lines on the grid. (Position coordinates are approximately 273, 220.)

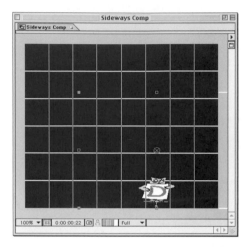

7 Move the current-time marker to 01:07. Start dragging horizontally, press and hold Shift, and then drag the illustration to the left between the third and fourth vertical lines on the grid (approximately 175, 220).

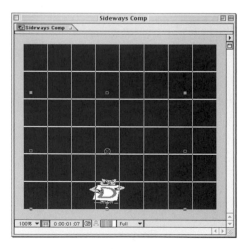

8 Move to 1:22. Start dragging horizontally, press and hold Shift, and then position the layer on top of the fifth vertical line (approximately 250, 220).

9 In the Time Layout window, select the keyframes at 01:07 and 01:22, copy them, and then move to frame 2:07, and paste.

10 Move to 3:07, and position the layer on the center line of the grid (approximately 200, 220).

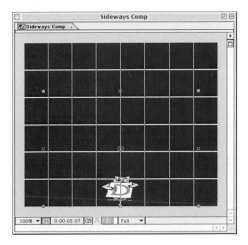

11 Save the project. In the Time Layout window, drag the right work-area marker in to 04:00 seconds, and press Alt-0 (Windows) or Option-0 (Mac OS) to preview. Since this is a nested composition, you won't see the alpha outlines—you'll see a rectangular shape instead.

12 Select the Motion Blur switch for the layer, but do not select the Enable Motion Blur button above it.

Creating the swinging rotation

Now set up the rotation motion in the same composition.

1 In the Time Layout window, make sure that the outline is collapsed so that the transform properties are not displayed.

2 Move the current-time marker to 00:07, press R to display the Rotation property, set an initial Rotation keyframe, and then set the Rotation value to **9** degrees.

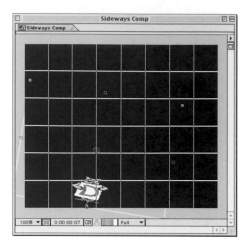

3 Move the current-time marker to 00:22, and set the Rotation to **–11**.

4 Continue moving the time marker and use the following table to enter Rotation values. Since there are keyframes already set up for the Position property, you can use the keyframe navigator or press the K key to move from keyframe to keyframe.

01:07	7°
01:22	-8°
02:07	4°
02:22	-9°
03:07	0°

5 Turn off the proportional grid by pressing Alt (Windows) or Option (Mac OS) and clicking the safe-zones icon in the Composition window.

6 Collapse the outline in the Time Layout window and save the project.

7 Preview the motion, and then close the Composition window and the Time Layout window.

Nesting the Bounce composition into the Sideways composition

Now you will exchange the letter comps with respective sideways comps. You'll end up with comps called K/Side, I/Side, D/Side, and S/Side.

1 In the Project window, click the create folder icon (🗀), name the new folder **Side Comps**, and then drag the Sideways composition into the new folder, and click the triangle to expand the folder.

2 Select the Sideways composition in the Project window, and choose Edit > Duplicate.

3 Duplicate two more times, until you have four Sideways compositions, one for each letter in *KIDS*.

4 Rename each of the four Sideways comps K/Side, I/Side, D/Side, and S/Side, respectively.

You will exchange the artwork with the appropriate letter composition, just as you did when creating the Bounce comps.

5 Open the K/Side composition, and in the Time Layout window, select the D/Bounce layer. In the Project window, open the Bounce Comps folder and select the K/Bounce composition.

6 Hold down the Alt key (Windows) or Option key (Mac OS) and drag the K/Bounce composition into the K/Side Composition window (or Time Layout window).

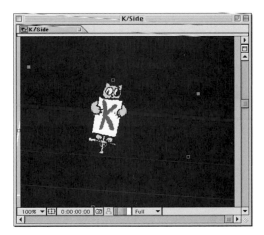

The new art replaces the original, but all the motion remains the same.

7 Close the K/Side Composition window and Time Layout window.

8 Open the I/Side composition, and in the Time Layout window, select the D/Bounce layer. In the Bounce Comps folder, select the I/Bounce composition.

9 Hold down the Alt key (Windows) or Option key (Mac OS) and drag the I/Bounce composition into the I/Side Composition window (or Time Layout window).

10 Close the I/Side Composition window and Time Layout window.

11 Repeat steps 8 through 10 to create the S/Side composition.

12 Save the project.

Staggering the animation

In this section, you will assemble the Side comps into the final composition, staggering the animated letters so they begin at different times and enter the frame from different angles.

1 Double-click Final Comp in the Project window, and set the current time to 05:12.

2 Drag the Side Comps folder from the Project window into the Time Layout window. All the layers are stacked on top of each other in the Composition window, so you will see only the top layer until you move them.

Now you'll set scale and position keyframes for the layers you just added to Final Comp.

3 Make sure all the Side layers are selected in the Time Layout window, and press the S key to display the Scale property.

4 Click the Scale value for any one of the layers, enter **50** for Scale, and click OK.

5 Press the P key to display the Position property, and then move the current-time marker to 12:00.

6 In the Composition window, click the safe-zones icon to show the action-safe and title-safe zones. Make sure to place the letters within the action-safe zone.

If you have a small monitor, reduce the Magnification to 50%. This will ensure that the letters stay in the composition.

7 Deselect all the layers, and then select the K/Side composition layer in the Time Layout window.

8 In the Composition window, start with the K/Side composition, and move the four Side comps to the positions where you want them to end up. Use the last frame of the final movie as a reference.

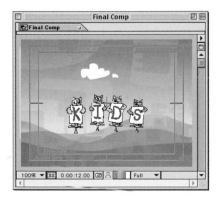

It's easier to select a layer in the Time Layout window and then move it in the Composition window.

9 In the Time Layout window, set Position keyframes for all the layers so that each has a fixed keyframe at 12:00, representing its final position.

10 In the Composition window, move the current-time marker to 5:20, which is where each character will first land. Position all the characters in slightly different positions from their ending positions. In this way, they will move around between this point and the end point.

11 In the Time Layout window, move the current-time marker to 05:12, and then deselect all the layers. In the Composition window, position each individual character outside of the frame (you may need to change the magnification) so that each appears to jump in from a different area.

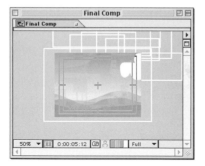

Make sure that you have Position keyframes set for all four layers.

Staggering the In points

The D/Side composition starts seven frames after the big cat in the beginning jumps out of the frame. It should land and bounce twice before any of the other pogo jumpers appear.

1 Leave the D/Side composition In point positioned at 05:12, and then set the current time to 05:26.

2 Drag the I/Side layer duration bar so that it starts at 05:26. Be sure to drag inside the duration bar, not on the In- or Out-point handles.

3 Stagger the other letters by dragging the layer duration bars in the Time Layout window. Make sure that all the letters compositions (except for the D/Side composition) start after frame 05:26.

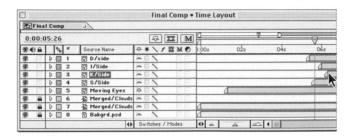

4 Set the current time to 12:00, and then align all the last keyframes at 12:00 so that the letters line up properly. (Drag a keyframe close to the current-time marker, and then press the Shift key to snap the keyframe into position at 12:00.)

5 Save the project. You may want to create a draft movie to preview your work.

Importing a movie

To complete the pogo stick cat animation, you will import a movie in which the animation for the rest of the letters (*Network*) has been created for you.

1 Activate the Project window and right-click (Windows) or Control-click (Mac OS) in an open area of the Project window. Choose Import > Footage File, and select NetCat.mov in the 06Lesson folder.

2 Position the current-time marker at 05:00, and then drag the NetCat.mov footage file into the Final Comp Time Layout window.

The NetCat.mov footage was created by setting up compositions like the compositions you just created. The final composition was rendered with an alpha channel that makes the background transparent, allowing you to superimpose the QuickTime movie in the current composition.

3 Save the project.

Editing a motion path

Finally, you will place the blimp image and edit the motion path in the Composition window.

1 Activate the Project window and right-click (Windows) or Control-click (Mac OS) in an open area of the Project window. Choose Import > Footage File, and select the Blimp.ai file in the 06Lesson folder. In the Blimp.ai dialog box, leave Merged Layers selected and click OK.

2 Set the current-time marker to 08:08, and then drag the Merged/Blimp.ai footage item into the Final Comp window.

3 With the Merged/Blimp.ai layer selected in the Time Layout window, set the Scale to **20**.

4 In the Composition window, position the blimp off the left side of the screen, with the top of the graphic even with the top of the action-safe zone.

5 Set an initial Position keyframe in the Time Layout window.

6 Move the current-time marker to 11:14 and in the Composition window, position the blimp near the center of the screen. Another position keyframe is created.

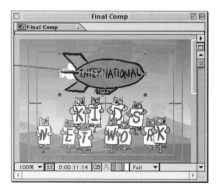

You'll edit the movement by using Bezier curves, making the blimp appear to float down into the position.

7 If necessary, choose 50% from the Magnification menu so you can see the whole motion path.

8 Locate the direction handle for the first motion keyframe and drag it up to create a gently rising curve (as shown in the following illustration).

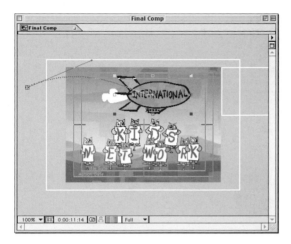

9 Now drag the direction handle for the final motion keyframe down to create a backward S curve.

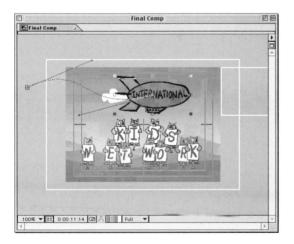

10 If the current-time marker is not at 11:14 in the Time Layout window, move it there, and then select the Position keyframe at that time.

11 Choose Layer > Keyframe Interpolation, and choose Continuous Bezier from the Temporal Interpolation menu. Click OK.

12 In the Time Layout window, expand the Position outline for the Merged/Blimp.ai layer and drag the ease handles to create a smooth downward motion from the first keyframe to the second. This alters the velocity, so the blimp appears to gradually slow to a stop.

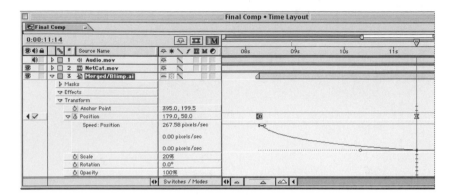

13 Click the triangle to collapse the Speed graph.

14 Save the project.

Importing the sound

The audio for the project consists of a combination of "boing" sounds created with a jew's-harp, plus giggles, and a cat's meow sound effect. Since the focus of this lesson is animation, you will import the completed sound track as a finishing touch.

1 Activate the Project window and right-click (Windows) or Control-click (Mac OS) in an open area of the Project window. Choose Import > Footage File, select the Audio.mov file, and click Open.

2 Set the current time to 00:00, and then drag the audio item from the Project window into the Final Comp window.

3 Save the project.

Rendering the final project

You have finished the animation and are now ready to render the final project.

1 Close all windows except the Final Comp and Project windows.

Select Final Comp in the Project window. Choose Composition > Make Movie, type **06Movie.mov** for the name, and save it in your Projects folder.

2 In the Render Queue window, choose Custom for Render Settings.

3 Make sure the Quality is set to Best and the Resolution is set to Full.

If you prefer, render a draft movie.

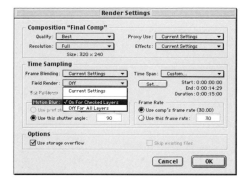

4 For Motion Blur, choose On For Checked Layers. This will render the movie with the Motion Blur that you specified for the Merged/CatPogo.ai character.

5 For Time Span, choose Length of Comp. Leave all other settings at their defaults, and then click OK.

6 For Output Module, choose Custom. For Format, choose QuickTime Movie.

Note: In a Mac OS, QuickTime Movie is the default format.

7 In Windows, the QuickTime settings dialog box appears. Leave Compressor set to Animation, and click OK. In Mac OS, leave the Video Output options at their defaults.

8 Select Import into Project When Done.

9 Select Audio Output to include audio in the movie, and then choose 22.050 KHz for the sample rate, 8-bit for the sample depth, and mono for the playback format, and click OK.

10 Click Render.

11 When you are finished rendering the movie, open the footage file that appears in your Project window and play the movie.

12 After watching the movie, exit from After Effects.

Congratulations! Cats off to you! Completing this project is quite an achievement.

Special Effects for Film

In this lesson, you'll create a short scene for a motion picture, working with high-resolution images, blue screen keying, and motion tracking.

The movie you create in this project depicts a short scene from a fictitious motion picture, requiring a number of visual effects.

In this lesson you'll explore compositing at film resolution, keying out a blue screen, and tracking motion to generate keyframes.

This lesson covers the following topics:

- Organizing a project
- Working with film-resolution images
- Creating and using proxies
- Using the Timecode effect
- Setting custom resolution
- Using the Cineon Converter effect
- Using the Production Bundle Glow effect
- Using the Production Bundle Corner Pin effect
- Creating a track matte
- Using the Color Key
- Using the Production Bundle Color Difference key and Motion Tracker Keyframe Assistant

At the end of this lesson you will have created an 8-second scene to be used in a motion picture.

It should take approximately 3 to 4 hours to complete this project.

Viewing the final project

Before you begin, take a look at the finished movie that you'll create in this lesson.

1 Double-click the 07Final.mov file in the 07Lesson folder to open the final QuickTime movie, and then click the Play button.

This scene with special effects consists of an actor who was filmed against a blue screen background and then composited over an old-fashioned still image of a feed store. An animated compact disc appears out of the sky and hovers over him. A glowing light also follows the motion of the actor's hand.

2 When finished, quit the MoviePlayer application.

Before you begin

This lesson uses several plug-ins from the Production Bundle version of After Effects. Before you start, make sure that you have installed the Glow and Corner Pin plug-ins according to the instructions in "Installing Production Bundle plug-ins" on page 4.

This lesson also uses two features that are available only in the Production Bundle version of After Effects, and that have not been included on the After Effects Classroom in a Book CD. These are the Color Difference Keying Effect and the Motion Tracker Keyframe Assistant. If you do not have access to the Production Bundle version of After Effects, follow the alternative steps that are provided.

Size and memory considerations

If you plan to copy project files from the CD-ROM to your hard disk, you'll need at least 450 MB of available space. First try the lesson without copying the files; if After Effects seems too slow, copy the files to the hard disk.

On Windows systems, you should have at least 64 MB of RAM installed. On Mac OS systems, you should assign at least 20 MB of RAM to After Effects.

The final goal of this project is to create a full-screen image for film. The original footage and final output size of this project is 2048 x 1536, usually referred to as *2K*. Part of the purpose of this project is to allow you to judge what your machine resources need to be to work with this kind of material, but you can work on almost any machine at a lower output resolution.

Several strategies are provided to help conserve memory and increase editing speed.

Getting started

1 To ensure that the tools and palettes function exactly as described in this lesson, delete or deactivate (by renaming) the After Effects preferences file. See "Restoring default preferences" on page 6.

2 Start After Effects.

Using a process flow

Before you start the project, you will open the completed project and examine some process flow issues.

1 Choose File > Open, and select the 07Proj.aep file in the 07Lesson folder.

2 Click OK if a dialog box prompts you that the file has been changed.

The Project window contains six numbered compositions as well as a folder containing QuickTime movies and still images.

In this project, compositions are numbered according to a process flow from 1, which is a Cineon file conversion composition, to 6, which is the final rendered movie.

Now you'll close the finished project and start constructing your own special effects for film. Instead of creating a new project, you open a project that has already been started.

3 Choose File > Open. You may need to click the Don't Save button to close the 07project file without saving changes. Select 07begin.aep in the 07Lesson folder, and click Open.

This project contains a Timing Script composition that has been set up for you and that you will use later in the lesson.

4 Choose File > Save As, name the file **07Work.aep**, and save it into your Projects folder.

Setting preferences

Before you get started, set a few preferences that will come in handy during the lesson.

1 Choose File > Preferences > Time, set the Display Style to Frames, and enter **1** for "Start Numbering Frames At." Do not click OK just yet.

All the time rulers will display in frame numbers instead of SMTPE timecode, and the first frame in the composition is numbered 0001 instead of 0000.

2 In the Preferences menu, choose Display. Select Disable thumbnails in project window.

If you select this option, After Effects doesn't generate thumbnail previews in the Project window, so you'll save time on screen redraw if you are working with high-resolution files.

3 Select Auto-Zoom When Resolution Changes.

This option will resize the window to match the resolution. For example, when you choose Quarter Resolution, the Magnification changes to 25%.

4 Select Synchronize Time of All Related Items.

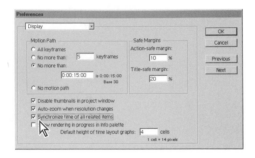

Since you will be creating a lot of different compositions, this option helps to synchronize the current-time marker in all related open compositions.

5 Click OK to close the Display Preferences dialog box.

Using the Timecode effect

In this section, you will examine the 1_Timing_Script composition, and then see how the Timecode effect is used to help analyze timing cues.

This composition is a record of how the film scene was originally conceived. There is a solid for each event in the sequence, numbered for the starting frame, and named for the event. There is also a marker for each layer, with further explanations. In addition, a composition-time marker (1–7) has been set at each event start point as a navigation aid. Because these layers are intended only for designing the project and contain no footage, the video for each of these layers is turned off.

To set up 1_Timing_Script, we used the Timing.mov file with timecode going through the movie frame by frame and setting composition-time markers at important parts of the scene.

1 On your keyboard, press the 1 key from the number keys (above the letter keys) to go to the first composition-time marker.

The first composition-time marker is set at frame 24, where the flying CD first enters. The name of the Solid layer includes the frame number and a description of the action at that time.

2 Press the 3 key from the number keys (above the letter keys) to go to the third composition-time marker. From frame 43 to frame 78, the CD will fly past the actor.

3 Continue examining the marker frames in the 1_Timing_Script composition. You'll use this composition again when you are creating the motion for the flying CD.

Now you will step through the process of adding timecode to the timing movie. You will superimpose frame numbers on the footage by applying the Timecode effect. The Timecode effect displays or encodes timecode or frame number information in the layer to which it is applied.

4 Press the Home key to go to the beginning of the composition. Choose Layer > New Solid, type **Timecode** for the name, set the size to **110** x **35** pixels, leave the color at the default gray, and click OK.

5 Choose Effect > Video > Timecode. The Timecode Effect Controls window appears.

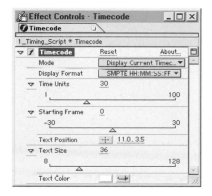

You can choose to display or encode the current timecode of your composition. For this composition, you will display the timecode since it will be used only to analyze timing cues.

6 Make sure Display Current Timecode is selected in the Mode menu.

You have the option to display SMPTE timecode (hours:minutes:seconds:frames) or frame numbers.

7 Choose Frame numbers from the Display Format menu.

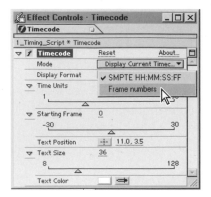

8 Since the frame rate of this composition is 24 fps, set the Time Units to **24**.

9 Set the Starting Frame to 1, and then set the Text size to **28** points.

10 In the Composition window, drag the solid down below the actor's feet.

It doesn't matter where you put the solid as long as it isn't obscuring the action and you can easily read it.

11 Close the Effect Controls window and save the project.

12 Preview the composition with RAM Preview by pressing the 0 key on your numeric keypad.

13 Close the Composition and Time Layout windows.

Now that you have seen how the 1_Timing_Script composition was created, you will begin work on the elements for the movie scene.

Understanding the Cineon file format

The standard professional picture file format for working in digital film is the Cineon format. Originally developed by the Eastman Kodak Company, the Cineon format is designed to contain all the picture information present in a frame of motion picture negative film, so that the artist has the maximum possible color correction range available. High-resolution motion picture scans can be very expensive, so one naturally wants to avoid rescanning footage because of wrong color correction choices. With the Cineon format, no choices need be made at the scanner, other than basic calibration to your film type.

Unlike most picture file formats, the Cineon format samples the image at 10 bits per channel, and encodes the data in a logarithmic scale which looks extremely low-contrast and washed out, as opposed to the normal-contrast linear scale images you're used to seeing.

After Effects 4.0 was designed to work primarily with 8-bpc (bit per channel) images, so some slight liberties have been taken with the normal footage importing process to allow you to choose (and even animate) the best possible 8-bpc conversion from the 10-bpc Cineon original.

The file-format plug-in presents the Cineon file to After Effects as if it were an 8-bpc image with an alpha channel. After placing the footage in a composition, it will look like bad television reception because there is a mismatch between the 8-bit and 10-bit channel widths. To properly decode the image, you must apply the Cineon Converter effect.

Once the Cineon Converter effect has been applied, you then have the choice of working in log or linear mode. Linear mode is the more familiar mode, but there are some advantages to keeping your Cineon images in log scale all the way through the compositing process. The most important benefit is that an end-to-end log scale composite will result in a higher-quality film recording, because it will have retained all the extended highlight information which is discarded in the conversion to linear.

The Windows and UNIX® three-letter file type extension for Cineon is .cin. In Mac OS, the file Type should be SDPX and the Creator FXTC for automatic recognition by After Effects.

The After Effects Cineon Converter is designed to make the task of color management in log scale compositing as easy and intuitive as possible.

Note: Only one real Cineon file is included with this lesson so that you can practice importing it. Due to the limited amount of space available on the CD-ROM, a high-resolution log scale QuickTime movie will stand in for a Cineon sequence in this lesson.

Creating a proxy for a high-resolution footage file

You will begin by importing high-resolution footage of an actor filmed against a blue screen. Next you'll create and assign a *proxy*, or lower-resolution copy, of the original footage to make working with the project faster and easier.

1 Choose File > Import > Footage File, and then select ActHiR01.cin from the 07Lesson folder. In the Interpret Footage dialog box, select Treat As Straight (Unmatted), and click OK.

2 Next, choose Composition > New Composition, type **2_Proxy** for the name, and choose Film (2K) from the Frame Size menu for a Frame Size of 2048 x 1536 pixels.

3 In the Composition window, choose Quarter from the Resolution menu.

Making a full-size composition at Quarter Resolution is far thriftier with RAM than making a 512 x 384 composition and shrinking the 2048 x 1536 image within it.

4 Set the Frame Rate to **24** fps—the standard frame rate for movies made in the United States. Set the Duration to **192** frames (8 seconds), and then click OK.

The Composition window opens with a Magnification of 25% and Quarter Resolution. The composition has the same dimensions and duration as the original footage, but it will be displayed and rendered at a fraction of the original dimensions. It's best with film-resolution images to make your proxy at about video resolution; 512 x 384 is close enough.

5 Drag the ActHiR01.cin footage file from the Project window into the Time Layout window.

6 The image should look like a mosaic. Choose Effect > Cineon Tools > Cineon Converter. The image should now look normal. This is a linear conversion. Note that the Conversion Type menu in the Effect Controls window is set to Auto Log to Linear by default. Experiment with the Black and White Point, Gamma, and Highlight Rolloff sliders.

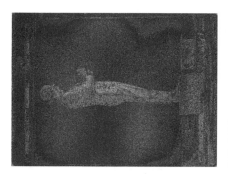 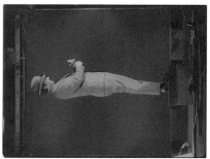

The original footage was shot sideways, but you'll correct that when you create a composition. (You want the proxy to be the same orientation as the original footage.)

If you don't have much RAM available you might get an out-of-RAM warning. You can lower the resolution of the image even more to conserve RAM.

7 To set a custom resolution, choose Custom from the Resolution menu, and then enter **8** for both horizontal and vertical pixels, and click OK.

This results in a Resolution of one-eighth, and a window size that is close to the 320 x 240 windows you've been working with throughout this book. It may take a moment to display the contents of the Composition window.

8 Since you'll be building a log scale composition, choose Auto Log to Log from the Conversion Type menu and note the slider settings. Note the very flat (low) image contrast. Apply a second Cineon Converter effect, leaving it at the default settings. The image has now been relinearized and looks correct. Apart from the loss of extended highlight information at the first linearization, you can convert between log and linear any number of times without harming the image.

9 When finished, delete the ActHiR01.cin layer, since it is only a single frame.

10 Choose File > Import > Footage File, and then select ActHiR.mov from the 07Lesson folder and click Open. Drag it from the Project window into the 2_Proxy Time Layout window.

ActHiR.mov is a high-resolution QuickTime movie made from the Cineon sequence using the Auto Log to Log Conversion Type. Although it is an 8-bpc file, it still retains all the dynamic range of the 10-bpc Cineon file, but with slightly less color precision. Later, you'll correct this by applying a log-to-log conversion with an adjustment layer. The movie was compressed using the standard QuickTime Photo-JPEG compressor, which is an excellent choice when you need to retain maximum image quality. At up to 10:1 compression, Photo-JPEG images are still very close to uncompressed quality, but at the expense of native playback speed.

11 Save the project.

If you were to render the project, you would use the following settings: Best Quality, Quarter Resolution, and a Frame Rate of 24 fps. The proxy for this lesson was rendered with the Photo-JPEG compressor at the High quality setting.

After rendering the proxy, you'll assign it to represent the original footage.

12 Close the 2_Proxy Composition window and Time Layout window.

Setting a Proxy file

Now you'll assign a proxy to the high-resolution footage.

1 Select the ActHiR.mov footage item in the Project window, and then choose File > Set Proxy > File, select ActPrx.mov from the 07Lesson folder, and click Open.

A small black square (called a *proxy indicator*) appears to the left of the ActHiR.mov footage item in the Project window, indicating that a proxy has been set. The name of the proxy appears next to the thumbnail in the Project window. If you need to switch between the original footage and its proxy, click the proxy indicator to turn it on or off.

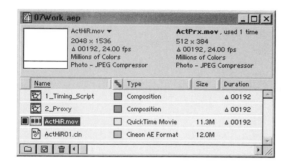

When you use the ActHiR.mov file in a composition, After Effects will use the proxy for display. Effects and properties applied to the proxy are applied to the actual footage when the movie is rendered with Use No Proxies selected from the Proxy Use menu in the Render Settings dialog box. Even though the proxy is 512 x 384, it behaves as if it's 2048 x 1536 in the composition.

Preparing the actor footage

Now you are ready to prepare the footage for the actor. You need to rotate and flip the layer, and key out the blue screen background.

1 Create a new composition, name it **3_Actor_Prep**, and then set the Frame Size to **600 x 1536** (this frame size serves to crop the layer).

2 In the Composition window, set the Resolution to Quarter.

Note: Depending upon the size of your monitor, you may need to set the resolution even lower by choosing Custom from the Resolution menu and entering a value, such as 8.

3 Make sure the Frame Rate is **24** and Duration is **192** frames, and then click OK.

4 Drag the ActHiR.mov footage item from the Project window into the 3_Actor_Prep Time Layout window. Even though you are using the ActHiR.mov footage, the proxy is actually being displayed.

Looking at the ActHiR.mov, you'll notice that the blue screen footage was shot sideways to maximize use of the frame for sharpness. This is typical of the kinds of tricks special effects supervisors come up with to improve the quality of their work.

5 Select the ActHiR.mov layer in the Time Layout window. Press the S key and then press Shift+R to display the Scale and Rotation properties. Click the underlined Rotation value, enter **90** for degrees, and click OK.

6 To flip the image, click the underlined Scale value, deselect Preserve Frame Aspect Ratio, and then enter **–100** for Height, and click OK.

7 Position the image of the actor inside the composition: click the underlined Position value and enter a position of **332** for X-axis and **792** for Y-axis.

Using color keys

The actor footage has been filmed against a blue screen. Because you want to superimpose the actor against the feed-store background in the final composition, you will *key out* the blue screen background.

The most common example of this procedure is your local news show. The weathercaster stands in front of a bright-blue screen. The image is picked up by the camera, but before it is broadcast, a keying process makes the blue screen transparent, allowing a computer-generated weather map to show through.

In After Effects, you use keying effects to make certain areas of an image transparent. Keying effects base the areas of transparency on particular colors, or on the luminance of particular colors. In this section you will use keying effects to key out the blue screen background.

Just like all effects in After Effects, all color keys are applied over time and can be animated. In this example you will create a key that is constant for the entire duration of the footage. If you encountered a situation where the lighting changed or the actor's movement caused shadows that affected the key, you could change your key values just as you animate any other property in After Effects.

Because you'll be working in Cineon log scale color, the color key is set up in a less direct way than if you were keying a linear scale image. The key will be applied to a linear version of the footage, which is then turned off as the resulting matte is assigned as a track matte to a log version of the footage.

Changing the Background Color to check the key

Before you apply a color key, you'll change the background color. A bright background makes it easier to analyze the effectiveness of your key.

1 Choose Composition > Background Color and click the swatch to display the color picker.

2 Choose a bright yellow color and click OK. Click OK again to close the Background Color dialog box.

Keying methods

The standard version of After Effects provides two keying effects: the Color Key effect, for keying out a color value, and the Luma Key effect, for keying out a luminance, or lightness value. The After Effects Production Bundle provides advanced keying effects with more powerful keying capabilities. The keys in the Production Bundle differ from the standard keys in that you can make some pixels partially transparent so that you can achieve more realistic-looking edges.

For this lesson, two methods are described. If you are using the After Effects Production Bundle, skip to "Using the Color Difference key—Production Bundle version users" on page 313. If you are using the standard version of After Effects, perform the following procedure to use the Color Key effect. Do not use both keying effects on the footage.

Both methods require you to apply the keying effects to a linear version of the footage first, since keyers are designed to work properly on linear images.

Using the Color Key effect—standard version users

1 With the ActHiR.mov layer selected in the Time Layout window, choose Effect > Cineon Tools > Cineon Converter, and set the Highlight Rolloff slider to 0.

2 Choose Effect > Keying > Color Key.

3 To match the existing blue screen color, click the Key Color eyedropper in the Effect Controls window, and click anywhere in the blue screen background to sample the color.

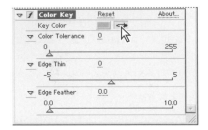

4 To increase the range of color that is keyed out, drag the Color Tolerance slider to the right. Experiment with the slider to see what happens.

As you drag the slider to the right, more and more of the actor becomes transparent. Your goal is to find the point where most of the background is keyed out but the actor remains opaque. Your final setting should be approximately 60.

5 To fine-tune the mask at the edges of the actor, adjust the Edge Thin values with the Edge Thin slider. This adjusts the width of the keyed area's border. To increase the transparent area and key out some of the blue at the edges of the actor image, set a positive value. Negative values spread the matte. Set the Edge Thin value to 1.

To get a more accurate look at the key effect, and especially at the edge pixels, you need to display the high-resolution image instead of the proxy.

6 Click the proxy indicator icon for the ActHiR.mov footage item in the Project window to replace the proxy with the high-resolution image.

7 In the Composition window, set the Resolution to Full.

If you don't have enough memory to display the high-resolution image, an out-of-memory warning will appear. If this occurs, try setting the Resolution to Half.

Press the Caps Lock key to stop screen refresh while you set the Resolution.

8 To soften the edge of the mask, set the Edge Feather value to 0.5. Higher values create softer edges, but take longer to render.

9 After refining the edge, close the Effect Controls window, click the proxy indicator icon in the Project window to turn the proxy back on, and set Resolution back to Quarter in the Composition window.

10 To restore the layer back to log, choose Effect > Cineon Tools > Cineon Converter. If a Cineon error message appears, simply click OK.

11 In the Effect Controls window, make sure you are looking at the second application of Cineon Converter, and change the Conversion Type menu to 8 bit Linear to Log and leave the sliders at their default values.

Skip the next section and go to "Setting a track matte to a log scale layer" on page 318.

Using the Color Difference key—Production Bundle version users

If you are using the Production Bundle version of After Effects, follow these instructions to use the Color Difference Key, Matte Choker, and Spill Suppressor effects.

1 With the ActHiR.mov layer selected in the Time Layout window, choose Effect > Cineon Tools > Cineon Converter, and set the Highlight Rolloff slider to 0.

Now you'll change a setting in the Cineon Converter's log to linear transform that will make the key easier.

2 Change the 10 bit White Point setting from 685 to 500.

This brightens the image considerably, washing out the actor. Since you'll be using this layer as a track matte, you can do what you want with the RGB portion of the image.

3 Choose Effect > Keying > Color Difference Key. The Effect Controls window appears.

The Color Difference Key works best with footage shot in front of a blue or green screen. Generally speaking, because of the way the color is recorded, blue works better for film and green for video. In this project the actor was filmed in front of a blue screen, so it should be fairly straightforward to key out the background. The Color Difference Key gives you the capability to key images that have semitransparent areas. Other keys included in the Production Bundle offer additional control for creating high-quality, animated mattes in film, broadcast, or interactive projects.

4 Resize the Effect Controls window so that you can see the previews.

5 Make sure that the alpha button is selected beneath the preview thumbnail.

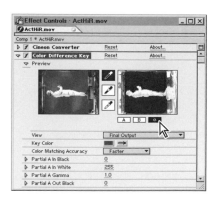

The ActHiR.mov layer is transformed into two grayscale components. The Color Difference Key generates a matte using a variation of the optical method used in traditional blue screening.

6 Leave the Key Color set to blue.

For the Color Difference key, the key color is used as a general guideline rather than a strict matching rule, so you don't need to change the color. The default will work for most shades of blue.

7 Click the A button in the Effect Controls window.

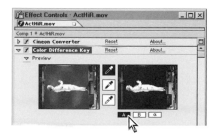

View A is a grayscale matte of color values that differ from the key color. All white pixels represent color values that are opaque; the black pixels are transparent; and the gray pixels are partially transparent. In View A, all colors very different from the key color are white; all colors equal to the key color are black; and colors that contain some amount of the key color are gray.

8 Click the B button in the Effect Controls window.

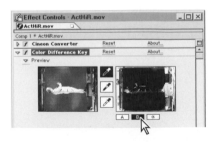

View B is a grayscale matte of the key color. Again, all white pixels represent color values that are opaque; the black pixels are transparent; and the gray pixels are partially transparent. In View B, all colors equal to the key color are white; colors very different from the key color are black; and colors that contain some amount of the key color are gray.

Combined, these two views offer separate control over the key color and colors very different from the key color. This has the effect of foreground and background control. You can edit the matte of the background (the key color) separate from the matte of the foreground (colors very different from the key color).

9 In this case, the best result is achieved by setting the input levels of both Partial A and Partial B to reduce grayscale before trimming the final matte stage. Experiment with various settings. We used the following settings.

Control	Value
Partial A In Black	35
Partial B In Black	35
Partial A In White	160
Partial B In White	160
Matte In White	200
Matte Gamma	1.5

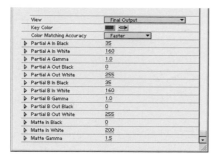

10 There is still some dark fringe on the key, which often happens, so choose Effect > Matte Tools > Matte Choker.

Matte Choker works on the principal that an edge can be redefined anywhere within the diameter of a blur by adjusting levels. Matte Choker has two stages, 1 and 2. Stage 1 Geometric Softness blurs the matte slightly, positive Choke values shrink the matte in, and Gray Level Softness sets the softness of the choke. Stage 2 gives you the ability to then respread the matte slightly, smoothing rough or irregular edges without cutting into the foreground too much. The Iterations slider sets how many times the two stages are to be performed.

11 The recommended settings for Matte Choker are shown in the table below.

Control	Value
Geometric Softness 1	1
Choke 1	75
Gray Level Softness 1	10%
Geometric Softness 2	2
Choke 2	0
Gray Level Softness 2	100%
Iterations	3

In this case, the Geometric Softness 1 is set to 1 rather than the default of 4 and the Iterations are set to 3 so that the choke is done a little at a time rather than all at once, to better preserve delicate edge detail. Geometric Softness 2 is being used here simply to soften the matte edge. Feel free to experiment; fewer iterations will result in faster rendering.

12 Close the Effect Controls window and save the project.

Setting a track matte to a log scale layer

Because you used the Cineon Converter to brighten the RGB beyond recoverable limits in order to get a better blue screen key, you will now have to use the keyed layer as a track matte source for a log scale layer.

1 In the Time Layout window, select the ActHiR.mov layer and rename it ActHiRKey.mov.

2 Drag the ActHiR.mov footage item from the Project window into the 3_Actor_Prep Time Layout window, and drag it below the key layer.

3 Click the Switches/Modes button at the bottom of the Time Layout window to display the transfer mode and track matte menus.

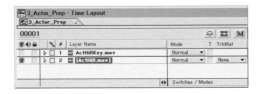

4 Choose Alpha Matte "ActHiRKey.mov" from the new layer's TrkMat menu. The key layer's visibility will automatically turn off and a dotted line appear between the two layers to indicate that the lower layer is using the upper layer as a track matte.

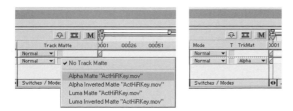

Notice that ActHiR.mov appears behind the track matte, but isn't aligned with it. You'll now rotate it and reverse it, just as you did when you created the track matte.

5 With the ActHiR.mov layer selected, press the S key and then press Shift+R to display the Scale and Rotation properties. Click the underlined Rotation value, enter **90** for Degrees, and click OK.

6 To flip the image, click the underlined Scale value, deselect Preserve Frame Aspect Ratio, and then enter **–100** for Height, and click OK.

7 Position the image by clicking the underlined Position value, and then enter a position of **332** for X-axis and **792** for Y-axis.

8 Select ActHiR.mov and choose Effect > Keying > Spill Suppressor, and leave the settings at their default values.

The Spill Suppressor effect removes any leftover blue color that might have been reflected onto the foreground. Since you are seeing only the image from the layer which received the track matte, that is the layer that needs Spill Suppression, rather than the key layer itself.

To see the finished image in natural linear color, you'll create a preview layer by applying the Cineon Converter effect to an adjustment layer.

9 Choose Layer > New Adjustment Layer, and then in the Time Layout window, rename it **Linear Preview**. Leave this layer at the top of the stack in the Time Layout window.

10 With the Linear Preview layer still selected, choose Effect > Cineon Tools > Cineon Converter. If you get an error message at this point, simply click OK. In the Effect Controls window, set Conversion Type to 8 Bit Log to Linear. Leave the remaining settings at the defaults, which are generally a good predictor of what the image will look like on film. Close the Effect Controls window.

Notice how the adjustment layer corrects the color of the other layers. This layer is for previewing only, and should be turned off before leaving the composition and before rendering.

11 In the Time Layout window, deselect the Video switch for the Linear Preview layer to turn it off.

12 Close the 3_Actor_Prep Composition and Time Layout windows, and save the project.

Creating the Handlight Composition

Now you will set up a composition that will serve as the hand light effect in the final scene. This composition makes a little radiating light that you will track to the actor's hand, giving the impression that the light is emanating from his palm. After creating a solid, you will apply a randomizing noise effect.

1 Create a new composition, type **4_Handlight** as the name, and set the frame size to **512 x 512**, the Resolution to Full, the Frame Rate to **24** fps, and the Duration to **32** frames. Click OK.

You'll start with a small solid, and then apply noise to it by using the Noise effect. Next you'll enlarge the dimensions of the solid to fill the frame and stretch the noise pixels to create shifting color bars.

2 Choose Layer > New Solid, name it **Handlight**, set the size to **64 x 1** pixels, and leave the default color as gray, and then click OK.

3 Use the magnifying glass tool to zoom in to 400% on the small solid.

4 Choose Effect > Stylize > Noise, and change the Amount of Noise Rate to **100**%. Deselect both Use Color Noise and Clip Result Values.

The Noise effect randomly changes pixel values throughout an image. (Like some other effects, the Noise effect does not require keyframes for animation.) Turning off the Color Noise option applies the same value to all the channels. The Clipping option determines whether noise colors will change once they reach their highest values. Since you want random noise based on luminescent values, both options are deselected.

5 Close the Effect Controls window.

6 Zoom back to 100%.

7 Press the S key to display the Scale property, and then click the underlined Scale value. In the Scale dialog box, choose % of Composition for Units.

8 Deselect Preserve Frame Aspect Ratio, enter **100** for both Width and Height, and click OK.

This technique creates a series of bars in random colors of gray.

9 Press the Home key to move to the beginning of the composition, and then press the spacebar to see how the noise creates a shifting grayscale composition.

If you hadn't created the small solid and stretched it with the Scale command, the noise would appear as pixels instead of gray bars.

Now you'll darken the layer by using a gray gradient.

10 Choose Layer > New Solid, name it **Gradient**, set the size to **512 x 512**, leave the rest of the defaults, and click OK.

11 Choose Effect > Render > Ramp. This creates a gray blend with white on the bottom and black on the top. Leave the default settings as they are, and close the Effect Controls window.

12 In the Time Layout window, click the Switches/Modes button to display the Transfer Modes panel, and choose Multiply from the Mode menu for the Gradient layer. The Multiply mode combines the two layers, and makes the top part of the hand light image darker and the bottom part lighter.

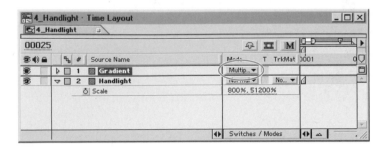

When you add this composition as a layer to the final composition, you will change its color and shape and apply the Glow effect.

13 Close the Composition window and Time Layout window, and save the project.

Positioning the elements for the final composition

Now that you have constructed all the elements that you need, you are ready to import the rest of the files and assemble the pieces into the final composition. You'll import the sky and feed-store images and the sky light effect.

Preparing a still image file for import into After Effects

Before you import a still footage item into After Effects, prepare the file as completely as possible. It is generally easier and faster to prepare a file in its original application; this also reduces rendering time in After Effects. You can use an image-editing application, such as Adobe Photoshop, to prepare the footage, and then use After Effects to manipulate only the image attributes you want to change over time. Before you import still image files into After Effects, consider doing the following:

• Set the pixel dimensions of the still image to the resolution at which you will use it in After Effects. If you plan to output to DV or D1, you can set the pixel dimensions to a smaller size. If you plan to scale the image over time, set image dimensions that provide enough detail at the image's largest size in the project. The maximum resolution you can use in After Effects is 4000-by-4000 pixels.

• Set the resolution to even numbers if working in a composition that uses even-numbered resolution (for example, 2048 by 1536). Likewise, set the resolution to odd numbers if working in a composition that uses odd-numbered resolution. This process prevents additional softening of images.

• Crop the parts of the image that you do not want to be visible in After Effects.

• Correct the contrast and color balance to ensure they are set correctly for broadcast video, if necessary.

• Create an alpha channel if you want to designate areas as transparent.

• If final output will be broadcast video, avoid the use of thin lines, for example, 1-pixel lines, for images or text because they may appear to flicker. If you must use thin lines, add a slight blur so the line or text displays on both fields instead of flickering between them.

• Save the file using the correct naming convention. For example, if you plan to import the file to After Effects on a Windows system, save the file using a three-character extension. If you plan to import the file to Mac OS, save the file with a name containing a maximum of 31 characters.

• Make sure the file format is supported in the operating system you plan to use.

—From the Adobe After Effects User Guide, Chapter 3

1 Choose File > Import > Footage Files, and then select Fds.psd in the 07Lesson folder, and click Open. In the Interpret Footage dialog box, select the Treat as Straight option, and click OK.

2 Select Sky.psd, and click Open.

3 Select the FX_HiR.mov file, click Open, and then click Done.

Both the Fds.psd image and the Sky.psd image are 2918 x 1946 in size, and both were scanned into Adobe Photoshop and saved as 72 dpi Photoshop files.

The FX_HiR.mov file is a 36-frame QuickTime movie of a lens flare.

You'll set proxies to speed up screen redraw.

4 Select Fds.psd in the Project window, choose File > Set Proxy > File, select FdsPrx.psd in the 07Lesson folder and click OK. Select the Treat as Straight option for the alpha channel, and then click OK.

5 Select Sky.psd in the Project window, and then choose File > Set Proxy > File, and select SkyPrx.psd in the 07Lesson folder.

Both the FdsPrx.psd and SkyPrx.psd files are smaller versions of the original Photoshop images. When used as proxies, they are scaled up to the same size as the original.

6 Select FX_HiR.mov, choose File > Set Proxy > File, and select FX_Prx.mov in the 07Lesson folder.

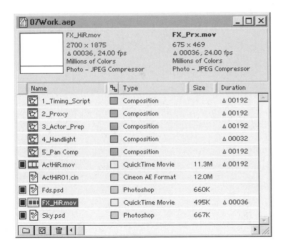

Positioning the layers

After positioning the feed-store and sky layers and rotating them slightly, you'll set Position keyframes for the Sky.psd layer so that the sky moves slightly from left to right. First, you'll create a new composition.

1 Create a new composition, name it **5_Pan_Comp**, set the Frame Size to **2700** x **1875**, and set the Resolution to Quarter.

2 Make sure the Frame Rate is set to **24** fps, and set the Duration to **192** frames.

3 If you need to conserve memory, select Custom in the Resolution menu, set both values to **8**, and then click OK. Click OK again to create the composition.

Now you'll add the files you just imported.

4 Drag both Sky.psd and Fds.psd from the Project window into the 5_Pan_Comp Time Layout window, making sure that Fds.psd is at the top of the stack.

Both Fds.psd and Sky.psd need to be rotated slightly.

5 With both the Fds.psd and Sky.psd layers selected in the Time Layout window, press the R key to see the Rotation property, and then press the – (minus) key on your numeric keypad to rotate the layers one degree counterclockwise. (You can use the + key to rotate clockwise in 1-degree increments.)

6 Deselect Sky.psd, press the P key, and set the Position value for the Fds.psd layer to **1268** for X-axis and **936** for Y-axis.

7 To move the sky, set the current time to 0001, select the Sky.psd layer, and click the stopwatch icon next to Position to set an initial Position keyframe. Then click the underlined value and enter **1284** for X-axis and **936** for Y-axis.

8 Go to the end of the composition, and change the Position value to **1212** for X-axis and **936** for Y-axis.

The Fds.psd layer needs some color correction. You'll use the Levels effect to do this.

9 Select Fds.psd and choose Effect > Adjust > Levels. In the Effect Controls window, choose the channel and enter the values from the following table.

RGB Input Black	26
RGB Gamma	0.8
Red Input White	250
Green Input Black	4
Blue Input White	251

Now you'll use the Noise effect to make the Fds.psd layer, which is a still image, look more like film. This effect adds random noise that can be used to simulate film grain. After applying the Cineon Converter effect to Fds.psd, you'll copy these two effects and paste them into Sky.psd.

10 With Fds.psd selected, choose Effect > Stylize > Noise. In the Effect Controls window, set the Amount of Noise to **2** percent.

Your final adjustment will be to apply the Cineon Converter to convert the linear Fds.psd image to log scale.

11 With Fds.psd selected, choose Effect > Cineon Tools > Cineon Converter. If you get an error message at this point, simply click OK. In the Effect Controls window, choose 8 Bit Linear to Log from the Conversion Type menu.

12 Select the Noise and Cineon Converter effects in the Effect Controls window and choose Edit > Copy.

13 Select the Sky.psd layer, and choose Edit > Paste.

14 You'll want to be able to see the composition in linear scale, so press the Home key to move the current-time marker to the beginning of the composition, choose Layer > New Adjustment Layer, and then rename the layer **Linear Preview**.

15 Choose Effect > Cineon Tools > Cineon Converter. Leave the settings at the defaults and close the Effect Controls window.

This layer should stay at the top of the stack in the Time Layout window. It should be turned off before leaving the composition, and before rendering.

16 Save the project.

Adding the FX_HiR.mov footage item

Now you'll add the FX_HiR.mov image to the composition twice to give the sky a glow.

1 Set the current time to 0004, and then drag the FX_HiR.mov footage item from the Project window into the Time Layout window. Display the Transfer Modes panel, and set the mode for the FX_HiR.mov layer to Screen.

The Screen mode keys out the black areas of the FX_HiR.mov image and leaves a glowing light over the sky. Unlike the other linear scale layers, you won't convert the Flare layers to log scale. Placed in a log scale composition, the highlight will render as brighter than the white point in a standard print.

2 With the FX_HiR.mov layer selected, choose Edit > Duplicate. The duplicate layer is displayed at the top of the layer stack in the Time Layout window. An asterisk appears at the end of the layer name to indicate that it is a duplicate. Drag the layer duration bar of the duplicate layer until the In point is positioned at frame 152.

3 To reverse the second layer's playback direction, select the layer that begins at frame 152 and press Ctrl+Alt+R (Windows) or Command+Option+R (Mac OS). The layer duration bar now has diagonal red stripes, indicating that it has been reversed.

The layer is automatically time stretched -100% and will play backwards from frame 152.

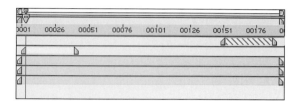

4 Save the project.

Adding the actor and creating his shadow

After adding the 3_Actor Prep composition to the 5_Pan Comp, you'll create the actor's shadow.

1 Set the current time to 0001. Drag the 3_Actor_Prep composition from the Project window into the 5_Pan Comp Time Layout window.

2 Press the P key to display the Position property in the Time Layout window, and enter **1728** for X-axis and **1164** for Y-axis.

Before creating the actor's shadow, you'll need to mask out the box on which the actor is standing. Because the object you want to mask out is small, you can save time by drawing the mask around the box and then reversing the mask.

3 Double-click the 3_Actor_Prep layer to open the Layer window. Select the pen tool from the toolbox and use it to mask out the box which the actor is standing on. When finished, close the Layer window.

4 With the new mask (Mask 1) selected in the Time Layout window, choose Layer > Mask > Inverse.

Next you'll use a solid to make the actor's shadow.

5 Choose Layer > New Solid, name it **Actor Shadow**, set the size to **1024** x **128**, and leave the color at default gray. Click OK.

6 In the Transfer Modes panel, change the mode for the Solid layer to Multiply.

7 Position the solid to the right of the actor in the Composition window (2204, 1812), and beneath the 3_Actor_Prep layer in the Time Layout window.

8 Double-click the solid layer to display the Layer window, and then create a mask to reshape the rectangular solid as shown below.

9 Press the F key to display the Mask Feather property in the Time Layout window, and then set Mask Feather to **10** pixels for both Horizontal and Vertical.

10 Close the Layer window.

Adding the 4_Handlight layer

Now you'll add the 4_Handlight layer to the composition and apply a variety of visual effects to turn the dull gray bars into glowing light.

1 In the Time Layout window, deselect the Video switches to turn off the video for all layers except the 3_Actor_Prep composition.

2 Go to frame 115 and drag the 4_Handlight composition from the Project window into the Composition window. Position the hand light on top of the man, obscuring his hands and face for the moment. (You will change the position later.)

3 Use the zoom tool to zoom in on the hand light area.

4 In the Time Layout window, display the Transfer Modes panel. Set the mode for the 4_Handlight composition layer to Screen.

Now you'll apply the Hue/Saturation, Corner Pin, Glow, and Fast Blur effects.

The Glow and Corner Pin effects are available only in the Production Bundle version of After Effects. However, both plug-ins have been included for you on the After Effects Classroom in a Book CD-ROM. To use the Corner Pin or Glow effects, make sure that you have installed both plug-ins according to the instructions in "Installing Production Bundle plug-ins" on page 4.

5 Display the Scale property and click the underlined Scale value. In the Scale dialog box, choose % of Source for Units, set the Scale value of the 4_Handlight layer to **75** for both Width and Height.

6 Choose Effect > Adjust > Hue/Saturation, and then select Colorize in the Effect Controls window. Now skew the gray ramp to blue: set Colorize Hue to **240**, set Colorize Saturation to **50**, and set Colorize Lightness to **−20**.

Next you'll apply the Glow effect.

7 Choose Effect > Stylize > Glow, and make sure that the glow is based on the Color Channels.

8 Enter **33** for the Glow Threshold and **25** for the Glow Radius. Leave the other settings at their defaults.

9 Choose Effect > Blur & Sharpen > Fast Blur, and set the Blurriness value to **10**.

Now you'll use the Corner Pin effect to turn the rectangular shape into a triangular shape that fits in the actor's hand.

10 Collapse the three effect outlines by clicking the triangles in the Effect Controls window. Save the project.

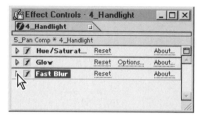

Using the Corner Pin effect

The Corner Pin effect distorts a layer by repositioning its four corners to simulate a perspective view. This is especially useful for aligning layers with elements in other layers. For example, you can use the Corner Pin effect to replace the video on a television screen. In this example, you will use it to create the directional glow effect.

1 Make sure the 4_Handlight layer is selected in the Time Layout window, and choose Effect > Distort > Corner Pin.

2 In the Effect Controls window, notice the four corner controls. Click the Lower Left crosshair. A crosshair appears in the lower left corner of the 4_Handlight layer in the Composition window.

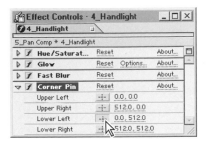 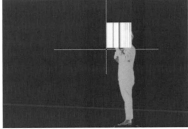

3 Click in the center of the layer in the Composition window with the crosshair.

4 Click the Lower Right crosshair in the Effect Controls window, and click again in the middle of the 4_Hand Light layer in the Composition window, but not in the exact same position as before. You will not get the desired effect if both positions are identical.

The effect becomes triangular in shape. If the shape is still rectangular, change one of the coordinates slightly in the Effect Controls window.

5 In the Time Layout window, drag the 4_Handlight layer below the 3_Actor Prep layer. In the Composition window, position the hand light behind the actor's left hand.

6 If you set a custom resolution to conserve memory when you created 5_Pan Comp, set the Resolution of the composition to Quarter. Close the Effect Controls window and save the project.

Using the Motion Tracker Keyframe assistant

You will use the Motion Tracker Keyframe Assistant to track the motion of the actor's hand so that you can match the motion of the glow to the moving hand.

The Motion Tracker and several other keyframe assistants are available only with the Production Bundle version of After Effects. The Motion Tracker keyframe assistant is not included with the After Effects Classroom in a Book. If you do not have the After Effects Production Bundle, skip to "Importing keyframes" on page 337.

Keyframe assistants are a set of plug-ins that generate and manipulate keyframes automatically. Other keyframe assistants include the Motion Stabilizer, which eliminates movement caused by a handheld camera; Motion Sketch, which captures a motion path you draw freehand with the mouse; and several others.

Setting up Motion Tracker options

In order to use the Motion Tracker, the composition must have at least two layers—one layer to track and one to attach to. At least one of the layers must be a movie or composition. In this example, you will track the position and rotation of the actor's hand and arm, and then attach the hand light to the actor's hand.

Note: *To ensure sufficient accuracy, you should turn proxies off when using the Motion Tracker in a production environment. To conserve memory during this lesson, leave the proxy on.*

1 Select the 3_Actor_Prep layer in the Time Layout window, and then choose Layer > Keyframe Assistant > Motion Tracker. The Motion Tracker window appears.

The Motion Tracker window contains an image of the selected layer, a time ruler, controls found in the Layer window, and the Motion Tracker controls.

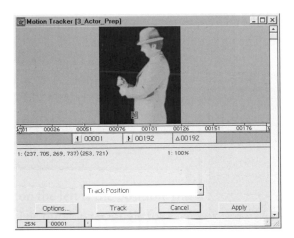

Note: *Although you cannot manually select different tools while the Motion Tracker is active, you can select them using the keyboard shortcut commands.*

4 Use the handles to resize the Search region (outer rectangle) to define the area that the Motion Tracker will use.

The Search region should be quite wide in this case, since at one point the actor moves his hand rather quickly. Make the Search region large enough to contain the greatest possible movement of the Feature region from one frame to the next, but no larger. Large Search regions slow down the tracking process.

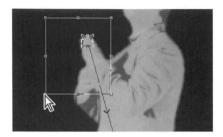

5 Use the handles to resize the Feature region (inner rectangle) to define the area around the top of the actor's left hand.

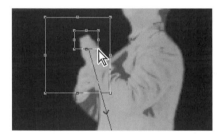

6 Drag the Rotation Feature and Search regions to the man's elbow. The Search region can be fairly close to the Feature region, which should cover about 50% of the elbow area.

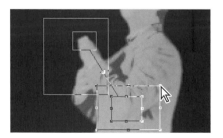

7 Make sure that you can see the actor's hands so that you can watch the tracking process, and then click the Track button.

A narrow black bar appears under the timeline to mark time regions that have been tracked. You can interrupt the tracking process at any time by clicking the mouse or pressing any key.

It can take up to 10 minutes for the Motion Tracker to track the motion for the 4 seconds that you have specified.

You may need to experiment with the positioning of the Search region and Feature region boxes before you are satisfied. Accurate tracking requires patience and a lot of trial and error. If you find that you don't have the time, you can skip to "Importing keyframes" and copy keyframes that have already been created.

8 After you have finished tracking, click the Apply button to generate keyframes.

Examining the keyframes

The Motion Tracker applies Position and Rotation keyframes to the 4_Handlight layer for every frame within the tracking region.

1 Display both the Position and Rotation properties of the HandLight layer: select the 4_Handlight layer, and then press the P key, and Shift+R. Examine the Position and Rotation keyframes that have been automatically created.

2 Set the work area to just the area where the keyframes are, and press 0 on your numeric keypad to preview the motion of the layer.

For more information on the Motion Tracker keyframe assistant, see the *Adobe After Effects 4.0 Production Bundle Guide*.

Importing keyframes

If you do not have the Production Bundle version of After Effects, you do not have access to the Motion Tracker. Instead, you can import a project that contains the 4_HandLight layer with the keyframes created for you. If you completed the previous section, skip these instructions and go to the next section, "Positioning the CD-ROM image."

1 Choose File > Import > Project, and then select HndKey.aep in the 07Lesson folder, and click Open.

2 Double-click the HndKey.aep folder in the Project window, and double-click the Handlight_Keyframes composition.

3 With the 4_Handlight layer selected and the Position and Rotation properties displayed, Shift-click both properties to select all the keyframes, and choose Edit > Copy.

4 Activate the 5_Pan_Comp window, make sure that the 4_Handlight layer is selected and the current-time marker is set to 0115, and then choose Edit > Paste.

5 If 4_Handlight has shifted so that the layer position no longer matches the actor's hand position, then Shift-click both the Position and Rotation properties to select all keyframes, and use the Arrow keys to nudge all the keyframes equally until the 4_Handlight layer is in correct position.

6 Close the Handlight_Keyframes Comp and Time Layout windows and save the project.

Positioning the CD-ROM image

The only layer left to add is an image of a CD-ROM, which was created in After Effects. To make the CD fly, you'll create a motion path and define Scale and Rotation keyframes.

Here's the flight plan you'll set up for the flying CD: it starts scaled down to nothing, flies out of the center of the light flare in FX_HiR.mov, increases in size and flies past the man, circles back, dives into his hand, and then jumps out and back into the light flare. Feel free to experiment with your own motion path.

First, import the CD footage item.

1 Choose File > Import > Footage File, select the CD.mov in the 07Lesson folder, and click Open.

You'll use the 1_Timing_Script composition to guide you in placing Position keyframes.

2 Set the current time to 0001, drag the 1_Timing_Script composition from the Project window into 5_Pan Comp Time Layout window. Hide the video for the 1_Timing_Script layer.

3 Double-click the 1_Timing_Script composition in the Project window to open its Time Layout window, and then click the 5_Pan Comp tab in the Time Layout window.

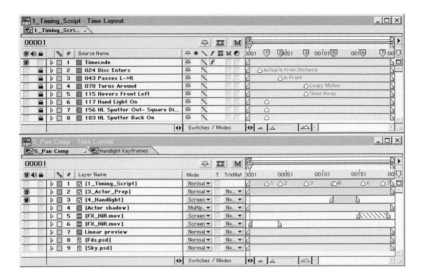

4 In the 5_Pan Comp Time Layout window, turn off the video for all the layers except 3_Actor_Prep and FX_HiR.mov that starts near the beginning of the composition.

5 In the 5_Pan Comp Composition window, set the Magnification to 25%, set the current time to 0008, and drag in CD.mov from the Project window.

Since you selected the Synchronize Time of All Related Items preference in the beginning of the lesson, the current-time marker will reflect the same time in both tabbed compositions in the Time Layout window.

6 Position the CD.mov layer in the center of the star shape (FX_HiR.mov), and then set a Position keyframe for it.

7 Click the 1_Timing_Script tab in the Time Layout window. According to 1_Timing_Script, the next important point is frame 0078, where the actor is looking to the right side of the frame, so click the 5_Pan Comp tab, set the current time to 0078, and set the position coordinates to 2437, 419.

8 Move the current-time marker to 0123, and set the position coordinates for the CD layer to 1421, 315.

9 Move the current-time marker to 0135, and position the CD.mov layer in the actor's hand.

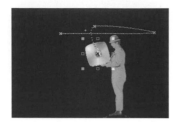

10 Move the current-time marker to frame 0151, and click the keyframe navigator check box to set a duplicate keyframe.

11 Move the current-time marker to frame 0183, and drag the CD.mov layer back to the center of the star shape, where it started.

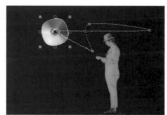

12 In the Time Layout window, make sure the CD.mov layer is selected, click the word *Position* to select all the keyframes, choose Layer > Keyframe Interpolation, select Bezier from the Temporal Interpolation menu, and then click OK.

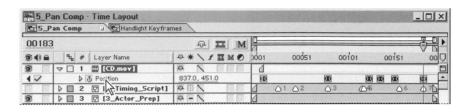

13 To pause the motion at frame 135, first deselect the keyframes you selected in the previous step, and then select the Position keyframe at frame 135 in the Time Layout window. Choose Layer > Toggle Hold Keyframe. This holds the position value until the next keyframe.

Note: Although the keyframes at frames 135 and 151 are identical, using Continuous or Bezier keyframe interpolation can cause slight motion. The Toggle Hold Keyframe command eliminates this motion entirely.

14 Now you'll create a smooth motion path at several keyframes. Select the keyframe at frame 0078 and drag the direction handles to create a smooth curve. Select the keyframe at 0135 and do the same.

15 Drag the work area markers so that the work area includes all the motion you just created, and then press Alt+0 (Windows) or Option+0 (Mac OS) on your numeric keypad to create a wireframe preview of the motion.

Setting the Scale and Rotation keyframes

Next you'll set the Scale and Rotation keyframes for the CD.mov layer.

1 In the Time Layout window, select the CD.mov layer, set the current time to 0008, change the Scale value to **1%**, and set a Scale keyframe.

2 Use the following table to set values for the Scale keyframes.

Frame	Scale
57	78%
78	60%
123	100%
135	10%
151	10%
162	80%
183	1%

3 Make sure the CD.mov layer is selected, click the word *Scale* to select all the Scale keyframes, choose Layer > Keyframe Interpolation, and then select Bezier from the Temporal Interpolation menu. Click OK.

Now you will set the Rotation keyframes so that the CD rotates 12 times during the course of its travel.

4 Move to frame 0001, and set a Rotation keyframe with a value of **0°**.

5 Move to frame 0192, and change the Rotation value to **12** revolutions, **0°**.

6 Press 0 on your numeric keypad to preview the motion.

Using the Basic 3D effect

Now add and animate the Basic 3D effect so that the CD will tumble in as it flies around.

1 Set the current time to frame 0008. With CD.mov selected, choose Effect > Perspective > Basic 3D.

2 Press the E key to display the Basic 3D effect in the Time Layout window, click the triangle to display the Basic 3D properties, and then set a Swivel keyframe and a Tilt keyframe.

The Basic 3D effect manipulates a layer in an imaginary three-dimensional space. Swivel controls horizontal rotation, and Tilt controls vertical rotation.

3 Change the Swivel value to **37°** and the Tilt value to **20°**.

4 Move the current-time marker to frame **188**, set Swivel to **60°**, and set Tilt to **1 Revolution** and **260°**.

5 To see the results of this effect, go to frame 0123 and toggle the Basic 3D effect off and on by clicking its check box in the Effect Controls window. When finished, leave the Basic 3D effect on.

Finishing the composition

To finish the composition, turn on some of the hidden video.

1 In the 5_Pan Comp Time Layout window, turn on all video except for the 1_Timing Script layer and the Linear Preview layer.

2 Click the 1_Timing_Script tab in the Time Layout window, and then click the close box on the right side of the tab to close the window.

3 Close the 5_Pan_Comp, Time Layout, and Effect Controls windows and save the project.

Creating the final composition

To finish the project, you'll create a new composition, set up a slate to identify the beginning and end of your composition to the film output service bureau, add the 5_Pan_Comp, and set Position keyframes to simulate a camera panning the image.

1 Create a new composition, name it **6_Final_Render**, and choose Film (2K) from the Frame Size menu to set the size to 2048 x 1536.

2 Set the Resolution to Quarter, the Frame Rate to **24** fps, and the Duration to **194** frames. Click OK.

This composition is two frames longer than the others to leave room for one-frame *head* and *tail* slates.

3 Choose Layer > New Adjustment Layer and name it **Linear Preview**. Choose Effect > Cineon Tools > Cineon Converter, leave the settings at the defaults, and close the Effect Controls window. If you get a Cineon error message at this point, simply click OK. This layer, like the other linear preview layers, is for preview only; it should be turned off before rendering, and should remain at the top of the layer stack.

Creating a slate

It's good practice to *slate* (include a labeling frame for) one's work, to avoid confusion with your client and output service bureau over the version and contents of a particular composition, as well as providing process control charts. The head slate typically contains the shot, version, and date information while the tail slate indicates the end of the composite to provide a positive indication that all the frames were recorded to film. Usually only one frame each is used because of the cost of film recording. An example of a standard slate has been provided.

You will import a standard slate frame and apply the Basic Text effect.

1 Choose File > Import > Footage File and select Adobe_slate.cin from the 07Lesson folder. In the Interpret Footage dialog, choose the Treat As Straight alpha interpretation and click OK.

2 Make sure you are at frame 0001, and then drag the Adobe_slate.cin footage item from the Project window into the 6_Final_Render Time Layout window.

3 Rename the Adobe_slate.cin layer **Head Slate**.

4 You'll use the Linear Preview layer later in this exercise, so drag it back to the top of the layer stack in the Time Layout window.

5 Choose Effect > Cineon Tools > Cineon Converter and then choose Auto Log to Log in the Conversion Type menu.

6 Select the Head Slate layer and choose Effect > Text > Basic Text. Enter on separate lines the client, production name, shot number, composite version number, length exclusive of the slate, and date. How the text is arranged on screen and the font used are up to you, but quick and easy readability will be appreciated by others. Click OK.

7 In the Effect Controls window, make the text color black and select Composite On Original.

Note: *Turn the Linear Preview layer on and off and observe the grayscale patches on the left side of the slate frame. Both the 1023 and 685 patches are white when the Linear Preview is on, and differentiated when it is off. Likewise, the 95 and 0 patches are black with Linear Preview, and differentiated without. That's because the standard linear transform specifies black at 95 on the 10-bpc 0–1023 scale (10 bits contain four times as many discrete values as 8 bits, which is 0–255).*

Even though the differences between these two groups of patches shouldn't be visible in a print from the film recording, the difference between the 1023 and 685 patches particularly should be visible in the film negative. Thus, a slate like this is a good indicator of whether your composition was properly recorded to film.

8 To make the tail slate, first duplicate the Adobe_slate.cin layer by choosing Edit > Duplicate. Then switch the Effect Controls window to the duplicate layer by pressing Shift+Ctrl+T (Windows) or Shift+Command+T (Mac OS). Click the underlined Options in Basic Text, delete the version and date information after your shot number, and type **END COMPOSITE** on a new line.

9 In the Time Layout window, rename the duplicate Adobe_slate.cin layer **Tail Slate**.

It's not necessary to have version information on the tail slate, but it is useful to signal to the film recording operator that this is the last frame of the composite.

10 Select the head slate layer (a bottom layer) and, with the current time set at 0001, trim the layer to a single frame duration by pressing Alt+right bracket (]) (Windows) or Option+right bracket (]) (Mac OS).

11 Select the Tail Slate layer, set the current time to 0194, and then trim the layer to a single frame duration by pressing Alt/Option+left bracket ([).

Adding 5_Pan_Comp

1 Go to frame 0002, drag the 5_Pan_Comp from the Project window into the 6_Final_Render Time Layout window, and then drag it below the Linear Preview layer.

2 Display the Transform properties, and set the Scale value to **90**%. Because you won't be animating the scale, you don't need to set a keyframe for this property.

To create movement simulating a roving camera, you'll set some position keyframes for the 5_Pan_Comp layer.

3 Set the current time to 0025 and set the Position values to **1200, 827**. Set an initial Position keyframe.

4 Move the current-time marker to 0079, and change the Position values to **844, 735**.

5 Finally, move the current-time marker to 0193, and change the Position values to **1196, 700**.

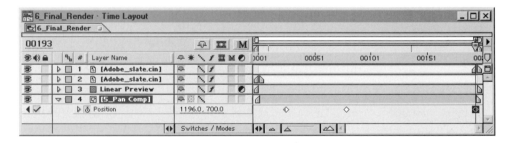

6 Select all three Position keyframes choose Layer > Keyframe Interpolation, and choose Bezier from the Temporal Interpolation menu. Click OK.

7 Save the project.

Rendering the project

Now you are ready to render the project. Since this project uses high-resolution images, you will use proxies when you render the project.

1 Choose Composition > Make Movie, name it **07Movie.mov**, and save the file in your Projects folder.

2 In the Render Queue, choose Custom for Render Settings.

3 For Quality, choose Best. For Resolution, choose Quarter for a size of 512 x 384.

Note: *You may prefer to render a draft movie.*

4 For Proxy Use, choose Use All Proxies. Make sure Time Span is set to Length of Comp. Click OK.

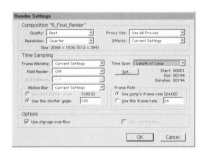

5 For Output Module, choose Custom, and for Format, choose QuickTime Movie.

6 In Windows, the QuickTime settings dialog box appears. Set Compressor to None, and then click OK. In Mac OS, leave the Video Output options at their defaults.

7 Select Import into Project When Done, and click OK.

8 Click Render.

9 When you are finished rendering the movie, open the footage file that appears in your Project window and play it.

If it doesn't play smoothly, then create a new composition at 512 x 384 pixels, Full Resolution, and 194 frames Duration. Drag the Final.mov footage item from the Project window into the Time Layout window and click the RAM Playback button. If you have enough RAM available, the movie will now play smoothly.

10 Save and close the project, and quit After Effects.

To render the entire project for film output, you would turn proxies off and render at full size as Cineon files, using the Full Range preset. (To render a file of this size would take more than 150 MB of RAM and 2.4 GB of hard drive space.) You would then take it to a motion picture film output service provider, where it would be recorded onto motion picture film. To transport such a large file sequence, you could use Exabyte 8mm, DAT 4mm or DLT format tapes, or a large removable hard drive.

For more information, see "Rendering for film" on page 363 and "Video transfer issues" on page 361.

Congratulations! This ends the lessons. You've accomplished quite a bit since you began setting keyframes and creating simple compositions. As you continue to work with After Effects, you might want to refer to specific lessons in this book to remind yourself of particular procedures, or to remember how to create a specific effect.

In the next several pages, you'll find a special "Technical Information" section on working with dynamic media and digital video. It includes information on pertinent issues including video-to-film conversion and production. You can read it at your leisure, or use it as a reference.

Technical Information

This appendix provides in-depth technical information on various film and video topics, which may be particularly helpful if you don't have a background in film or video.

This special appendix will familiarize you with several technical issues relating to dynamic media. You'll also find tips for using Adobe After Effects features related to these technical areas.

This section covers the following topics:

- Frame rate issues
- Video safe zones
- NTSC color space
- Video aspect ratios
- Interlace issues
- Video transfer issues
- Rendering for film
- Audio issues

Frame rate issue

A fundamental difference between Adobe After Effects and a program such as Adobe Photoshop is that in addition to composing an image, images in Adobe After Effects can change over time. To show this animation, time must be broken up into individual frames that are shown in order. The speed at which these frames are played back is known as the *frame rate*. The choice of a frame rate depends on the medium where the final output will be displayed.

In general, the higher the frame rate, the smoother are the changes and motion you create. However, you usually cannot pick an arbitrary rate. Video, film, and multimedia all tend to have different inherent frame rates. Video itself has different frame rates, depending on the format used. PAL (Phase Alternation Line) format video, as commonly used in Europe, has a frame rate of 25 fps (frames per second). NTSC (National Television Standards Committee) color video, the standard in the United States and Japan, has a frame rate of 29.97 fps. Many refer to this as 30 fps, since it is more convenient to say and to deal with than 29.97 (and because black-and-white NTSC used to run at 30 fps).

In some cases, you can get by with rounding 29.97 fps up to 30 for your work in Adobe After Effects. However, there are some specific instances when you will run into trouble if you do this. The most common problem results from using source footage that was shot and digitized into the computer at 29.97 fps, and the source clip is labeled as such, but you build your compositions and render your final output in Adobe After Effects at 30 fps. The result is that every one-thousandth frame will be repeated (making up for the 0.1% speed difference between 29.97 and 30), and there will be a stutter in the motion of this original footage. Mixing source footage with labeled frame rates of 29.97 (such as captured video) and 30 (as in a 3-D animation) will also result in a frame being lost or repeated when these two different rates are mixed together. If you choose to work at 30, you conform your source video footage to 30 fps in the Interpret Footage dialog box for the clip. Alternatively, you could choose to work at 29.97 and conform to that. Just avoid mixing and matching.

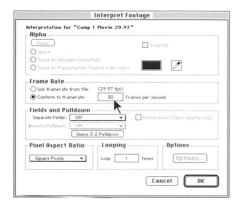

Note: When you change a source's frame rate in its Interpret Footage dialog box, you are not adding or subtracting frames to or from the source; you are merely telling Adobe After Effects that each frame in the source should be interpreted as having a duration of (1/[frame rate]of a second).

Although 30 fps is an easier timebase to conceptualize, there is a strong potential downside to using it for video work. Depending on your output device, if you render a movie labeled at 30 fps but play it through a system that is very strict about being at 29.97, you may skip every one-thousandth frame on playback. In this case, you will want to conform everything to 29.97 fps, and make sure you use 29.97 for the frame rate in your Composition and Render settings.

Film is much simpler. Although some special formats have their own frame rates, most film is shot and projected at a frame rate of 24 fps. Note that it is also possible to shoot normal film at other frame rates that might be more video-friendly, such as 25, 30, or 60 fps (the last yielding one separate film frame per field of NTSC video). On the other end of the extreme, multimedia clips can have virtually any frame rate, and the frame rate you choose will depend on your image size, playback platform, and any of a number of other issues that are beyond the scope of this discussion. As a general rule, 12 fps is a good minimum (this is the same frame rate at which most animations, such as cartoons, are created); 15 fps is common; 25 or 30 fps will yield video-like results.

Note: A video frame displayed on an interlaced monitor is usually divided further into two fields, each having a duration of half a frame. Therefore, the field rate is twice the frame rate, and as far as smoothness of motion is concerned, yields results similar to doubling the frame rate. See "Interlace issues" on page 356.

Video safe zones

On a computer monitor, you typically can see the entire image projected by your video card, with a black border around the outside. On a video monitor or television set, or through most film projection systems, however, you do not see the entire image. The outer edge is cropped, in a process akin to the printing practice of bleeding an image off the edge. This is called *overscanning*.

TVs and projection systems are often imperfect; you cannot guarantee that the image is centered and scaled properly. Due to the nature of these systems, the outer limits of the image area may also be blurry or distorted compared with the center of the screen. Therefore, these systems are built with overscan in mind so that the viewer is not distracted by borders or distortions around the edges.

The most significant point about overscanning is that the viewer will not see the entire image area that you see in your Composition window inside Adobe After Effects, so you must design with this in mind. The easiest way to ensure that the vital information in your program is not cut off is to keep it inside *safe zones*, predefined areas of the screen in which visual information is not obscured by overscanning.

Video has two sets of safe zones—action safe and title safe. The action safe zone is what you can usually count on your viewer being able to see. Do not set up any significant motion outside of this area; the viewer may miss it. On the other hand, it is not safe to leave unwanted images on-screen but just outside the action-safe zone; some TVs might actually show them. The title-safe zone is inset from this to get away from possible distortions at the edges of many television screens; it is a good idea to keep any text or important objects inside this additional safe zone. The action-safe zone is inset 5% from all edges of the image (resulting in a total loss of 10% of the height and width of the displayable image area); the title-safe zone is inset another 5% on all sides from the action-safe zone.

To help you, Adobe After Effects can overlay an outline that shows the safe areas of your destination. Both the action- and title-safe zones are overlaid on a blank Composition window in the following illustration.

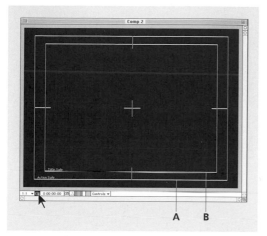

A. Action-safe zone B. Title-safe zone

To display the safe areas inside Adobe After Effects, click the safe-zones icon in the bottom left corner of the Composition window. Click again to turn the safe areas off. You can also enter custom safe area percentages inside the Display Preferences dialog box.

If you will be displaying captured video either on a computer monitor or inset into an image (picture-in-picture), you often will need to crop the image beyond the action-safe zone. This is either because it contains irrelevant image area that is not intended to be seen, or because there may be some distortions or unwanted lines (particularly along the bottom of the image) in the video capture.

NTSC color space

Adobe After Effects works in an RGB color space (named for its red, green, and blue component colors), where colors are defined by the intensities of their red, green, and blue components. Broadcast video formats, however, use different color spaces (YUV or YIQ), where colors are described in terms of luminance and chromatic components.

When designing for broadcast formats such as NTSC, it is important to consider the limitations of the final color space. The 24-bit RGB color space used by Adobe After Effects has a different range of possible colors than the spaces used by broadcast formats. NTSC does not reproduce very saturated colors well and has particular problems with subtle color gradients.

The simplest solution is to create your designs from the beginning with these limitations in mind. Many people place their main Composition window on a properly calibrated broadcast monitor. (In Windows, pressing Ctrl + Shift + \ expands the Composition window to fit the size of the application window. In Mac OS, pressing Command + Shift + \ expands the Composition window to fit the size of the monitor.)

Adobe After Effects does provide a Broadcast Colors plug-in that can reduce the range of colors used in a layer, but it's best used as a fix for material that is beyond your control. However, it is instructive to show the colors that can cause problems for broadcast encoding.

Video aspect ratios

The frame aspect ratio of an image is its horizontal size divided by its vertical size. The frame aspect ratio of television is normally stated as 4:3, or 1.33:1. Most video images, whether for broadcast or multimedia, are based on this 4:3 frame aspect ratio.

Most computer-based desktop video systems define a full-screen NTSC image as being 640 x 480 pixels, which exactly fits a 4:3 frame aspect ratio. (This is also the most common image area size for a 13-inch monitor.) A full-screen PAL image is usually defined as being 768 x 576 pixels. However, much professional NTSC digital video follows the CCIR-601 standard (which defines most professional-format digital video, such as D1) of 720 x 486 pixels. This is the most common size for NTSC D1 video frames. Its corresponding definition for PAL is 720 x 576 pixels. (A third common NTSC format is 648 x 486 pixels, because it retains all 486 horizontal scan lines of D1 video and maintains the normal square-pixel 4:3 aspect ratio that computer users often prefer.)

Note that 720 x 486 does not give the same 4:3 ratio as 640 x 480. This is because D1 pixels are not square—they are only about 90% as wide as they are tall. This causes some image distortion when moving between the two systems.

A D1 NTSC video frame displayed on a normal square-pixel computer screen will appear slightly wider than in reality; an image that looks correct on a computer screen will look slightly narrow when displayed through a D1 system. (PAL D1 pixels, in turn, are wider than they are tall, and will have the opposite appearance.) It is important not to ignore these pixel aspect ratios when working with D1 video.

Adobe After Effects offers a Pixel Aspect Ratio option in the Composition Settings dialog box to compensate for the rectangular pixels of a D1 image. To change the Pixel Aspect Ratio, choose Composition > Composition Settings, then choose D1 NTSC from the Pixel Aspect Ratio pop-up menu.

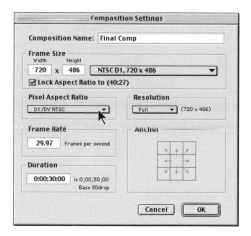

Some new PC digital video and the new digital video cameras support an image area of 720 x 480 pixels. This standard, called DV (for digital video), has the same pixel aspect ratio as D1.

Interlace issues

A computer monitor draws its pixels horizontally across the screen one line at a time, from top to bottom. This is called *progressive scanning*. Video works differently. It draws every other horizontal line on its way down and then goes back to the top and fills in the lines in between. Each half-image is called a field, and fields are drawn at 59.94 per second for NTSC video—double the speed of the well-known NTSC 29.97 frame rate. Combining the fields is called *interlacing*. The most important point to remember about interlacing is that one frame contains pixels from two different instances of time, and that you don't want to get the time order wrong.

For more information on interlacing, see the After Effects User Guide.

Handling interlace on input

Here are some tips on how to handle interlace issues for stills, video, film, and animation.

• *Stills*. Still images, unless they are frame grabs from video, are usually not interlaced. Therefore, they do not need to be treated specially in Adobe After Effects. If the stills did come from video frame grabs and you notice scattered lines around moving objects where every other line seems to be displaced horizontally from those around it, then you will need to remove one of the fields. This is usually done when initially preparing the frames in Adobe Photoshop, using the De-interlace filter. Which field you remove is not very important in this case; choose the one that seems to give the best-looking results.

• *Video*. Full-screen captured video is most likely interlaced (i.e., 60 fields). In most cases, you will want to set the Separate Fields option in the Interpret Footage settings to match your video clips. If you don't, whenever you scale, move, rotate, or otherwise treat a video clip, pixels that are supposed to appear on one field (set of lines) will also appear on another, resulting in a scrambling of the time order of the pixels in each frame of the clip.

The one case in which you do not have to separate video on input is when the clips will have the same field order on output as they had when originally captured; the clips are centered in the comp of the same size; and you do not move, scale, rotate, or distort them, or apply a filter that rearranges the position of pixels. Most experts recommend that you go ahead and use Separate Fields in this situation, just to be on the safe side.

To properly set the Interpret Footage dialog box for a video clip, you will need to know the field order of the clip. This means knowing whether the even- or odd-numbered horizontal lines inside a frame are meant to appear before the other in time. Hopefully, either the manual for your video capture card or the person who supplied you with the video clips will identify the correct field order. As a general rule, most JPEG capture cards tend to be upper field first; most digital disc recorders (such as those made by Abekas) tend to be lower field first.

If the field order of video clips is unknown, you can determine it by observation. Set the field order for your clip to Upper Field First from the Separate Fields pop-up menu in the Fields and Pulldown section of the Interpret Footage dialog box. Open the footage directly in the Project window by holding down the Alt key (Windows) or Option key (Mac OS) and double-clicking the footage item.

This will open a special Adobe After Effects Footage window. Locate a portion of the movie that contains motion, and step through it frame by frame using the Time Controls palette or the right arrow key on your keyboard. If it seems to stutter back and forth (for example, two steps forward, one step back, another two steps forward, and so on), then the field order is set incorrectly and must be changed. Otherwise, it is set correctly. If you do not notice any motion every other field, then the original clip did not have fields recorded—only entire frames.

• *Film.* Film transferred to video also often has fields and a field order to worry about. When 24-fps film is transferred to 29.97-fps video, the following occurs: The film is slowed down by 0.1% to match the odd video rate better, and then film frames are spread across video fields in a repeating 3:2 pattern. This means the first frame of film is copied to fields 1 and 2 of the first frame of video, and also to the first field of video frame 2. The second frame of film is then spread across the next two fields of video—field 2 of video frame 2 and field 1 of video frame 3. This 3:2 pattern is repeated until four frames of film are spread over five frames of video, and is then repeated. This technique is known as *3:2 pulldown* (see page 210). Again, you will need to set your field order correctly to use these clips.

Setting the field order correctly will allow you to properly scale, rotate, and distort video that came from film, but you might notice some staggering in the motion as a result of the 3:2 process—especially if you time stretch or compress a clip. This is where the Remove 3:2 Pulldown option in the Interpret Footage dialog box comes in.

The Remove 3:2 Pulldown option converts the sequence back to 24 full frames per second. If Adobe After Effects is to remove the pulldown, though, it has to know where the first frame of your footage starts; it may not start with a whole (W) frame. Adobe After Effects is able to start its removal at different phases in the pulldown cycle. You can either specify the phase manually or have Adobe After Effects attempt to guess the phase. To analyze the footage, select the footage item in the Project window, then click the Guess 3:2 Pulldown button in the Fields and Pulldown area of the Interpret Footage dialog box. Adobe After Effects will analyze the first 10 fields and suggest a suitable Phase.

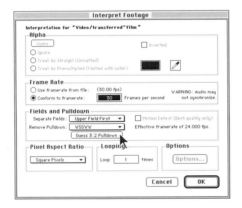

• *Animation.* Some 3D animation programs are capable of creating field-rendered material that simulates the field interlacing of normal video; some do not. In the former case, treat the material as video. In the latter case, try to have the animations output at 59.94 or 60 frames per second, and set their frame rate to match in the Interpret Footage dialog box in Adobe After Effects. Do not set any field order for them, because each field exists as a whole frame.

If you have an animation that was rendered as a 60-fps movie, and you are compositing it with 29.97-fps video, conform it to 59.94 fps inside the Interpret Footage dialog box as well, so that fields are not skipped to resolve this frame rate difference.

Interlace interpolation

When you're working with interlaced source material and attempting to de-interlace it, it is important to understand the difference between de-interlace and separate fields options.

The De-interlace command in Adobe Photoshop actually discards data from one of the two fields, and either copies or interpolates data from the remaining field to make up for the removed field. The result is a reduction in resolution. You should de-interlace still captures from video; you should not de-interlace moving video (unless preparing the clip for multimedia).

The Separate Fields option in the Interpret Footage dialog box in Adobe After Effects 4.0 actually splits fields into two independent frames. Each new frame has only half the information of the original frame, but none is actually thrown away. You should separate the fields of moving video; you should not do this to still captures from video.

Handling interlace on output

If your output is intended for full-frame video, then you will need to interlace your movies. You tell Adobe After Effects whether or not to interlace a movie in the Render Settings dialog box for each composition set up in the Render window. In the Time Sampling area of the window, under Field Render, you can set your choice. The choices are Off, Upper, and Lower. You should set this to match your output destination or device.

As mentioned earlier, different video output devices have different field orderings. As a general rule, JPEG computer cards tend to be upper field first and DDRs tend to be lower field first. Some frame buffer cards allow you to set the field order on output.

To determine the field order of your output device, it may be necessary to render a pair of test movies. To do this, create a small solid and animate it to move quickly around a composition. Render a movie of this at full resolution, set to Upper Field First. Then render the same movie again set to Lower Field First. Play them back through your output system. One should exhibit smooth motion; the other will exhibit jerky motion. The smooth one is the setting you want.

If your final output is intended for film or multimedia, then you should turn off the Field Render option. However, you will still want to separate the fields of interlaced footage on input; otherwise, their fields might cause jerkiness and other artifacts on playback. By turning off the Field Rendering option on output, only the first field is used and interlaced clips are de-interlaced automatically.

Designing to reduce interlace flicker

One strong disadvantage of interlaced display systems is their difficulty in displaying objects with thin horizontal lines. If a line from an object appears on one field but not the other, the line will appear to flicker as the monitor displays the field with it and then the field without it. Note that some NTSC output cards for computers feature *convolution* or *de-flicker* circuitry to reduce flickering in computer images. Some of these cards, however, may turn this feature off when playing full-motion video, which may cause flicker to return.

You have several options to prevent this unwanted flickering. The first is to avoid designing graphics with thin (i.e., 1-pixel) horizontal lines. Sometimes this cannot be avoided—for example, when computer screen captures are incorporated into video. The quick solution here is to shift the image horizontally up or down by a half pixel, causing any 1-pixel lines to appear on both fields.

A third solution is to blur the image slightly to spread thin lines across fields. This technique is the only cure for some problems, such as vertically scrolling text with sharp horizontal edges (sometimes these edges hop between fields, causing some flickering). Adobe After Effects features a Reduce Interlace Flicker filter specially designed for this application. A setting of 1.0 is a good starting point for this filter.

To apply the Reduce Interlace Flicker effect, select choose Effect > Video > Reduce Interlace Flicker.

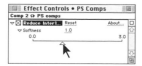

Video transfer issues

Before you begin your animation, you should decide on the method to be used for transferring the final rendered frames to videotape. The hardware choice will usually determine the maximum frame size and the field order.

In general, the most popular methods for transferring movies to tape use either real-time JPEG-compressed video, or frame-by-frame uncompressed video, using either a video card or a digital disc recorder.

• *Real-time video.* With a relatively inexpensive video card installed in your system, you can capture and transfer 30-fps/60 fields JPEG-compressed video to tape. The less expensive boards offer Composite and S-Video outputs, with the high-end boards adding component output for BetaSP decks. If you plan on doing long-form pieces that need perfect synchronization, look for a system that offers 16-bit audio genlocked to video. For the best results, expect to add a SCSI accelerator card and a disk array. (Check to make sure that it is one that is recommended by the video card manufacturer.) Examples of video cards worth checking out include those from Matrox (DigiSuite), Truevision (Targa2000), and Data Translation (Media 100).

Digital video in DV format can be imported directly through an IEEE 1394 (FireWire) port.

If you're providing graphics for use in an Avid editing environment, it may be possible to supply images or movies that can be imported directly to the Avid and converted to Avid compression. This is useful only if the production is being finished on the Avid. If the Avid is being used off-line only, the editor will need the graphics supplied on a tape with SMPTE timecode.

• *Frame by frame.* This transfer method features uncompressed video output and is offered as a service by many postproduction houses. Although you won't need expensive disk arrays with this method, you will need a lot of storage. (Estimate 900K maximum per frame for 640 x 480, and 1.1 MB maximum per frame for 720 x 486.) You can even use software-only movies for proofing purposes, or your regular JPEG hardware. For rendering, save as an image sequence and take your hard disk to a studio that has the equipment to transfer a sequence to tape.

Estimate 3-seconds-per-frame layoff time. Most studios charge by the hour, not the frame, so resist the urge to conserve disk space by saving the frames with a slow compressor (such as Apple JPEG). If you have many short animations, the layoff will go more quickly if you render them using the same filename and sequential frame numbers and place them in one folder. All frames must be the same size. Due to current Finder limitations (Mac OS), avoid creating folders with more than about 900 frames (30 seconds) per folder.

Still frames can also be laid off with this method. To expedite the layoff, number the stills sequentially and tell the operator how long each frame of the image sequence should play.

Note: You can find renaming utilities that will change filenames and frame numbers quickly and easily. (One such utility is called Renamer and is available on many online services.)

• *Digital disk recorder (DDR).* Popular digital disk recorders include those by Abekas and Accom, and the newer models are intended to be connected directly to the computer via SCSI or Ethernet. After Effects 4.0 includes the Accom plug-in that enables reading and writing to some DDR models directly. Another plug-in that supports other DDR models is available from Diaquest. See the After Effects User Guide for more information on DDR support.

For those who do not have in-house access to a DDR and professional tape deck, most postproduction houses offer *Exabyte-to-Abekas transfers* for laying off uncompressed animation to any analog or digital tape format, including BetaSP, Digital Betacam, D1, and D2. (Some service providers are also set up to transfer to a DDR from your hard drive.) The results are of the highest quality, but you'll need an additional application, such as Knoll Software's Missing Link and an Exabyte 8mm tape drive. To ensure that the whole process works without a hitch, ask the postproduction house to output a short field-rendered test file (3 seconds of both Upper Field First and Lower Field First), and check which field order looks correct.

When transferring your footage to and from video, use the highest quality signal available from your hardware setup. The choices consist of the following:

• *Composite video.* Before a signal can be broadcast, it must be sent as a composite signal because all standard televisions accept only composite. Because the color signal is combined with the luminance signal and sync pulses in composite video, the quality is not very high and it doesn't hold up well to duplication. Most tape decks and monitors offer composite inputs and outputs.

• *Y/C.* Commonly referred to as *S-Video* and *S-VHS* (although it is not tied to any specific tape format), Y/C is available on many S-VHS and Hi-8-format consumer camcorders and tape decks, as well as on more professional recorders. The luminance and color (Y and C, respectively) signals are kept separate in this signal, which yields better resolution and color than does composite video.

• *Component video.* The highest quality signal is component video (often referred to as YUV). In component video, three separate signals are used for Luminance (Y), Red-Y, and Blue-Y, which result in superior color and image quality. Considered a broadcast-quality signal, analog component video is available on MII and BetaSP decks, with digital component video available with D1 and some other emerging digital formats.

Some tape decks also feature their own dub connectors that may carry variations on Y/C and component video. Because they tend to be specific to manufacturers, we will not cover them here.

Rendering for film

The process of scanning and recording back to film can vary somewhat among postproduction houses, so it's critical to work closely with your client and the service provider. You will want to plan your disk space, RAM requirements, and budget carefully.

When working in Adobe After Effects at film resolution, you'll find the ability to work at half and quarter resolution very useful to conserve screen space, update time, and operating memory. Set the comp frame rate and the Preferences > Display Frame Rate to 24 fps and the Display Style to SMPTE, Frames, or Feet & Frames. In Preferences > Import, set the Default Frame Rate for the Newly Imported Sequences option to 24 fps.

Film basics

The most common aspect ratio in the United States is Academy Aperture, or 1.85:1 (*referred to as one-eight-five*). The *American Cinematographer Manual* describes this 35mm format as follows:

Full Aperture (or *camera aperture*) refers to the total area between the 35mm perforations, including the area normally reserved for the soundtrack.

Academy Aperture refers to that area of the negative excluding the soundtrack area.

The following illustration shows a film frame as it might appear on a contact print for projection. The extra areas at the top and bottom will be visible only when the movie is transferred to video or shown on TV. They will not be seen at the theater.

Film is scanned to fit the final output. If you need Academy Aperture output, only the image area of the source footage is scanned. Likewise, if designing CGI for Academy Aperture, there's no need to create files at Full Aperture size. Recommended pixel sizes can vary among service providers, and typical sizes include the following:

- Full Aperture: 2048 W x 1536 H (9 MB per frame)
- Academy Aperture: 1828 W x 1332 H (7 MB per frame)

Although 1828 x 1332 is roughly a 4:3 aspect ratio (not 1.85:1), you will usually want to work with the extra pixels so that when the movie is shown on TV or video, it won't be letterboxed (formatted so that the full width is shown but with black bands across the top and bottom). Titles and important action should stay within the 1.85 safe zones. Here you see both 1.85 and TV safe zones overlaid on an Academy 1828 x 1332 frame.

An Academy RGB frame of 1828 x 1332 pixels takes up 7 MB of RAM per frame, so at 24 fps, 1 second of film consumes close to 168 MB of disk space. The RAM requirements are not small: You'll need nine times the amount of RAM for film as you would for a similar design at 720 x 486. Consider 100 MB to be a minimum for simple compositing, though many large nested comps may necessitate 256 MB or more.

Getting film scanned

Make a log of the frames that need to be scanned by reading the key-code numbers on the film and making a note of the In and Out points for each clip. If you plan on doing a rough cut first, have the film transferred to video with the key-code numbers window burned in; you can then easily log only the frames to be scanned once the design is approved. You can request that the scanned footage be converted from 10 bits to 8 bits per channel for use on your system, and determine the best method of file transportation. Another way of dealing with conversion is to use the Cineon format so you can make conversion decisions yourself in After Effects.

Film frames viewed on an RGB or NTSC screen can look very different from the original footage. However, your service provider will thank you if you suppress the urge to do any color correction—their color lookup tables should restore the frames to the original color and gamma when recorded back to film. If you do need to do creative compositing or to add CGI elements, agree with your provider about how to tackle the color correction tasks and render output tests as you go.

Making video proofs

Although you can't view the film frames easily at full resolution, you can use a JPEG hardware board to make high-quality real-time video proofs. Render at half resolution, and in the Output Module select the Stretch To option to make a 640 x 480 or other size.

File and tape formats

Because most film recorders and scanners are connected to a Silicon Graphics machine, you may find yourself dealing with UNIX file formats that are not native on your system, and transferring files via Tar (Tape ARchive) on Exabyte. Fortunately, it's relatively simple to convert image sequences to and from SGI files, and some programs such as Knoll Software's Missing Link can read and write Tar. The step-by-step process is as follows:

1 In the Render Settings dialog box, choose Best Quality, Full Resolution, 24 fps. Set field rendering off, and set the other pop-up menu items as desired.

2 In the Output Module, select an image sequence for the final film frames. To also render a video proof version, select Composition > Add Output Module and edit the second output settings to render a movie using your compressor of choice and changing the Stretch To settings to 640 x 480 (or as needed).

3 Determine the file format favored by your service provider for their UNIX platform. SGI-RGB is quite common, along with TIFF and Targa. (SGI-RGB files can be saved as compressed or uncompressed. The compressed version is lossless and preferable if the postproduction house accepts it.) With After Effects 4.0, you can directly output to SGI-RGB format.

Missing Link can be used to transfer the SGI-compatible files to Exabyte tape by using Tar.

4 In Missing Link, specify the *block size* requested by the postproduction house. Be aware that a small number like 16 or 20 is the size in *physical blocks*; multiply by 512 to get the *logical block* size. Your service provider will have a preference for whether the One Archive Per File option should be checked or not.

5 You can back up the image sequences and delete the disk space-consuming SGI files. By doing this, you'll need only two free partitions to perform the final render.

Audio issues

In digital audio, vibrations in the air (or electrical impulses traveling down a wire) are converted to a string of numbers that a computer can store and replay at a later time. This is done by sampling the air pressure or signal level at regular intervals. The frequency of these intervals is known as the *sample rate*; it is similar to the concept of pixels and dots per inch in a digitized image. Each sample is converted into a number. The precision of these numbers is usually 8 or 16 bits per sample; this is known as a sample's *resolution* or *bit depth*. The concept is similar to one in graphics—the more samples and bits you have, the more accurate the sound.

Audio resolution

Every bit of resolution in an audio file closely corresponds to 6 decibels (dB) of signal level, with the decibel being the common unit used to measure audio loudness. Older systems had 8-bit audio resolution. This translates roughly into a 48 dB signal-to-noise ratio, which isn't very high—roughly the equivalent of noisy AM radio. Newer systems use 16-bit resolution, which translates roughly to a 96 dB signal-to-noise ratio. This is the same as used by audio CDs, and is very good. The Audio Level palette in Adobe After Effects displays audio level as both decibels and percentage of full scale. Adobe After Effects performs linear fades in units of decibels, not percentage.

Eight-bit audio often sounds "noisy." This noise is actually *quantization distortion*, caused by not having enough bits of resolution to describe the audio signal. The lower the level of the sound, the fewer the bits that can be used to describe it, resulting in more distortion and apparent noise. Sixteen-bit audio rarely exhibits this noise, since even very quiet sounds still have sufficient bits left over to describe them.

If your application demands that 8-bit audio be used for your final output, you should attempt to keep the sound levels consistently loud to reduce the apparent effects of quantization distortion. One way to do this is to animate audio levels to raise the level of an audio track at the points where the sound itself is lower in volume. Remember to lower the level back to normal during louder sections of the audio track; otherwise, it will overload and give an unpleasant clipping distortion. Mixing in additional background sounds such as music and sound-effects tracks can also help even out the overall level of audio. There are also dedicated audio-processing programs and audio plug-in filters for Adobe Premiere that can even out the level of an audio clip, by using functions known as *compressing* and *limiting*. These techniques are also useful for some television and video production, to keep the audio level of your movie even and above the noise floor of the listening environment.

Audio sample rate

Sample rate directly corresponds to how high a frequency can be accurately captured. The higher the sample rate is, the higher the frequency that can be captured. The highest frequency that can be theoretically captured is half the sample rate. For example, you need to sample audio at a rate of at least 40,000 times per second to capture an audio frequency of 20,000 cycles per second (often referred to as the *upper limit of audibility*).

Common professional sample rates are 48,000 Hz and 44,100 Hz (samples per second). Audio CDs use 44.1 kHz; digital audio tape (DAT) decks tend to use 48 kHz (1000 Hz = 1 kHz). Personal computers tend to use lower rates for most of their audio. Older systems used to use rates of 22,254 and 11,127 Hz; today, most systems tend to use rates of 22,050 Hz and 11,025 Hz (which are simpler divisions of the CD rate of 44.1 kHz). Most of the audio you hear on interactive CD-ROMs is either 22 kHz or 11 kHz. The result is less frequency response and slightly more noise, but also less room taken up on the CD. Lower sample rates can be acceptable for audio sources without high frequencies, such as voice; 44.1 or 48 kHz are almost always used for professional applications such as broadcast TV.

Note: A side effect of sample rate is that the higher the rate, the lower the distortion and apparent noise in the sound as well. This doesn't have as much effect on noise as the sampling resolution does, but it does help.

Figuring out how much room a sound file is going to take is a simple function of math:

(sample rate) x (bytes per sample) x (number of channels) x (time) = size

The size of a sound file that is recorded at 22.254 kHz at 8-bit (1 byte) resolution, is monophonic (one channel), and is 30 seconds long is calculated as follows:

22,254 x 1 x 1 x 30 = 667,620 bytes
(÷ 1024 ≈ 652 KB)

The size of a sound file that is recorded at 48 kHz at 16-bit resolution (2 bytes per sample), is in stereo (two channels), and is 3 minutes (180 seconds) long is calculated as follows:

48,000 x 2 x 2 x 180 = 34,560,000 bytes
(÷ 1024 = 33,750 KB)

The very rough rule of thumb is that stereo CD-quality (44.1 kHz, 16-bit) audio takes up 10 MB of space per minute. For lower quality files, divide by 2 for monophonic; divide by 2 for 8-bit; divide by 2 for 22 kHz.

Many software programs can convert between different sample rates, but the quality varies considerably between different programs. For professional audio, it is a good idea to sample-rate convert all of your audio sources to the final output rate you will need, using higher-quality dedicated audio software or hardware. After Effects 4.0 can perform high quality anti-aliased resampling when Quality in a layer is set to Best.

Pull up and pull down issues

A properly configured audio-video studio has the audio sample rate and video frame rate clocks locked together. However, there can still be some drift problems between audio and video. To fix them, you may need to vary slightly (*pull down*—or sometimes, *pull up*) the sample rate of the audio.

The most common mistake is to create a movie at 30 fps with audio at 44.1 kHz, and then to play back the video at 29.97 fps. The result is a slight slowdown in the video, while the audio (depending on your hardware) may still be playing at the correct rate and therefore will seem to get ahead of the video. The difference between 30 and 29.97—1.001:1—is a "magic number" that comes up often in synchronization problems. This ratio works out to 1 frame per 1000 frames, or 1 frame per 33.3 seconds (just under 2 frames per minute). If you notice audio and video drifting apart at about this rate, it is probably the result of a 29.97 versus 30-fps issue.

The best solution is to build all of your video and animation at 29.97 frames per second. The second-best solution is to alter your audio sample rate. If your hardware allows itself to be slowed down by 0.1% (for example, from 44.1 to 44.056 kHz), this will cure the problem. A third solution is to render audio at a rate that is 0.1% fast— 44.144 kHz versus 30 fps; this will stay in sync when played back through hardware that plays video at 29.97 fps and audio at 44.1 kHz.

Film is often recorded at 24 frames per second. It is not unusual to record the original audio in the field, slaved to the film camera, in a DAT recorder at a sample rate of 48 kHz. But when the film is transferred to video, it must actually be slowed down by 0.1% to 23.976 frames per second (so that 24 film frames can be interwoven into 30 video frames). If you leave the DAT at 48 kHz, the audio will run faster than the video. The DAT needs to be slowed down 0.1% when transferring the audio into the computer to make sure everything realigns. (The best solution is for the person recording the audio to have a special DAT deck that will record 0.1% fast, at 48,048 samples per second, when slaved to the film camera.)

If a DAT tape of the audio is recorded at the same time as the original video or film, you may be asked to transfer it into your computer to work with. If you do not have a DAT that can be slaved to video, you may be tempted to sample-rate convert it to force it to the "correct" rate while recording. However, performing this conversion after the DAT recording will not change the speed of the DAT; it will freeze in memory any speed errors present in your DAT player.

Another magic ratio you have to be concerned with when dealing with multimedia is the ratio between the older sample rate of 22.254 kHz and the now more-common rate of 22.050 kHz, which works out to a ratio of 1.00925:1. This is a much larger error and will appear much more quickly—almost 1 frame per 100, or 1 frame every 3.3 seconds (roughly 17 per minute). If you plan to be working at these lower rates, for CD-ROM production, for example, try to work at 22.050 rather than 22.254 kHz.

Index

Project designers

Tour: Bonnie Lebesch

Bonnie Lebesch is a digital artist working in dynamic and interactive computer media. Her vision of creating an intuitive CD-ROM for children resulted in *Stella and the Star-Tones*, the recipient of five international design awards and two educational software endorsements. As art director and designer, Bonnie has worked with MSN's Interactive Music show, Rifff, where she collaborated with musical artists including B. B. King and Cyndi Lauper. Her other projects include software instructional design for Adobe Premiere, Adobe After Effects, and Adobe InDesign and numerous CD-ROM titles for Microsoft. She also creates interactive art for installations and performances, collaborating with various musical artists in the Seattle area.

Lesson 1: Trish Meyer

As an entrepreneur moving from a background in print media to 2-D animation, Trish Meyer uses Adobe After Effects to deliver high-quality animation at a reasonable cost. Trish and Chris Meyer own CyberMotion, which specializes in motion graphic design, sound design, and digital compositing for film and video. CyberMotion creates animated videos for corporate and commercial clients.

Music by Kurt Wortman, Hidden Spot Music. Painted Background image from *Painted Backgrounds* CD-ROM by Digital Stock Corp. Music Score image and Composers images from "Music—Business and Industry Series, Vol. 2," CD-ROM by Planet Art.

Lesson 2: Beth Roy

Beth Roy has a degree in Visual Arts/Graphic Design and English from Brown University. She began working for CoSA when the first version of AfterEffects was in development. Beth organized events and managed in-house design projects for CoSA. As a Project Manager with the Dynamic Media Group at Adobe, she produced demo reels and developed training materials, focusing mainly on After Effects marketing and training programs. She consulted with Adobe to provide on-staff quality assurance for After Effects for Windows.

Beth now works as a freelance motion graphics designer and After Effects educator, and has taught After Effects courses all over the U.S., Canada, and Puerto Rico. She is the owner and lead designer of Toast Factory, a motion graphics design firm whose projects include work for commercials, film titles, corporate and educational video, CD-ROM, and the web. Contact Toast Factory via email at toastf@aol.com.

Ballet footage courtesy of the Oakland Ballet.

Lesson 3: Lynda Weinman

Lynda Weinman is the founder of lynda.com, LLC, and the Ojai Digital Arts Center, a training facility devoted to professional digital arts. She has worked in design and animation for the past 18 years, and has been teaching digital design for the past 10 years. She has taught at Art Center College of Design, San Francisco Multimedia Studies, American Film Institute, UCLA, and at numerous conferences and workshops throughout the world before founding her own training facility in Ojai, California.

Lynda is the author of a series of books on web design, and writes for numerous magazines, including *MacWorld, How, Adobe Magazine, Step-by-Step Graphics, Web Techniques, Dynamic Graphics, Animation, Full Motion, New Media,* and *Diem.*

Above all, Lynda loves to teach. She has conducted private classes for many corporations, including MSNBC, Microsoft, Capital Group,

CBS, NBC, Genentech, and Apple Computer. You can check out her training materials (books, videos, and classes) at www.lynda.com.

Lesson 4: David Biedny and Nathan S. Moody

David Biedny is the President & CEO and Nathan Moody is the Director of Entropy of IDIG (Interactive Digital Intelligence Group), Inc., a polymedia production group based in San Rafael, California. They have created digital special effects for the motion picture "Spawn," and are coauthors (with Bert Monroy) of the critically acclaimed *Photoshop Channel Chops* (New Riders Publishing), as well as the *Photoshop Inside & Out* video learning series. They can be reached at www.idignet.com.

Music by Chris Meyer, CyberMotion.

Lesson 5: Brian Maffitt

Brian Maffitt is the Chief Software Designer for the Atomic Power Corporation, creators of Evolution and Psunami, two high-end effects packages for Adobe After Effects 4.0. You can find out more about Atomic Power's products at www.AtomicPower.com, or by calling 760-516-9000. Brian is also creative director of Total Training Inc., and is the author of several video-training courses for computer-graphics professionals. Brian first released the award-winning *Total AE*, a comprehensive training series for Adobe After Effects 3.1, and followed that up with series on ICE'd Final Effects Complete, Adobe Premiere 5.0, MetaCreations Painter 5.5 (with Jeremy Sutton), and Atomic Power's Evolution and Psunami packages. Brian hosts the New York After Effects User Group (www.otown-media.com/nycaesig), which meets monthly in Manhattan. You can find out more about Brian's Total Training products at www.Total-Training.com, or by calling 760-858-0590.

Lesson 6: Bruce Heavin and Lynda Weinman

Bruce Heavin is an acclaimed painter and illustrator, who works expertly with traditional and electronic media. His clients include Adobe, MSNBC, E! Entertainment Television, *Outside*, *Computer Life*, *MacUser*, and *Keyboard*. He has designed graphics for numerous Web sites and CD-ROMs, including pieces for DreamWorks SKG Interactive's Web site.

Bruce is a graduate of Art Center College of Design in Illustration. He is the co-author of *Coloring Web Graphics*, a Web design book devoted to Web-based color aesthetics and technical issues. Bruce is the co-founder of the Ojai Digital Arts Center, a training facility devoted to the professional digital arts. Visit the center at www.digitalartscenter.com or Bruce's portfolio site, www.stink.com, to see and learn more.

Lesson 7: Tim Sassoon

Tim Sassoon is Creative Director of Sassoon Film Design. He has produced special visual effects for feature films such as *Deep Impact*, *George of the Jungle*, and *Doctor Doolittle* as well as IMAX films like *Alaska - Spirit of the Wild* and *T-Rex - Back To The Cretaceous*. "After Effects has really changed the visual effects landscape," says Tim, "These days it's personal skill that counts, not how much money one has to spend. After Effects Cineon Tools actually provides more flexibility for film compositing than is available in most of the high-priced solutions."

Erica Schisler

Erica Schisler has a B.A. in filmmaking from Evergreen State College in Olympia, Washington, where she specialized in optical printing and traditional cel animation. Erica has worked for Aldus and CoSA. She currently works for the Dynamic Media Group of Adobe Systems as a Product Marketing Manager for After Effects. Erica worked with the designers to bring this book together.